MEASURES OF SCIENCE

Northwestern University

Studies in Phenomenology

and

Existential Philosophy

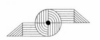

MEASURES OF SCIENCE

Theological and Technological Impulses in Early Modern Thought

James Barry Jr.

Northwestern University Press
Evanston, Illinois

Northwestern University Press
Evanston, Illinois 60208-4210

Copyright © 1996 by Northwestern University Press
All rights reserved
Printed in the United States of America

ISBN cloth 0-8101-1424-0
     paper 0-8101-1425-9

Library of Congress Cataloging-in-Publication Data

Barry, James, 1955–
    Measures of science : theological and technological impulses in early modern
thought / James Barry, Jr.
        p.   cm. — (Northwestern University studies in phenomenology and exis-
tential philosophy)
    Includes bibliographical references and index.
    ISBN 0-8101-1424-0 (cloth : alk. paper). — ISBN 0-8101-1425-9 (pbk. : alk.
paper)
    1. Science—Europe—Philosophy—History—17th century.   2. Descartes,
René, 1596–1650—Contributions in philosophy of science.   3. Bacon, Francis, 1561–1626—Contributions in philosophy of science.   4. Newton, Isaac,
Sir, 1642–1727—Contributions in philosophy of science.   I. Title.   II. Series:
Northwestern University studies in phenomenology & existential philosophy.
Q174.8.B375   1996
501—dc20   96-26448
                                                                            CIP

The paper used in this publication meets the minimum requirements of the
American National Standard for Information Sciences—Permanence of Paper
for Printed Library Materials, ANSI Z39.48-1984.

A real science recognizes and accepts its own history without feeling attacked.

—*Michel Foucault*

Contents

Acknowledgments

This project has accumulated many debts. I owe much to many people, perhaps too much to fully acknowledge. My four years of study in the State University of New York at Stony Brook department of philosophy represent the bulk of this debt. Hugh Silverman, Don Ihde, and Patrick Heelan indulged a dissertation project that turned to out to have at least two books within it. I am grateful for their patience and encouragement. Their very different philosophical styles and projects encouraged me to find my own voice while instilling within me an appreciation of approaches different from my own.

Don Ihde deserves special thanks for keeping this book project alive. As editor of the Indiana University Press "Philosophy of Technology" Series, it was his encouragement that gave me the hope necessary to spend three grueling summers putting together the initial manuscript. Beyond this, it was as mentor that he helped bring this book to press.

Jacques Taminiaux's willingness to serve as outside reader on my dissertation, as well as his guidance of my dissertation work during the year I spent in Belgium on a Belgian-American Education Foundation fellowship, gave me the confidence to believe that my work was significant.

Mary Rawlinson gave me the gift of careful criticism. To her I owe thanks for much of my ability to see my own work as insightful but in constant need of improvement.

My debt to Hugh Silverman goes beyond this book. His reliance upon me in many projects instilled in me the importance and goodness of collegiality. He has taught me much about the business of philosophy in which we both live.

Perhaps my greatest debt is owed to the graduate students who shared with me the intense light and desire of the Stony Brook department of philosophy in the middle eighties. The intimate friendships that were forged there are sorely missed. To friends like Gary Aylesworth, Jim Carmine, James Clarke, Jim Hatley, Sharon Meagher, Michael Nass, and Brian Seitz I owe a sense of philosophy as a warm collective project, one that is alive and very well. We would make a powerfully diverse department of philosophy.

I owe much to Bill Rumsey and Curt Peters for their acceptance of the rambling ideas of a younger, rougher colleague. We have made a good, if sometime raucous, philosophical team.

Rick Kennedy was a source of friendship, support, and intellectual stimulation in a sometimes hostile environment.

The administration of Indiana University Southeast also offered financial support for this project.

John McCumber, both as editor of the series within which this book is appearing and as fellow father, has had a crucial role in the reality of this book. I also appreciate the efforts of Heather Kenny on my behalf.

Finally, I owe a debt of mind and heart to Elizabeth MacNabb. How she has accepted me for the strange thing I turned out to be I cannot say. However, if she had not done so, this book (and my human children, Cameron and Seamus) would neither exist nor thrive. Her nurturing of this project, her willingness to read and criticize it, is yet another form of love I only barely deserve. May we grow old together in love and laughter.

Somewhere near Crandall, Indiana, Winter 1995

Introduction

The history of science is not clear. The history of that form of science—modern science—which defines itself in terms of the strictest form of clarity is least clear of all. If this is so, then no study that takes modern science solely on its own terms can hope to uncover what makes modern science that singular clarity born of less than transparent stock. Without doubt, modern science is that subtle and opaque project by which thought gives itself a better body. And yet, no matter how clearly the structures of this new body—its tissues, organs, and systems—may be presented, the impulses and reasons of modern science betray the clarity of its appearance.

It might be this failure of clarity is not the fault of modern science itself, but rather stems from the sources over which it has only partial control—and this is to say nothing of the legacies over which it would seem to have no control whatsoever. Many historians and philosophers have argued in this way. Many have concluded from this problem of limited control that science must be taken at face value, while others have claimed that science must be taken down from its tower and seen for the ordinary activity that it is. Few historians or philosophers concerned with science have seemed to be able to resist choosing one of these paths, and fewer still have offered a sustained reading of modern science that portrays it as more than just one more human enterprise, or less than that singular human project which outstrips all other forms of human thinking or achievement.

At the same time, it is only by taking the texts of early modern science at their word that any study of modern science can even begin to succeed. We must read these texts with high empathy to understand modern science; yet in so doing we are caught up in the power and scope of their projects. If we refuse to be drawn into the project of modern science, if we arm ourselves before the fact, before the reading, with an armor of suspicion and distrust of its motives, then how can we begin to know its aims and reasons? Somehow one must read modern science without taking it at face value on the one

1

hand, or rejecting, even destroying, it on the other. An impasse seems unavoidable.[1]

What, then, is the best way in which to proceed? Again, it depends upon our objectives. If we aim primarily at promoting the greatness of modern science, then we will choose to practice what is called the "internal history of science." Alternatively, if we seek to show the violence inherent in the advent and development of modern science, then we will remain outside looking in, taking science as a sort of pathological curiosity to be studied, but only at a distance. However, if we want to see modern science as a project whose accomplishments are only exceeded by its audacity, then we must refuse to read modern science solely from the inside or the outside. Instead, we must struggle to remember that modern science has, in fact, three sides: a past, a present, and a future.

Or rather, it would be more accurate to say that it is, for us, a double three-dimensional event. For those who actually conceived and practiced modern science, it had a tradition, a contemporary context, and promises of what it might come to be. To read modern science now, it is necessary to try to grasp that other three-dimensional form as well as our own. In other words, we have to view it both from the inside (what it was for those who practiced and conceived it at that moment) and from the outside (as a project that is now, in some sense, finished, though still not fully understood). For this double reading—science "inside out" and science "outside in"—to be possible, there must be a third position (beyond science as truth and science as pathology), a way of reading modern science as still at play though not as it once was, as neither quite alive nor quite dead. In other words, this third reading begins and ends by the recognition that modern science is the singular project it is because, in the richest sense of the word, it is historical. To read modern science in this way means to take it as an intellectual, spiritual, and moral form, but one which transforms its own defining precedents. The task, then, is to see the forms which precede modern science both as they shape modern science and as they are retroactively shaped by modern science.

Perhaps, in reading modern science in this manner, one risks not only the failures intrinsic to this approach but also the combined failings of the internal and external histories of modern science as well. However, with this risk of failure comes an opportunity to see in modern science the frequently ambiguous play between its ambitions and its reasons, its impulses and its accomplishments. With this risk of failure comes the possibility of seeing beyond the limitations of total clarity, of seeing beyond a science that disappoints the world or a world that disappoints science. Such a reading would measure modern science not only by what it has claimed and denied, but, more importantly, by seeking to understand how its claims and denials are sibling activities, two sides of the same transformative intellectual project.

All of the foregoing leads me to admit that, in some important sense, this book begins and ends with the work of Alexandre Koyré.[2] This statement should not be seen as a confession, leaving the reader to wonder why this project is significant, for Koyré's reading of the advent of modern science is not a narrowly limited effort but rather one that opens up a new field of questions. Thus, my work here begins with some of the questions bequeathed by Koyré. Among these questions I would stress the following: How can modern science's announcement of itself as *the* radically new science represent both audacious rhetoric and powerful accomplishment? What makes the new mathematical science, unlike its failed predecessors, so productive that it sweeps away prior science as bad philosophy (and prior philosophy as bad science)? How is it that what began as a tremendous conflict of views and projects finally came to be a singular modern scientific vision?

If I have taken Koyré's work in a direction that some would consider illicit, that is, against Koyré's own leanings, this is only because he framed the opening which I used to the advantage of my own project. Even the very structure of my book is a result of this mixed hermeneutic inheritance, for Koyré leaves Bacon in a sort of wasteland, neither fully modern nor fully nonmodern. Since Koyré (and others) taught me long ago that modern science depended as much upon what it denied as what it proposed, Bacon's odd position seems to me an indication of his importance to the project of early modern science. In other words, sometimes in order to follow Koyré it is necessary to go against him.

Koyré's work on modern science demonstrates that it is possible for the careful reader to resist the siren song of scientism without resorting to a full-scale rejection of the modern scientific discourse. He offers us a way to begin to take a fuller measure of modern science, because he is able to read the texts of early modern science as both revealing and concealing, both productive and seductive. To read the texts of early modern science in this way, one must also read what is denied in the very same texts. Thus, if one is to follow Koyré's lead, taking measure of modern science requires that we accept the measures early modern science uses to identify itself and that we seek out those measures which early modern science denies. To take measure of science is always a plural task: to take measure of science we must also take measure of its measures.[3]

DESCARTES'S RECTIFICATION OF NATURAL APPEARANCE: THINKING OVER PERCEPTION

1

Platonic and Aristotelian Anticipations of Descartes's God of Infinite Productivity

R eplying to Henry More in a letter dated February 5th, 1649, Descartes writes:

> The first question was why I defined body as extended substance, rather than perceptible, tangible, or impenetrable substance. However, notice that by calling it sensible substance, you defined body by its relation to our senses, and thus we explain only a certain property of it, instead of the essence of bodies in their entirety. The latter certainly does not depend upon our senses since it could exist even though there were no people. Thus, I do not see why you say that it is absolutely necessary that all matter must be sensible. For, on the contrary, there is none of it which might not be entirely nonsensible, were it to be divided into bits much smaller than our nerves, and if any given body moved in a sufficiently rapid manner.[1]

Descartes seeks to identify the essence of bodies, not their sensorial trivia. In his view, it is not perceptibility, but intelligibility, which funds this essence. Thus, only mental perception, not the perception of the senses, can serve as the foundation for the Cartesian science, a science whose ambitious goal involves the acquisition of a power and legitimacy necessary to delimit the general nature of bodies. The senses have a part in this delimitation of the true essence of matter only insofar as they are channels opening onto bodies, but they must be guided by the mind's vision, for by themselves they are not capable of grasping the essence of *res extensa*. This strange Cartesian matter—part extension, part motion— lies beyond the proper realm of sense perception, a realm populated as much by things belonging to illusion and opinion, that is, to *doxa*, as by more dependable entities. Thus, inasmuch as his new science seeks to grasp what is essential concerning the things about him, Descartes must be cautious, prudent, even suspicious in his use of perception.

The Cartesian project provides the solution to a very old problem. Descartes's epistemological fervor, his commitment to knowing what is most true, most real, and most essential, even if it means denying the obvious and the everyday, aims to break down the barriers that have held science back for two thousand years. Descartes's project is revolutionary, not so much because it flies in the face of traditional science and philosophy, but rather because it represents a radical appropriation of central tenets of the tradition against the backdrop of this denial of what was most obviously real, if ordinary. Even Galileo is not protected from this denying and appropriating claim. Descartes's epistemological ambitions are so great that everything is swept away, even the ontological underpinnings necessary to knowledge, leaving him to remake not only the realm of human knowledge and experience, but also the existential realm that serves as its backdrop.[2]

This unrestricted effort to rebuild the realms of knowing and being that swirls in the complicated depths of the Cartesian revolution have almost everything to do with what Alexandre Koyré has called the Cartesian quest for a total geometrization of space, his *géométrization à outrance.*[3] In his account, Koyré outlines the abyss which separates the Galilean and Cartesian views of the relation of perceptual and scientific experience, an abyss formed by the radical way in which Descartes "solves" the problem of the nature of motion. As Koyré shows, Descartes succeeds where Galileo had been to some extent stymied, because the former disallows certain traditional strictures that the latter implicitly honored concerning the relationship between the real and the mathematical. Following Koyré, I wish to show that the "success" of Descartes's effort is significant for much more than the history of mathematical physics. This success story marks the emergence of a crucial historical decision concerning the status of nature and perception in the emergent discourse of early modern science. What is at stake is a radical reorganization of the structures that relate and distinguish the natural realm and the technical realm. What makes this shift difficult to detect is its intimate involvement with what Koyré has characterized as Descartes's vision of the "intellectual primacy of infinity."[4]

In the *Regulae ad Directionem Ingenii,* Descartes extensively delineates the method one must employ in order to attain the great clarity to which the mind is entitled by birthright. Following Galileo, he contends that a process of analysis and simplification will explicitly reveal what has been clouded and blurred in the confused mass of everyday thought:

the simple nature of things, once exposed and fathomed, facilitates the understanding of composites. That is, by incessantly dividing things until one reaches the simplest essences (and thus the most clear and distinct ones) and then ordering and enumerating these simple forms, one can achieve a greater knowledge of these simple absolutes and their relative composites. Thus, these simple natures serve as the mathematically engendered bridge between the intellect and extension. Such intellectually simple natures can be "either purely intellectual, purely material, or finally common to both."[5] It is clear from Descartes's response to Henry More that this simplification exceeds the powers of sense perception, leaving the intellect the sole independent authority empowered to decipher these distilled essences. What can be perceived by the senses is only a pale reflection of the force of truth to which the mind is privy; the latter is of an entirely different dimension than the former.

Something very different with regard to the play of perception is maintained in Aristotle's work—both in the texts which take up the question of science directly, as well as those writings which set forth the structures which make knowledge possible. For example, in the opening lines of *Peri Hermeneias*, Aristotle offers a schematic for the general flow of experience: *grammata* as *symbola* of *phonai* as *symbola* of *pathemata* as *omoiomata* of *pragmata*: written words as symbolic of spoken words as symbolic of mental affections as likenesses of things-in-the-world.[6] From Aristotle's point of view, this chain of experience—and therefore of possible knowledge—is unbreakable. What is *pathemata*, translated so poignantly here as "mental affection"? It is the active complex of *nous* and *aisthesis*, a complex arising from the play of the soul and beings. In order for this to be a viable structure there must be a pole of a priori receptivity, that is, *aisthesis*. This "mental affection" should perhaps be read as "mental-affection." As Aristotle writes in *On the Soul*, "a man can exercise his knowledge when he wishes, but his sensation does not depend on himself—a sensible object must be there."[7]

Aristotle's point (or the trajectory of the translation) could be amended by saying that one's ability to perceive sensibly is a function of both the soul *and* things in the world. Central to the question of this capacity of perception is the issue of natural appearance as more than the repository of true structures mixed with error or illusion. According to Heidegger, only when appearance stands as something more than this pejorative force is something like the play of perception as experienced by the Greeks revealed:

> That which is [*Das Seiende*] is what emerges and opens itself, which, as what presences, comes over the human which itself presences, i.e., comes upon

the human which itself opens up to what presences insofar as it perceives it. That which is does not arise or emerge simply because the human first looks upon it, in the sense of a representation such as a subjective perception. Rather, the human is the one conceived by that which is. . . . Greek human being *is* as the one who perceives [*der Vernehmer*] that which is.[8]

According to this view of Greek experience, perception qua *aisthesis* stands as a central and indispensable link in the chain of apprehension. To render it inessential or suspect would be for Aristotle as absurd as diminishing the equally central and indispensable role which *nous* plays in experience. It is the play of *nous* and *aisthesis* in the face of what comes upon them that is Aristotelian perception in the most radical sense. The fact that Aristotle's physics is drawn directly from this chainlike schema is borne out by the fact that he seeks as much as possible to reconcile his physical science with common sense.[9]

Early modern science grounds itself in an understanding of perception and natural appearance quite different from that upon which Aristotle based his physics. Koyré suggests that this new ground which early modern science struggles to find is not "ground" at all, but actually "sky."[10] Aristotle's physics involves a careful set of distinctions between terrestrial and superlunar entities and states, while the physics which begins with Galileo, and finds a new level fulfillment in the work of Descartes, represents an accomplishment of extraordinary proportions: to understand the essence of motion on earth, it is necessary to detach oneself from the everyday, or what might be called typically terrestrial movement. Instead, one must look to stellar motion, which reflects more faithfully the regularity of all true movement, thus learning to ignore the all too quotidian tendency to accept what one sees immediately as the true nature of things.

Ultimately, of course, all motion—sublunar or stellar—will be subjugated to a single set of physical laws, laws which take neither stars nor the earth for their most rigorous model. What one perceives in the world about oneself can be delusion, unless one understands the essential language which underlies it. According to early modern science, the "Book of Nature" is written in the language of mathematics, and the extent to which the power of this language has been revealed marks the profound difference between Galileo and Descartes. I will characterize this growing mathematicization of nature in terms of a double movement: on the one hand, an homogenization of things—a rendering of material objects as essentially identical and therefore replaceable the one with the other; and on the other hand, the sterilization of space—an essential eradication of any bearing or influence of things upon the sites in which they come to stand. Out of this double movement the subordination of sensible perception and natural appearance to the powers of thought reaches a new level of manifestation. This manifestation can be introduced very clearly, but by no means exclusively, in a reading of Descartes's accounts of the essence and existence of material things and the divine power which brings them into being.

The Platonic Vision of Descartes's New World Order

In the *Meditations*, Descartes claims to seek that one Archimedean point which can sustain something like a set of positive sciences, for nothing like the new science can occur without this one certain point.[11] Via his initial *skepsis*, Descartes finds the immovable fulcrum necessary for a new scientific certainty. He describes this fulcrum in terms of a specific idea of God. Aside from his overt theological concerns, Descartes finds in this idea of God a way of grounding his new science; he discovers an extremely effective metaphysical foundation for his essentially mathematical sciences.[12] In sum, the Cartesian God is the infinite generative source of an indefinite, but certain, realm which comes to be called the universe. In Descartes's notion of God he finds the set of rational formulae which render the extended universe at once thoroughly questionable and essentially fathomable.

However, what of Descartes's passing reference to Archimedes? Is it only that, a passing remark? Or does this reference in fact bear directly on the central aims of the Cartesian project of science? Descartes undoubtedly held Archimedes in almost as much esteem as had Galileo, both finding in the ancient Syracusan an ancestor whose mathematical prowess was of heroic and inspiring proportions. This reference is all the more significant since it represents one of Descartes's few laudatory citations of ancient scientific efforts. Little surprise that the ancient figure Descartes (and Galileo) embrace was himself fiercely committed to mathematical investigations.

What world is Descartes going to leverage with his Archimedean fulcrum? If we ask this question in terms of his earliest work, *Le monde, ou, traité de la lumière*, the answer is given clearly enough: not this world but another, imaginary, one. Descartes is willing to concede that this world will not lend itself to such movement, but asks his reader to consider another world, one in which the very substance of things is best described in mathematical terms. In this admittedly imaginary world

Descartes finds a solution to, perhaps even an escape from, the Galilean dilemma concerning the multiplicity of nature and the natural language of geometry. In this new world the Archimedean talent for translating geometrical principles into the natural world takes on new promise, for the movement of translation is reversed, the natural world is now superimposed on a geometrical grid.

Descartes's *World* involves a "feint." While granting that the philosophical doctors know much more about the actual qualitatively driven world, he appropriates their idea that an infinite number of imaginary spaces are possible to establish a world driven by number, quantity, and extension. His new world is not real because it is only imaginary, but it is an imaginary space of a special kind in that it frees Descartes from the strictures of everyday life through its analytically geometrical essence.[13] This "free world" allows Descartes a metaphysical and epistemological license in his search for the true essences of matter and mind.

What is the relation between these two worlds, the one real and the other imaginary? Is there any correlative situation which might inspire this Cartesian double worldview? A clue to this question is found in an examination of the Platonic roots of Archimedean apocrypha. Archimedes is said to have left no writings regarding his engineering achievements for these efforts paled in importance beside the study of pure geometry. That is, no terrestrially bound work can rival the attainments of geometry, for the latter only escapes the imperfection of everyday life in its alliance with astronomical existence: geometry is closer to the world of sky than to the world of earth. Thus, to make inroads in the realm of geometrical truth one must leave behind the everyday world for the sky. Plato knew this, Archimedes knew this, and Descartes knows this.

The fact that Descartes appeals to Archimedes, while largely ignoring Plato, reveals his essential commitment to an active science. However, Descartes will go further than Archimedes on the Platonic track, for the former is a philosopher while the latter a mathematician and engineer. Pure geometry gives way to analytic geometry, the new form involving a logistic power which is not content with geometric description or technical excellence, but with wholesale transformation of how the world is understood. The Cartesian feint, this fable of the "new world," is the lever which engenders this transformation which will do much more than break the Roman siege of Syracuse. Although less immediately dramatic or effective, the Cartesian effort is more global in that it depicts what it would mean to live in a world dominated by one set of laws for earth and sky, everyday life and the life of the mind. It provides ordinary experience and mathematically guided experience with common justification by unilaterally prioritizing one side of each binary over the other.

Archimedes breaks the siege by Rome, but Descartes breaks the siege of Doxa.

At the heart of Descartes's scientific project lies an appeal to the primacy of the heavens. As he writes at the beginning of *The Meteors,* "We have naturally greater admiration and astonishment before things which are above us than the things which are beside or below us."[14] The appeal to sky is, of course, not new; it forms the guiding motif in Plato's cosmological account in the *Timaeus* and in his allegory of the cave. It is the preworldly heaven of ideas that inspires the Demiurge to perform the act of creation, and it is the sun that symbolizes the Good toward which humans by their essence are drawn. Thus, both gods and mortals derive their reasons from the sky, though the former live in more intimate proximity to it.

One finds in the *Timaeus* an interesting anticipation of Descartes's fable of the new world. Here Plato describes the appearance of the world in a double account: the first part laying out the development of the unchanging structure and form of the world, its permanent reasons, and the second part describing the changing aspects of the world with regard to this unstable site on which it is erected. In other words, the first account is of the ideal shape of the world, the second of its unavoidable debt to the shifting and shapeless *chora*. In the middle of this ambiguous double creation stands the Demiurge. His creation of the visible world is not ex nihilo, but rather mitigated by the inspiration of the heavens and the pliancy of the *chora*. That is, the task of the Demiurge is not to make something out of nothing, but to make visibility through the combination of the invisible and previsible. The Demiurge has a heavenly template upon which to draw for insight, a template whose form he must cajole the *chora* into assuming. The image offered by Plato is clearly that of a divine craftsman working some primordial clay into a definite but inspired form.

Plato's two-world schema in the *Timaeus* sets a metaphysical and theological standard which asserts a direct and essential influence on both Galileo and Descartes. However, its most powerful influence on them stems from Plato's description of the essence of the visible world (i.e., "world spirit") as a mathematically constructed entity. Both the movement of the heavenly bodies *and* the composition of earthly entities are defined by the best approximation that the Demiurge could muster of the goodness of the eternal world of intelligible forms, the geometrical structure of the visible world as heaven and earth.

An examination of the imagery of the sun in Books VI and VII of the *Republic* serves to further emphasize Descartes's theological debt to Plato. Socrates tells Glaucon to suppose that "the sun is the offspring of the good . . . as the good is to the intelligible and what is intellected, so the sun is in the visible region with respect to sight and what is seen."[15] Thus, the good is the source and mediating power of all intelligible things, and the sun is its child, source and mediating power of a somewhat lesser realm, the visible.

Socrates stresses the inferiority of the sun and the sunlike (i.e., light and vision) in the face of the good, but goes to even greater lengths to stress the subordinate position of knowledge and truth in relation to the good: "Therefore, say that not only being known is present in the things known as a consequence of the good, but also existence and being are in them besides as a result of it, although the good isn't being but is still beyond being, exceeding it in dignity and power."[16] The good lies beyond being known and even beyond being itself, for it is the king or father of the invisible and the father of the king or grandfather of the visible. Plato playfully avoids calling the visible (*houratou*) the heavens (*ouranous*) and in so doing makes it clear just how seriously he takes this image of familial lineage. By its age and overwhelming power, the good engenders the intelligible and the visible heavens.

Something very close to this Platonic appeal to a perfect, ideal, and unchanging goodness of the world lies at the heart of the Cartesian feint in *The World* as well, though the two-world schema of Plato has now been replaced by a single world with a necessarily quantitative substructure. As a matter of fact, Descartes's fable of the new world represents precisely the moment of collapse of the two worlds into one level of being, for Descartes will eventually conclude that because of the infinite power and goodness of God something very much like his imaginary world represents the essence, that is, the truth, of the real world. Descartes's new world is the old world shed of its illusory and inessential qualities, qualities which deny the adequacy of a mathematical perception inspired by his study of the sky. Descartes appropriately concludes *The World* by showing that "the face of the heavens of this new world must appear to its inhabitants exactly the same as that of our own."[17] Rather than a "likely story" or a "city in speech," Descartes asserts the legitimate right of this ideal world to exist.

Aristotle's *to theon* and the Method of the Cartesian Leap

Descartes is quite critical of Aristotle for taking Plato's method for searching out first principles as his own while at the same time making the ingenuous claim that the method is uncertain.[18] Be this as it may, Descartes makes it quite clear that he embraces the Aristotelian notion of God as "prime mover" as a basic logical necessity which must be heartily embraced.[19] God is, indeed, the initiating principle which must be at work in order for something like this world to exist. This is not to say that Descartes is an Aristotelian, but only to suggest that one finds very much alive in his work certain basic Aristotelian tenets. In fact, these tenets undergo a remarkable transformation which renders their similarities to Aristotelian (and certainly Aristotle's) metaphysics and science, in large part, problematic. This transformative appropriation, seen in a comparison of the idea of God maintained in each position, reveals much about Descartes's method, even when apparently isolated from any direct theological concerns. In fact, the method of the Cartesian leap depends upon the development of a new theological perspective.

For Aristotle, God is *to theon*. With this concept, Aristotle is able to establish a fundamental requirement for coherent scientific inquiry, a nonregressive ground. Indeed, *to theon* could be considered, in some respects, a precursor of the Cartesian God, because Aristotle's appeal is to a pure principle, a formal principle which lies to a certain extent beyond the senses and beyond experience while at the same time providing the absolutely necessary ground for all life, heavenly and earthly.

However, Aristotle goes further than this. He points out that God is not a merely empty concept, but like Plato's sun shares in life along with all the living beings which it engenders and supports:

> If, then, God is always in that good state in which we sometimes are, this compels our wonder; and if in a better one this compels it yet more. And God *is* in a better state. And life also belongs to God; for the actuality of thought is life, and God is that actuality; and God's self-dependent actuality is life most good and eternal. We say therefore that God is a living being, eternal, most good, so that life and duration continuous and eternal belong to God; for this *is* God.[20]

Small wonder that Aristotle stimulated the imagination of so many Christian thinkers. On the basis of metaphysical inquiry, Aristotle demonstrates the necessity of God as the entity unlike all other entities, the being which funds the existence of all other beings. God is the absolutely necessary formal principle which also lives, is present, in the world.

First philosophy must be, by its very nature, theological in its orientation, for what it seeks to establish is a science of "the causes that operate on so much of the divine as appears to us."[21] In the passage from which this quotation is taken we find striking proof that Descartes is very much mistaken in his claim that Aristotle simply borrows from his teacher. More importantly, we have profound evidence of the very different decisions made by Aristotle and Plato with regard to the theological question, a difference which bears directly on the Cartesian approach to the same problem. Indeed, Plato appeals to *helios*, the visible sun, in order to conjure up the best possible image of the purely intelligible Idea of the Good. In other words, Plato invokes the visible to open up a means of access to that which lies completely *beyond* the visible. Aristotle's theological appeal, on the other hand, is always at one and the same time to the visible heavens *and* the purely formal principle of the unmoved prime mover:

> For Plato it is precisely these things that do not exist for themselves, but rather, only the ideas. The divine—like the good—is beyond being (*epekeina tes ousias*), in a sense that prohibits its being called an existent thing. For Plato, eidetic or noetic constructs, for example, numbers, lines, and so forth, are to be separated from phenomenal existence, not fused with it as the Pythagoreans held. For Aristotle, the physei onta are inseparable from their ti estin (what-it-is). . . . But that means, conversely, that the eidos is not to be separated from its phenomenal appearance and, thus, this it is an *enhylon eidos* (materialized form).[22]

Where Plato ultimately subordinates the visible to the intelligible and mathematical, Aristotle tries to maintain them as coeval and mutually supportive. *To theon* is the pivotal moment in Aristotle's endeavor.

To theon is also for the Greeks the heavens, that set of superlunar beings which surpass all terrestrial beings in the radial perfection of their movements. Aristotle seeks to reconcile the oldest Greek attitudes concerning the existence of divine being with the sensible apprehension (*aisthesis*) of the sky, of the heavenly phenomena, in order to show how deep the theological aspect of thought (*nous*) runs. He finds a new and serious significance in the doxic pun concerning the similarity of *houratou, ouranous,* and *nous*:

> Our theory seems to confirm experience and to be confirmed by experience. For all men have some conception of the nature of the gods, and all who believe in the existence of gods at all, whether barbarian or Greek, agree in allotting the highest place to the deity. . . . If then there is, as there certainly is, anything divine, what we have just said about the primary bodily substance [being eternal and circular in its movements] was well said. The mere evidence of the senses is enough to convince of this, at least with human certainty. For in the whole range of time past, so far as our inherited records reach, no change appears to have taken place either in the whole scheme of the outermost heaven or in any of its proper parts.[23]

Sense perception and mental perception, visibility and divinity, find common ground in the face of the primary bodily substance, the heavens. Aristotle finds in the venerable past an important clue for his new science. This common ground embodied in the pure motion of *to theon* allows the possibility of a theoretical knowledge that need not shun natural experience so much as begin with it. Symbolized as the divine, pure motion serves to show the ancient and common heritage of questions regarding the physical and the theological realms. Distinct as they may be from one another, these questions are bound together by their essentially cosmic subject matter.

Aristotle's principle of the "unmoved mover" represents the quintessence of this most perfect motion, the pure actuality of radial motion, in need of nothing to render it complete in its reality. The symbolic perfection of this motion lies in the fact that it reconciles being and becoming at a single stroke: the heavens appear as the always moving which never moves. More than any other perceivable possibility, the heavens are the reconciliation of appearance and being, and of *aisthesis* and *nous*. This one self-sufficient and immovable substance, symbolized by the movement of the heavenly bodies, is the most perfect subject of the first theoretical science, *prote philosophia*, the study of being qua being. In this sense, the Aristotle of the *Metaphysics* holds that first philosophy is theological, because it contemplates beings which are the most whole, the most perfect, and thus the most overwhelming.[24]

Although drawing from the work of Aristotle quite freely, Descartes's God operates according to a distinctly different measure or ground than that found in Aristotle's divine substance or pure principle. Unlike Aristotle, Descartes's appeal to God is not to a pure act. Aristotle's "prime mover" is the final point at the end of an ontological gradient of motion; it provides the logical support, but not the creative ground, for all motion. For Descartes, on the other hand, God is not the most perfect being nor pure act, but "this first and sovereign being,"[25] the sole creative ground on which his new metaphysics *and* his new physics depend. Only in relation to this God-substance are *res extensa and res cogitans* at all substantial. What is for Aristotle a pure and necessary act which serves as a means of structuring inquiry into *kinesis* in accordance with its subject matter becomes for Descartes *the* substance which grants to all things their radically contingent possibilities.

Aristotle and Descartes are a chasm apart, a chasm that opens initially with the Cartesian vision of all things as propelled into existence and sustained there by a God of infinite productivity. Descartes leaps beyond the limits of cosmic thinking, beyond the limits of a world and mind that are classically finite. As Koyré, for one, has shown, this leap signifies the opening of the modern world and the final closing of its long-standing, long-suffering ancestor. More than this, the Cartesian leap announces the emergence of a double form of the infinite God and his not quite infinite world. Ultimately, and nestled behind all of these notions, lies yet another more radical aspect of the leap, for this Cartesian concept of God and world brings with it an analogous double, mind and body. Descartes may chortle at More's crude idea of the world as God's body, but it is not so much a chortle of rejection as a nervous response to More's crude recognition of this analogy of infinite mind and indefinite mind, of God and the human essence.

The God of Infinite Productivity and His Indefinite World

God is not a peripheral concern for Descartes, but rather close to his project's Archimedean point. Descartes comes to the conclusion that God's infinite productivity includes the capacity to act productively through his own creations, both extended nature and mind: "And first of all there is no doubt that everything that nature teaches me contains some truth. For by nature, considered generally, I now understand nothing else than God himself, or at least the order and the disposition that God has established in creation. And my nature in particular I understand as nothing other than the complexion or the assemblage of all the things that God has given me."[26]

Descartes's recurrent definition of God is essentially Archimedean, that is, actively Platonist, evoking an image of God as infinitely productive which we come closest to comprehending in a deep appreciation of the mathematical essence of creation. Aristotle would grant that mathematics is indeed a wonderful discipline, not because it can tell us much about the natural world or its necessary first principle, but rather because it allows us to manipulate the natural world within certain limits; it engenders a certain kind of technical realm. Where Descartes radicalizes the importance of mathematical understanding beyond even its broad Platonic limits, positing it as the model for all rational thought, Aristotle and his followers point to the crucial difference between the sky and the earth, as well as the technical and natural,[27] with regard to the usefulness and propriety of mathematical understanding.

The most profound difference between these two conceptions of God, however, stems not so much from the divergent definitions of God per se, but rather from the role which each initiating force or principle plays in the structuring of the world. As he writes in *The World*, Descartes is more than willing to accept that "there is some prime mover, who rolling around the world with an incomprehensible speed, is the origin and source of all other movements which one finds there,"[28] but what he takes movement to be in its essence is limited to one form of movement, that is, local, rectilinear movement. All the other forms of movement which Aristotle considers under the general notion of movement as *kinesis*, that is, movement understood as qualitative change, are abruptly set aside by Descartes. Where for Aristotle it was the radial motion (of the heavens) which best revealed the perfection of God, in the Cartesian vision God as the prime mover will be the initiator of rectilinear motion. Radial motion gives way to rectilinear motion as the best evidence of God's perfection, a perfection which is now defined as infinite.

Aristotle had placed the changeless and divine beauty of radial motion in the heavens, for here was where God belonged. Where is this realm of rectilinear motion which would seem to be the rightful home of Descartes's God? Certainly it is not the earth, for one cannot find a single example of true rectilinear motion there. Nor is it the heavens, for here circular, or at least elliptical, motion in all appearance holds sway. Neither of these places seems appropriate to the God who posits the primacy of rectilinear motion. Where then does this God reside? Descartes tells us in his response to More's second letter which raised a question closely akin to this one. It is a response that shows that Descartes's outlook is Platonic in a way which completely escapes his Neoplatonist correspondent:

> It is repugnant to my concept to attribute any limit to the world, and I have no other measure than my perception for what I have to assert or to deny. I say, therefore, that the world is indeterminate or indefinite, because I do not recognize in it any limits. But I dare not call it infinite as I perceive that God is greater than the world, not in respect to His extension, because, as I have already said, I do not acknowledge in God any proper [extension], but in respect to His perfection.[29]

Descartes's point is clear: God exists nowhere in the world. God's rightful realm is nowhere in the earth or the heavens, but in a third realm which grounds both of these as real, a realm which for lack of a better description we can call mathematical.

Here then is Descartes's radicalization of the Platonic project: to render Plato's eternal realm of ideal forms directly and completely equivalent to a purely mathematical space. This third space is the first space according to Descartes, for it this pure space of intelligibility which precedes and engenders the essence and true existence of all material things. Thus, when Descartes chastises More for claiming that all matter is necessarily sensible in nature he is simply trying to initiate him to the true source of matter, its intelligible and quasi-geometrical immateriality. As Descartes quite rightly points out, the only alternatives to his own doctrine are to imprison God in the impure space of the doxic world or exile God in the abstract space of a simple-minded Platonic heaven. Descartes wants no part of More's notion that the material world is the "body" of God.

It is Descartes's notion of God as the infinite creator of an indefinite world which decisively reveals the new form of Platonism which emerges in the his work. The Cartesian God is a hybrid of the Demiurge and the model which inspires him, the all-perfect Living Creature of Pure Intelligibility. Both craftsman and pure intelligible model, Descartes's God is the perfectly self-sufficient being that produces an indefinite world of visibility. The similarity of Descartes's account of the world's creation to that given in the *Timaeus* is still evident in his last major work, *Principles of Philosophy*:

> In order to philosophize correctly about [the general structure of the visible world], two points must be noted to begin with. The first is that we must bear in mind the infinite power and goodness of God, and not be afraid that our imagination may overestimate the vastness, beauty and perfection of his works. On the contrary, we must beware of positing limits here, when we have no certain knowledge of any, on pain of appearing to have an insufficient appreciation of the magnificence of God's creative power.[30]

Goodness, beauty, and truth are all locked deep within the structure of the visible world. The demiurgic power of Descartes's God is only matched by his powers of self-legitimation. Both powers are at play in the true essence of the visible world, though not always presenting themselves clearly to everyday comprehension.

At the same time, Descartes's notion of God outstrips its Platonic precursor, for the God of the former *is* the model for the structure of the visible world, while the image of the God of the latter is of a great craftsman standing before an even greater model. The goodness which inspires the Demiurge gives way to a self-enclosed infinite productive force which determines goodness in the very act of creation. There is no mistaking the deep influence of certain Platonic images on Descartes's vision of God, but Descartes critically distances himself from Platonism by his denial of the emanation of the truth of things out of God: "Because it is certain that [God] is also truly the Author of the essence as well as the existence of all creatures; however, this essence is nothing other than these eternal truths, which I do not conceive as emanating from God like the rays of the sun."[31] Thus, the Cartesian God is not like his creation, but is wholly other. Descartes goes to great pains to make this point, as seen in his attempt to convince More that God is infinite while the world is indefinite. God is everything that Plato and Aristotle had demonstrated him to be, but also much more; he is the great Craftsman and the First Principle of a world, but not of a world to which he belongs. Descartes's God transcends the heavens, both literally and symbolically, because his perfection is one of power and production, not of harmony or finite order.

What is more, Descartes's God does not dwell in the heavens any more than on the earth. God does not dwell anywhere, for everywhere is his creation. He has, in short, no need to be in any given place. On the contrary, it is every given place and thing that has need of God.[32] Further, it is on the basis of God's infinite perfection and "placelessness" that Descartes proclaims the new world. As he shows in his *World*, any world that might be imagined will in the end necessarily be of the same essence and form as the one we inhabit, for all possible worlds arise out of the ideal world structure created and supported by God. Stemming from the perfect and infinite productivity of God, certain relations, proportions, or ratios come into being. Chief among these essential proportions is the bifurcation of *res extensa* and *res cogitans*, with the latter having an existence distinct from, but allied with, the former. God cannot be extended matter (as More maintained), since to be extended means, at least conceivably, to have limits. From the Cartesian perspective, God cannot possess, in fact, is bound not to possess, any limitations, especially of the conceivable variety. Even the universe, which Descartes allows can be virtually infinite (i.e., indefinite) is not essentially infinite like God: "He is a pure mind, an infinite mind, whose very infinity is of a unique and incomparable non-quantitative and non-dimensional kind, of which spatial extension is neither an image nor even a symbol."[33]

Nature in the most general sense is the collective handiwork of the infinite productive power of God. Accordingly, it bears the mark of its creation or production. However, it is not just any creation, for there is a rectitude of creation or production in the Cartesian account. If in the world all things are directly or indirectly the product of the infinite producer, they come into being with a divine imperative of precision and regularity. It is this direct or indirect bequest of rectitude which God gives to the mind that is the source of all truth. All error stems not from this proper source, but from an improper mingling of natures. Just as in the case of motion, where all the qualitative Aristotelian varieties give way to the single locomotive and rectilinear form, what Descartes cannot reconcile with God (i.e., optical illusions, the idea of a void, and so forth) is attributed to this impropriety which arises as a result of the human conjunction of mind and body. Aristotle's God, the pure act which will grant the reconciliation of being and appearance, is replaced by Descartes's God of infinite productivity. If the reconciliation of divine nature and physical nature is a concern for Descartes as it once was for Aristotle, it is a reconciliation of a radically new and appropriative sort: what cannot be rectified is to be denied.

2

The Destruction of the Cosmos in the Homogeneity of Things

Without a doubt, the concept of *ens infinitum* is much older than Descartes. The notion is a fundamental one for virtually all of medieval thought and is an appeal as old as the ancient Greeks. However, the notion takes a significant new turn with Descartes, because through this appeal to an infinite and radically original productivity he stakes a claim to the primacy of a new order. The medieval notion undergoes a transformation in the work of Descartes, a transformation which bears decisively, if not directly, on the roles which natural appearance and perception will play in the emergence of the new science.

This transformation from the God of *to theon* to God as *ens infinitum*, from an inspiring, but essentially ubiquitous, perfection to a perfection which renders all beings contingent and nonessential, except in that they resemble it, stems from a basic perceptual shift. It involves the virtual destruction of an essentially qualitative world order and the intervention of a metaphysical structure which is not bound by the same separations and differentiations as those of the old world.[1] Chief among the old world's demarcations was the distinction between the sublunar and heavenly realms, earth and sky each possessing specific and characteristic forms of motion and existence. What things are and how they can be experienced depends on which realm or place they inhabit. Through their medieval interpretations, Aristotle's physics and metaphysics come to stand as the formalization of this basic way of seeing and understanding the world as an evidently and hierarchically ordered realm. Thus, with the coming of the Renaissance, and then the early modern age, it will be the Aristotelians who play the part of the preservers and the Platonists the questioners of this extremely old perceptual faith and order.

Double Genesis and the Architecture of Divine Persuasion

The advent of the new world involves the emergent collapse of the cosmos. Whereas before, astronomy and physics had dealt with respectively autonomous and essentially different subject matters, now the field of the former becomes more and more the gauge against which the concerns of the latter will be measured. The cosmos gives way to "a universe in which, in contradiction to the traditional conception with its distinction and opposition of the two worlds of Heaven and Earth, all things are on the same level of Being."[2] I would emphasize that all things are on the same level of being, *except* the author of this being, the *ens creans et infinitum*, for it is only with the impetus of something like Descartes's God (the great "leveler") that the ancient distinction between earth and sky could be fully overcome. His God is neither literally nor symbolically an exemplar of heavenly perfection, that is, a being qua *ens finitum* which reveals superlunary perfection. Rather, the Cartesian God represents the demand for the precision which one finds much better approximated by the sky than the earth, because the sky conforms much more closely to the ideal (i.e., the geometrical) than does the quotidian realm.

Descartes's Platonist roots are again evident in this divine demand of precision. It is a demand that originates in the cosmological account of a double genesis found in the *Timaeus*, one genesis describing the works of reason, *nous*, the other the works of necessity, *anagkais*. For Plato, it was necessary to explain the necessity of becoming and the becoming of necessity if one is to account fully for the order of the world. Despite his appeal to the primacy of the forms, Plato goes to great lengths to account for everyday appearance and change. That is, although Reason (the Demiurge inspired by the perfection of the eternal intelligible realm) ultimately persuades the Nurse of Becoming to submit to and engender the visible world, Plato makes it clear that "the creation of this world is the combined work of necessity and mind. Mind, the ruling power, persuaded necessity to bring the greater part of created things to perfection."[3]

This profound notion of a double genesis is not lost on the multiform tradition of Renaissance Platonism, much less on Galileo and Descartes. What is needed is a new science that can fully fathom this world by exploiting its own double nature. In other words, a technique of persuasion must be applied to questions of terrestrial phenomena to render them thoroughly comprehensible, a technique which simulates the persuasion which God used in forming the world. The straightforwardly rhetorical projects of their Renaissance predecessors will give way to a new kind of rhetoric of the moderns, a form that leaves behind the weak and sloppy rules of ordinary grammar for a more powerful syntax.

In Plato's account, God's persuasion takes the form of number and rhythm. The Platonists of the sixteenth and seventeenth centuries grasp this story with a new spirit of seriousness, eschewing the Aristotelian opinion that mathematics has a very limited purview and positing the primacy of the mathematical in the real. The degree of seriousness with which the Platonists took up this project concerning the mathematical essence of nature in opposition to the orthodoxy of the Aristotelians is captured in Galileo's *Dialogue Concerning the Two Chief World Systems*:

> *Extensively*, that is, with regard to the multitude of things to be known, which are infinite, the human understanding is as nothing. . . . But taking [it] *intensively*, I say that the human intellect does understand some [propositions] perfectly, and thus in these it has as much absolute certainty as Nature itself has. Of such are the mathematical sciences alone . . . in which the Divine intellect indeed knows infinitely more propositions since it knows all. But with regard to those few which the human intellect does understand, I believe that its knowledge equals the Divine in objective certainty.[4]

Like the Demiurge's persuasion of the shimmering realm of the previsible, the persuasion of becoming by Reason, Galileo calls for an intensive, mathematical science to grasp the real. The real will be defined intensively, that is, in relation to what can be known propositionally and with certainty. The multiplicity of things, their overly rich appearance, must be harnessed to be understood, particularly if human reason is to approach its quasi-divine potential.

Galileo declares his Platonist commitments very early on in the *Dialogue*. It is a declaration which takes the form of an architectural metaphor, a metaphor aimed directly at the cosmic presuppositions which underlie the physics of Aristotle and his followers: "Moreover, it appears that Aristotle implies that only one circular motion exists in the world, and consequently only one center to which the motions of upward and downward exclusively refer. All of which seems to indicate that he was pulling cards out of his sleeve, and trying to accommodate the architecture to the building instead of modeling the building after the precepts of architecture."[5] The Platonic allusion is unavoidable: the Demiurge built the world according to the architectural precepts of his model, pure intelligibility. Indeed, there is another side to the genesis of the world, that of a materiality and spatiality which are necessary to its essence as a visible world, but one must be clear concerning which genesis takes priority. In other words, one must grasp the direction in which the flow of persuasion moves, from reason to necessity, from the ideal to the material, from the unchanging to the changing, from truth to appearance.

Descartes's appeal to the double genesis of the world follows a similar Platonist line, but he goes even further than Galileo in his call for a new understanding of the world. In Part Two of Descartes's *Discourse* he takes up the same metaphor, that of architecture, and for much the same reason: to show that the construction of the world (and the sciences) must have a single architect if it is to be thoroughly rational in form. The regimen of Cartesian Platonism exceeds that of Galileo in its stridence, for the latter still strove toward the reconciliation of old world with new world, while the former demands the clearing away of the old world entirely to make way for the new.

> Let us not deceive ourselves. It is a true scientific revolution that is announced in the reticent and prudent phrases of the *Discourse*. It is a question, put most simply, of making a blank slate of all that had been up to now, of commencing anew, of reasoning "as if nobody had yet done anything," and of reconstructing or more exactly of constructing, for the first time, and once and for all, the true system of the sciences and the true system of the universe.[6]

The old, haphazardly built town of the tradition, of scholastic science, must be torn down and replaced by a scientifically structured city that does justice to the divine architect who brought into existence and still continues to order the true shape of the world. Standing alone before the blank slate of the new world, Descartes is sure that he will have profoundly luminous access to the principles and structures that ground all sound knowledge of the world.

Thus, a destruction is in order. If one is to begin anew, then what was before must be demolished and erased. Descartes stresses repeatedly that his project is a positive one, that all the apparent skepticism and strident doubt is just a means to an end, part of the preparation necessary for an essentially constructive effort. Galileo's hesitation to appeal to pure mathematics in the face of natural phenomena is, from the Cartesian point of view, unnecessary. Descartes points to this Galilean hesitation to destroy the "digressions" and the "particular effects" as the reasons why Galileo is not able to go further in laying out the "first causes of nature," and thus constructed his science "void of foundation."[7] These Cartesian building blocks, the "first causes," can only be detected by the removal of the doxic debris that covers them up.

Descartes subscribes to the notion of double genesis. He does not doubt that the world has two sides, one certain and one shaky, one true and one doxic. The fact that humans have labored for so long within the world of *doxa* stems from their misunderstanding of the priority of the double genesis; they put the second creation before the first, or, in Galileo's words, they put the building before the laws which made it possible. However, Descartes realizes something that Galileo did not, something that makes Descartes a new kind of Platonist: It is not enough to expose the prejudices which provoke the inverted world of the cosmos, one must venture to provide the metaphysical grounds for sweeping them away. The new science cannot be an essentially skeptical form of knowledge, but it must break down what has gone before, so that the new can be erected.

To establish a new metaphysics, this is the construction project of Descartes. Such an ambitious project has its risks, for in so doing Descartes must tear down not only a world but a tradition as well. In order to fend off criticism, but also in the name of something like intellectual honesty, Descartes tells us that he will keep some of the planks from the old building, the old tradition, incorporating them into the new structure. Put differently, Descartes is conceding an important fact: these new grounds which he has discovered are in fact as old as the world and the tradition. Ultimately, the Cartesian project throws away precious little, for in the end even the doxic debris upon which the everyday mind lives its life is a result of the same persuasion which shaped the world, the persuasion of mind over matter, of spirit over body.

The Simulation of Pure Mind and the New World Order

Central to the Cartesian version of Platonist Creationism is the relation of the two forms of worldly substance, *res cogitans* and *res extensa*. Descartes posits the former as the stuff of mind and the latter as the material stuff which best conforms to the persuasive primacy of pure mind, God. While only God is excused from corporeity and spatialization, *res cogitans*, as the mind to which human experience belongs, does enjoy the possibility of what Descartes terms a sort of "limited" perfection, a perfection which is reminiscent of Galileo's claim that the human mind can enjoy a sort of *intensively* perfect understanding.[8] Descartes would seem to agree with Galileo since he holds that this perfection only manifests itself through an ongoing examination of the extended world, that is, through the discovery of laws and principles which offer hints of God's power.

However, a crucial disagreement exists between Descartes and Galileo concerning the relation of intensive and extensive knowledge, for the

Galilean world is a unitary structure while that envisioned by Descartes is a double, hierarchized form. For Galileo, the dividing line between human knowledge and divine knowledge involves the infinite multiplicity of things in the world. The Cartesian denial of the actual infinitude of the world renders this distinction problematic, even nonsensical. Now extensive knowledge of the world is grounded in intensive knowledge, just as surely as extension is predicated on a logically prior substance, mind. For Descartes, the line between human knowledge and divine knowledge is not so much a barrier as a signpost leading the way to the rightful power of his new science. In other words, the discovery and examination of the material world once removed, that is, the world as extended substance, provides a new means for limited mental substance, the human essence, to discover its own purity.

The Cartesian division between *res cogitans* and *res extensa*, between mental and nonmental substance, stems from a vision of human under-standing as most powerful when it simulates the purity of the infinite intelligible force which gives rise to all substance, mental or otherwise. It is this vision of purity that lies at the heart of Descartes's strident denial of More's attempts to reconcile spirit and matter. Thus, when More challenges the Cartesian notion of extended substance as being so broad and abstract that "it seems, indeed, that God is extended substance," it is precisely to the purity of incorporeality that Descartes appeals in setting him straight:

> And though our mind is neither the measure of things nor of truth, nonetheless it must be the measure of things that we affirm or deny. In effect, nothing is more absurd or more thoughtless than the desire to pass judgement on things which, by our own admission, we will never be able to perceive.
>
> . . . you imagine beyond this . . . a certain divine extension, which would stretch farther than the extension of bodies, because this is to suppose that God has *partes extra partes*, that He is divisible, and, that the very essence of bodies entirely befits Him.[9]

Descartes proceeds to reassert that God is positively and intensively infi-nite and therefore necessarily incorporeal. His desire to distance himself from the sort of pantheistic tendency inherent in More's letters arises from Descartes's conviction that the radical purity of mind is the key to pushing the power of the human faculty of judgment to its essential but still distant limits.

Descartes's vision of science stands or falls with the primacy of mind and the correlative concept of extended substance. Thus, More's refusal to accept the Cartesian claim that the omnipresence of God's power does not require the omnipresence of God is more than a theological difference of opinion. For Descartes, God is not limited by some sort of requirement of extended presence in the world simply because he can act on any given thing at any given moment. In his last letter to More, Descartes makes the point as bluntly as possible: "I have said that God is extended in power because this power is visible or can be rendered visible in the extended thing; and it is certain that the essence of God must be present everywhere in order that his power could be revealed in things. However, I declare that this is not true in the same manner as are extended things."[10] The essence of God is everywhere but the body of God is nowhere, because God has no body, no extension, no motion. God's essence must be incorporeal in order for his power to be visible everywhere at once. For Descartes, God is the one exception to the law of pure mechanism which otherwise rules the universe, the one exception that makes this total law possible.

More is not convinced by Descartes's argument, essentially because he conceives of Cartesian *res extensa* as matter, a substance akin to the Lucretian tactile substance, and *res cogitans* as spirit, that is, as the divine substance which penetrates matter. Thus, More's God creates the world in order to exist, to live, within it. He even goes so far as to resurrect the images of heavenly bodies as intelligible beings in his effort to describe his notion of God: "And for the *Adoration* some them doe to the *Sun* and *Moon,* I cannot believe they doe it to them under the notion of mere *Inanimate Bodies,* but they take them to be the habitation of some *Intellectual Beings,* as the verse does plainly intimate to us, *Helios Theos pant' ephora kai pant' epakouei. The Sun that hears and sees all things*: and this is very near to the Notion of a God."[11] Unlike Descartes, More sees no need for a harsh and strict division between mind (or better, spirit) and matter. Certainly, the former substance is more advanced than the latter, but their kinship is guaranteed by the existence of God within both spheres. Like the sun and moon, we can see God with our eyes almost as well as we can with our minds.

Again, it is not simply the fact that More suggests a world schema in which ghosts might be as real as optical laws that distresses Descartes. More importantly, the Cartesian quest for a physical realm based on certainty is severely threatened by More's notion of the commonality of spirit and matter in God, a notion that Descartes must have seen as a throwback to the mystical line of ancient Platonism. Descartes's vision of the extended world as a vast order of purely mechanistic effects is grounded firmly in the primacy of mind, a primacy which stems from the radical alterity of mind and matter. Pure mind gives rise to the pure order of extended substance; a mind which exists within the world, something like More's spirit, would be infected by the nature of the material. Only a mind beyond all the things of the world can guarantee the new world order posited by Descartes. Any other conception of God, and especially one such as More's, limits the creative and conservative power of God and thus denies the possibility of a truly rational material order.

Descartes's growing antagonism to cosmic queries is one of the reasons for his rebuff of More's conception of God. He recognizes behind the issues raised by More the specter of the old world and its God. This old world is characterized by the familial mingling of spirit and matter and the attendant richness and confusions of these realms. The new world is a realm of strict and principled structures, one in which confusion and fuzziness is a function of misperception or misunderstanding rather than natural tendencies. In the new world pure mind is more than a fable, it is the creator and monitor of all that is real and true. Thus, Descartes's quest for a God of pure mind is a search for a new God upon which to ground his new world.

Descartes points out that the manifestations of God's power, which provide indirect evidence of God's perfection, can be fathomed consistently only by way of a methodical analysis such as his own. This Cartesian method has its hallmark in the proper regulation of things through the ideas the human mind clearly, that is, most purely, perceives. Descartes appeals again and again to the priority of ideas, to the unshakable clarity and purity of certain ideas in contrast to the always untrustworthy nature of what is seen with the eyes. The mind must regulate the senses in order to facilitate an escape from the fuzzy travail of appearance. In this manner, *res cogitans* stands as intermediary between God and extended matter, enjoying neither the sovereign force at God's disposal nor the abject quietude of the objects of *res extensa*. Mental substance resides in the rather precarious place, for it requires the continued support, the benevolent dispensation, of the divine light as well as the relative obedience of the objects of its scientific preoccupations. In its quest for certainty, the Cartesian mind is bound from above and from below.

The Cartesian triangle of God, finite mind, and extended stuff is scalene, the relations between the three sides exist as three separate ratios. God's relation to nature is one of producer to produced, while God's relation to finite mind is one of creation in the sense of parent and child. However, what of the relation of finite mind and nature? Following the other two ratios, this third relation represents the interaction of the two forms of creation, one production and the other generation. Human mind enjoys a relationship with extended substance that is reminiscent of that between God and nature. In short, finite mind, the condensed analogue of infinite spirit, finds its essential and legitimate power in the recognition of the condensed essence of nature qua *res extensa*. The Cartesian project represents a persuasion of nature by the human mind that is analogous to that established and maintained by God.

The Cartesian project has a second goal intimately involved with this persuasive identification of "true nature" and extended substance: the persuasive conflation of finite spirit and mental substance. They are in fact the one and the same effort, for without the reinterpretation of spirit, a new definition of its powers, rights, and obligations, nature would remain a rich but unmeasurable world unto itself. Further, only by the limitation and recasting of nature as extended stuff can finite mind now find its essence as the measuring force which can both ascertain the fundamental principles of nature *and* manipulate these principles to its further advantage. Descartes utilizes this binding of finite mind from above and below to free it for new degrees of apprehension and power. What had ben a restriction of the human mind is converted in such a way that the human mind enjoys a binding power all its own.

In Descartes's vision, cosmic order or harmony as the paradigmatic form gives way to a material regime productively engendered and imposed by God. The essence of this structure cannot be denied, according to Descartes, though it can be obscured by improper thinking, a thinking which depends too much on the vagaries of natural appearance and everyday sense experience. But the nature or essence of extended substance lies awaiting its release by thought, a release clearly foreseen from the beginning by God. Indeed, the extended universe encourages that mind which endeavors to ferret out the clarity and distinctness of ideas. However, the project committed to rendering this discovering power of clarity consistently efficient requires an unrelenting faith in the necessary rewriting of the fundamental structures of nature, truth, and existence.

What was a harmonious order for Aristotle, an order exemplified most profoundly by the well-rounded motion of the heavens, is now a universe well versed in its obedience to the will of its all-perfect, because all-powerful, conceiver and preserver. It is no longer a question of a world which inspires the virtue of aspiring to perfection, but rather of a universe which requires, as the undeniably immense evidence of divine power, an increasing mental precision, above all taking the form of thought as the regulation of natural appearance. "Nature will no longer have any secrets for us. It will not offer any resistance nor will we experience any strangeness in it."[12] Thoroughly stripped of its strangeness, nature ceases to be cosmic; it is no longer the companion of spirit in its quest for understanding. The new nature, the nature of *res extensa*, will be the indefinite mechanical relic of an infinite and therefore necessarily pure coherent production. Strangeness is eradicated by the total comprehensibility of the principles that made this natural relic true and real. The myth of the cosmos is dismissed once and for all by the discovery of extension that had resided alongside of it since Plato.

The development of the fundamental human ability to simulate pure mind and this methodical examination of the quasi-material world of extension and motion (that is also a total transformation of the very same realm) are inextricably caught up with one another. They are in fact two aspects of the very same project: the quest to show the technical homogeneity of all natural entities. Within the play of this project, all research ultimately assumes that what one will discover as the guiding principle of the new world is the common primacy of idea and power. The realization of this common primacy is itself a chief ambition of the Cartesian project. A new realm of truth will appear out of this ambition, a realm that for lack of a better term might be called "technical truth." With its appearance, certain traditional issues and questions will pass away along with the cosmos they once inhabited.

Technical Vision and the Homogenization of Things

Descartes "succeeds" in proving the existence of material things in the Sixth Meditation by an application of the essential precision and regulation of mind to the material realm. It is not an easy existence to prove, since matter has been reduced to the play of two essential aspects, motion and extension; the existence, the *quiditas* of a thing, thus becomes exceedingly difficult to ascertain. In other words, and this is the sort of question that More and others repeatedly put to Descartes, what is it that exists as a material thing in the Cartesian account? Matter as some hard and durable stuff is susceptible to an infinite reduction or miniaturization (at least by the mind), according to Descartes, and we must therefore look elsewhere for the essential existence of nonmental substance. Further, such a proof is not necessary in Descartes's examination of the faculties of pure thinking, but only when he comes to the confused faculties of imagination and, in particular, sense perception, faculties which are confused precisely because they sense something *like* durable material bodies:

> Further, I encounter in myself a certain passive faculty of sensing, that is, of receiving and understanding the ideas of sensible things. But it would be useless to me, I would not be able to aid myself with it in any fashion, if there were not also in me, or in others, another, active faculty,

capable of forming and producing these ideas. However, insofar as I am only a thinking thing this active faculty could not be in me, since it hardly requires my thought, these ideas often being represented to me without any contribution on my part and even sometimes against my will. Therefore, a substance must necessarily exist which is different from me. . . . And this substance is either a body, that is, a corporeal nature . . . or actually God himself, or some other creature more noble than the body, in which the objective reality of these ideas is eminently contained.[13]

As Descartes goes on to point out, since God has not given us a clear and distinct idea of his immediate involvement in sense perception (or that of a third agent like an angel), it must be concluded that bodies do have a provisional reality. However, their reality is always only provisional or doxic, since Descartes's relentless drive toward scientific precision forces him to call into question everything which seems to challenge God's thoroughly consistent power, goodwill, and truthfulness.[14]

Extended things, bodies, are purely mechanical beings. They truly exist only to the extent that they fulfill the strict requirements of this mechanistic law. Descartes has no problem demonstrating the essence of extended things (Meditation V), because it is in this essential existence that they clearly obey the strictures of mechanical life. The whole of Meditation VI involves Descartes's attempt to show that the line dividing the truth of extension from its error is precisely the end of mechanistic fact and the onset of qualitative fiction, a line which can be drawn properly or improperly by the mind. Bodies are the automata that Descartes is so fond of using as an "image" to illustrate their essence, little machines which emulate the great machinery of universal production. It is only a story, Descartes tells us, but one that is extremely useful. It is so useful a story that it virtually dominates Descartes's thought from the time of *The World* to that of *Principles*:

I do not detect any difference between machines made by technicians and the many bodies of nature, except that effects of machines . . . are always so great that their figures and movements can be seen, while the shafts and springs which cause the effects of natural bodies are ordinarily too small to be perceived by our senses. Further, it is certain that all the rules of mechanics belong to physics, and in this way, all artificial things are natural. Thus, for example, it is no less natural for a clock to mark the hours by means of the wheels of which it is constructed than it is for a tree to produce fruit.[15]

The difference between the technical device and the natural entity lies principally in the size of the parts which make them up. Or rather, since Descartes warns against the dangers of a too extreme view of matter as *partes extra partes*, the principles involved in the human-made machine and those contrived by divine nature are essentially the same, though they may be different in scope and capacity.

Thus, Descartes's criticism of More's notion of the essential sensibility of all matter stems not from some simple intellectualist bias in favor of mind, but rather because Descartes understands that if one is to assert all matter was produced by God (as both he and More wish to do), then one must grasp the necessity of a thoroughgoing mechanism of Nature. That is, the production of the world by God instills an order into all its forms, including the corporeal, an order which flies in the face of the ordinary understanding of material existence, since this understanding mistakes the effect for the cause in its assumption that matter is real and geometrical and mechanical structures abstract or artificial. The real is the artificial for Descartes, or at least those things made by human hands and minds resemble in an essential way the things made by God, an essential similarity which is often occluded by the qualitative appearance of things. As Nicolas Grimaldi describes the Cartesian attitude, "things can be *produced* completely different than they appear to the naïveté of our perception, in such a way that they all conspire to cause *reality to appear as the dissimulation of an artifice.*"[16]

Natural appearance is far from being an adequate ground for Cartesian science: it does not inspire Descartes as it did Aristotle, but is rather the most dangerous source of error. And yet, the Cartesian characterization of corporeal appearance as extended matter is at one and the same time the new solution and the new problem. As *res extensa*, things should not appear except in their essential precision. The fact that they normally exceed this imperative is proof for Descartes that their appearance must be regulated: what does not fit within the measure of this precision is relegated to the realm of unicorns, mirages, and the like. The natural models for this necessary and essential exercise of precision is offered by Descartes without qualm or hesitation: "all things, generally speaking, which are understood as the objects of analytic geometry."[17] Only rectified appearance, the essence of things which can be addressed as at least quasi-mathematical, will be granted admission to the permanent structure which Descartes sees as the proper abode of human thought.

Descartes appeals to God's perfection to dispel the dangers of the all too common errors of perception and appearance. He seeks that form of human thought which most closely resembles divine understanding.

He finds such a steady and determined form of mind in the precision and clarity of a vision shaped by geometrical understanding. In this geometrical vision he finds protection from the virtual convictions which appearance and perception tend to force upon the otherwise unguarded mind. This protection against *doxa* is afforded by a disciplined method of thinking certified by the similitude of such thinking to the necessary order of the extended world imposed by God.

It is precisely this certification of the similitude of the respective orders of his geometrical vision and the material regime with which Descartes struggles in attempting to bring the *Meditations* to an effective close. The primacy of mind was fairly easy to maintain as long as one was only dealing with the realm of ideas, but once it is a question of conclusively demonstrating the necessary and essential resemblance of the material order to this mental realm, difficulties begin to mount. Further, simply denying the reality of the phenomenal aspect of this order is counterproductive, since Descartes is trying to lay out the methodology for a universal science which is as concerned with increasing human power as well as understanding. In short, Descartes's program is techno-logical, because it seeks to penetrate the secrets of the material realm in order to manipulate them.

As Grimaldi points out, Descartes is making use of an "image of an image" in this comparison of technical and nature entities.[18] That is, Descartes explains the essence and existence of the natural entity (the one produced more or less directly by God) by an appeal to the machine (an item produced by a being who is itself produced directly by God). The central role of this "epistemological inversion" helps explain why Descartes has such a problem demonstrating the existence of material things: the difficulty is not so much that material things are doxically rich as it is that a certain image of them is already at play long before Descartes reaches the sixth and final Meditation. What is more, the Cartesian aversion to *doxa* stems in large part from the already operant play of the technical realm pushed to a new transcendental extreme.

The analogies discussed in terms of God's double productivity in the previous section come together in this subtle appeal to a transcendental mechanism. The new scientific vision depends upon the intrinsic correla-tion between these theological and technical analogies, and the Cartesian project can maintain itself only through the steadfast assumption that the productive nature of his active scientific method mirrors the productive nature that had already set the natural realm before it. Grimaldi sums up the intimate dance performed by these crucial analogies in terms of the double front of the method of thought and technical reality: "As logic institutes a technique for thought, technique then institutes a logic for the real . . . *it is only a question of logic guaranteeing the certitude of science to the extent that it is a question of science guaranteeing the efficiency of technique. Because this is the raison d'être and the purpose of science."*[19] The ratio of divine mind to human mind and the ratio of divine mind to nature imply a third ratio, that of human mind to nature. To decode the third ratio, it is first necessary at least provisionally to grasp the essence of the other two ratios. Then, having accomplished these provisional discoveries, one can institute the means whereby the true and right third ratio is itself discovered.

Of course, the third ratio, that of human mind and nature, had always already been at play. This is the point, the conspiratorial point, of Grimaldi's claim about the "image of an image." The discovery of the true legitimacy of this third ratio is self-confirming, insofar as its "precedents" are themselves influenced by its own doxic version. In other words, the vindication of Descartes's active science is its practicality, and yet this practicality is always already at play, even when Descartes claims to be concerned solely with the relation of God to finite mind or God to nature. The doxic ratio of human mind to nature is the corrupt, and thus eradicable, ancestor of the technological vision that represents the fulfillment, the "proof," of Cartesian science. Everyday and age-old technical life is, or at least should be, superseded by technological vision: the slavish relationship between the human hand and matter gives way to a new human power, one which has at its disposal the underlying principles and structures of nature that it has had a powerful hand in making manifest.

This supersession is an unspoken motif in the recasting of mind as *res cogitans* and nature as *res extensa*, for by summoning a notion of God as pure mind that calls into being the indefinite realm of nature, a new form of vision that is at once controlling and exploratory is also summoned. The technological vision of Descartes is a response to the question of how the new world will differ from the old one, the answer being that the former will only arise through a science of discovery that is also a science of creation. Technology, as a chief impulse of modern science, makes its all too quiet appearance with this Cartesian double science. Jean-Luc Marion's concept of Cartesian "gray ontology" speaks to this doubly active science insofar as it suggests the mixed and suspicious nature of the project: "Gray ontology, because it does not declare itself, concealing itself within an epistemological discourse. But especially, because it bears on the thing in such a manner that it empowers itself to diverge from its irreducible *ousia* in order to take aim at an object, one submitted entirely to the exigencies of knowledge."[20] If presented nakedly, this sort of obscuring replacement of ontological categories by epistemological principles would lack credibility. Descartes's "gray ontology" operates according to less than directly presented principles and motives; it is driven by the Cartesian need for a new concept of power and knowledge, or, in short, a knowledge of power. It points to the ambitious modern principle that states that science is only science if it also empowers those who wield it.[21]

The modern concept of technology arises with this "grayness" of which Marion writes, announcing itself not as a means to power but rather as a new form of knowledge. Modern technology does in fact involve both a new technique of power and knowledge, but more than this it is the principle of creation cloaked as a form of discovery that drives both these techniques. All the new discoveries of modern science depend upon its power to cast forth "before the fact" the principles which it seeks, but always in such a way that what is found becomes a true object for its research. In other words, the doxic forms (e.g., secondary qualities, sense experience, etc.) which Descartes spends so much time pushing to the edges of the new world are being brought back into play at every moment in new shapes. The old world becomes the new world, and this transformative movement is not denied but simply never spoken. What we have yet to examine are some of the chief examples of this unspoken but essential shift from the exhausted cosmos to the new world of unforeseeable power and expanding vision.

3

The Measure of Space and the Rectification of Natural Appearance

escartes's description of the basic structure of his proper metaphysical dwelling in the *Discourse* involves a sort of provisional resting
place comprised of three or four moral tenets. Interestingly, it is
only within this temporary metaphysical lodging that Descartes expressly
grants natural appearance (*doxa*) anything more than a secondary status.
Indeed, it is the prescription of a certain mood in the face of natural
appearance that Descartes calls for in each of these tenets: moderation
with regard to opinion and the "inconstancy of the world," resoluteness
of decision in the face of the everyday, self-mastery before mastery of
nature, and faith in his method and vocation. In each of these codes the
basic mood is the same: a firmness of mind in the face of a wavering
reality. Descartes tells us that it is the mixed nature of human life, as
much if not more than the wavering aspects of nature, that require the
exercise of a radically constant doubt. Thus, natural appearance must be
met and secured by nonnatural apprehension, the doxic realm must be
challenged by the nondoxic force of thought. Only after having set forth
this provisional *ethos* with regard to appearance or opinion, that is, the
certainty of the mind before the uncertainty of everyday knowledge and
perception, does Descartes then feel prepared to blaze a path beyond
provisionalness and uncertainty, beyond the wavering aspects of nature
and doxic experience.[1]

A veritable conversion is necessary to accomplish this break with
natural appearance. Zeno Vendler has suggested the striking similarities between the Ignatian and Cartesian disciplines, claiming that the
Meditations is a special workbook, less concerned with developing a new
science than recommending a path for the conversion of mental spirit.[2]

Vendler claims that this project of conversion preoccupies Descartes from the time of his dreams in the German winter of 1619 through (at least) the writing of the *Meditations*. In making this claim, Vendler helps us to understand the massive scope of the Cartesian quest to ground the new science. Cartesian science is a project of conversion, not only of mind but of nature as well. That is, despite the significant debt he may have owed to St. Ignatius's spiritual and moral project, Descartes's own project of conversion is inextricably bound up with, even embodied in, his ambitious project to establish a new measure of experience and natural appearance, in short, a new science.

Indeed, like the project of Ignatius, Descartes's project is essentially a spiritual and moral one. And yet, at the same time, the Cartesian project also involves a conversion of what is meant by the terms "spiritual" and "moral." The Cartesian revision of the meaning of these terms bears directly on the rightful power of the new science, not only because these two terms undergo a radical revision, but also because they are bound together in a new manner. These two terms become virtually one, subsumed under the legitimating imperative of the new measure that drives the Cartesian project. What one should see is what one will see once the proper method is in force. The constant, though sometimes silent, moral edge to Descartes's radical epistemological project betrays its fiercely ontological ambitions. Where Ignatius urged a conversion of the "inner man" through spiritual exercise, Descartes calls for a *total conversion*, of spirit as mind, of nature as extended stuff, of truth as power.

One can see this project of total conversion at work quite clearly in the *Discourse*, as well as in the *Meditations*. Seen in this way, Descartes's provisional manufacture of a temporary shelter against appearance out of the very fabric of appearance reveals just how fundamental this movement of conversion is to his new science. Confronted by nature as an obscure or fuzzy form, Descartes seeks to show its illegitimacy, and the truth, utility, and goodness of a rectitudinal world. Sitting in his hut in the dead of the German winter, Descartes is insulated from the war and the cold, but also from the many distractions caused by the company of other people and things. The hut is his laboratory for the development of a method to cast aside all untested appearance, that is, all those things which cannot stand the acid test of radical doubt. His method of doubting is constructive, not skeptical, he tells us, and by it he intends to secure the unassailable foundations for a new science, a science unperturbed by the problems of error and illusion. The essential measure of doubt represents the moral conversion at which Descartes's science works. Grounded in the purity of a thought and insight which stems from the ever-present and all-powerful force which preserves the world, this science will be "appearance-proof."

Forming the quiet but crucial backdrop for Descartes's struggle with the questions of the rectitude of physical space and motion is another struggle, that involved in the enunciation of the measure which grounds science as the universal field of truth, a truth which is by nature at once moral and natural, spiritual and physical. Without this new and total measure of truth the new science remains trapped on the traditional grounds of doxic experience. Only with the completion of such a measure can both mind and matter be freed from these ancient grounds of error and exception.

True Doubt and the Quest for the Purity of Space and Motion

Descartes's metaphysical and scientific project has not simply a constructive, but also an essentially destructive, aspect. He affirms the new world, the quasi-mathematical world, by denying the primacy of the variegated world, the world of opinion and appearance. Descartes proclaims that he first encountered this fundamental truth at the same time that he discovered the legitimate purpose of doubt, during that fateful stay in the German hut. The fulfillment of his initial dreams of a "marvelous science" in 1619 depend on his ability to develop a program that will weave together the principles of pure doubt and pure materiality. He must institute a new method which will at once question the nature of matter and examine the matter of doubt. In short, both the purest form of mind and the purest form of material reality must be identified and then thoroughly interrogated, if this new science is to take hold.

Descartes tells us that radical doubt is the beginning of his new positive science, for by calling everything into question he finds those things which are most real. Doubt is only pure doubt when it finds an overwhelmingly positive entity or force which causes it to recoil and ultimately cease to be doubt. Proper doubt, then, is a propadeutic for science, because it serves to shunt aside untested objects and untested doubt; it clears the way of all wavering things, material and intellectual. Thus, the Cartesian science seeks a new positivity of matter and mind, even when it engages in the most destructive exercises of doubt.

Descartes's methodology of doubt calls into question the fundamental nature of material objects by showing how the common experience of them clashes with what is most certain and least doubtable about them, their mathematical essence. Only as *res extensa*, only as pure motion and extension, do material things withstand doubt and thus exist in the Cartesian sense. Cartesian doubt is not so much destructive as purgative. Thus, Descartes's methodology of doubt sets the stage for his project to uncover the mathematical essence of nature, both sharing in the principle of denying the reality of the merely qualitative and apparent by appealing to the purity of forms. The purgation of material reality must be accompanied by a reordering of the mental realm as well, for only by this appeal to the natural resonance of material and mental space can Descartes claim that his science will attain universal application and validity.[3]

At the heart of the Cartesian effort to establish a truly positive science lies the attempt to show the absolute purity of space. In its purity, space cannot be simply physical, since all physical entities are problematic amalgams of idea and extension. The effort to ascertain the purity of space beyond such mixed forms is a task assigned to methodical doubt, which goes about this purification process by eliminating all entities and forms that cannot withstand the test of its simplifying interrogation. For Descartes, then, pure space is comprised of those natural element(s) that can withstand the unwavering examination of pure doubt. Pure space will resemble pure mind in its unwavering nature, the two arising within the same explorative foray of doubt.

This familial purity of space and mind is uncoverable through Descartes's methodical doubt precisely because without the operant nature of this double purity doubt would be no more than a skeptical and destructive force. The purity of space and the purity of mind are the double ontological guarantees that make doubt the basic epistemological mechanism for the production of a wholly positive, and therefore productive, universal science. Ironically, the purity of doubt will find its final proof in this science, a science that will render doubt itself consistently dubious. The nonnegative, nondestructive, purity of doubt is the propadeutic for a project which will reveal and exploit the productive double purity of space.[4]

Newton's criticism of Cartesian space as the supposedly pure but not empty receptacle for extended things is well known. He wants nothing to do with the convoluted rationalism in which Descartes gets himself caught in an apparent effort to defend the old rule concerning the nonsensical nature of empty space.[5] Without question Descartes does make mention of this old philosophical principle, but the stakes are much higher for Descartes than simply defending a traditional notion. Empty space not only offends traditional physical concepts, it also severs the genetic intimacy of mind and space, or more accurately, *res cogitans* and *res extensa*. Thus, empty space threatens the success of the Cartesian scientific project because it omits the familial link between mind and space that serves as the gauge by which one can freely and rightfully treat physical entities as operating according to essentially mathematical principles. Without this positive link between the space of mind and the space of matter, doubt becomes something other than a means to a productive end: it threatens to become a destructive tendency that would undercut all scientific endeavor.

Pure space is the necessary companion of pure mind, and without both of them Descartes's quest for a science that can rightly claim to have universal explanatory power over physical nature remains stuck in the quandary announced by Galileo. This quandary testifies to the many problems bound up in the early modern search for a new measure for science. Whatever explicit form these troubling problems take, whether in the work of Galileo, Descartes, or Newton, they all turn on the question of what role *doxa* should or should not play in the new science. It falls to Descartes, the central member of this trio, to move beyond Galileo's "physical crisis" in establishing the proper territory for the new science, and consequently, also establishing the measure most appropriate to this new field of operations and truth. A brief look at Galileo's approach to the status of space and motion serves to better show the radical move undertaken by Descartes in staking claim to a new "scientific morality."

On the one hand, Galileo was convinced that mathematics was indeed the language in which nature articulated itself. On the other hand, he was hard-pressed to demonstrate this geometrical articulation in actual experimental studies and therefore found himself in a quandary concerning how to express the nature of a moving body in thoroughly mathematical terms. In other words, Galileo found it exceedingly difficult to reconcile what he took to be two equally central scientific concerns, a recognition of the geometrical nature of the world and a commitment to the phenomena under observation. The fact that he was able to at least provisionally reconcile these antagonistic concerns stems from what Feyerabend calls Galileo's "ad hoc procedure."[6]

Galileo exemplifies quite poignantly the difficulty involved in speaking of, or acting upon, the "phenomena under observation"; it is not enough to see with some pristine Euclidean vision. In his hesitation, one finds an implicit recognition that there are no pure phenomena, just as there are no pure theories nor pure space.[7] Galileo tolerates the difference between everyday experience and mathematical scientific experience, because he believes the two can and should coexist, just as he believes that Platonic and Aristotelian scientific convictions are not mutually destructive. It is a position of tolerance he assumes time and again, especially when struggling to account for the difference between ideal (i.e., rectilinear) motion and apparent motion. One even finds that Galileo's Platonist character in the *Dialogue*, Salviati, understands the reasons for Aristotle's denial of the primacy or "naturalness" of rectilinear motion in the world:

> Rectilinear movement is something which in truth cannot be found in the World. There cannot be any *natural* rectilinear motion. In effect, rectilinear movement is infinite by its nature and since the straight line is infinite and indeterminate, it is impossible that any movement whatsoever possessed, by nature, the principle of moving in a straight line, that is, towards a place it can never reach, since there is no end in infinity. And nature, as Aristotle himself said, never attempts to accomplish that which could not be done nor to endeavor to move towards that which is impossible to reach.[8]

Salviati does go so far as to follow Plato in suggesting that God may have begun by setting the heavens in rectilinear motion until they reached sufficient velocity and then converted this into pure radial motion, and, thus, maintains the possibility of a temporal primacy of rectilinear motion. However, Salviati also goes to great lengths to preserve the Aristotelian edict concerning the "perfect order of the world," an order which demands that all things have a proper, determinate, and qualitatively structured place toward which they tend.[9] Thus, the primacy of rectilinear motion is itself indebted to yet another primacy, one which is largely, if not essentially, compatible with the appearance of things.

Thus, Galileo, through his Platonist spokesman, softens the tension between natural appearance and pure mathematical space by this "partial primacy of rectilinear motion." In Koyré's terms, Galileo "did not know, or was not able to fully develop or accept, the inevitable consequences of the mathematicization of the real: the complete geometrization of space, which means the infinity of the Universe and the destruction of the Cosmos."[10] In other words, Galileo walked the fine line between everyday perception and appearance and a more certain form, mathematical vision, without making a decision that conclusively favored one over the other. He tolerated the tension between them by maintaining the viability of two levels of existence, one real and the other ideal and geometrical.

Descartes is not as sensitive to, or as tolerant of, the issue of natural appearance as Galileo, and through this insensitivity he stakes claim to the new territory of modern science. He may begin by struggling with Galileo's problems, but, having convinced himself that he is indeed ready to establish his metaphysical and scientific abode, the struggle is soon resolved. The Cartesian solution is simple and to the point. Descartes locates the source of Galileo's tribulations concerning the mathematical description of a body in motion precisely in the fact that Galileo seeks to describe moving *bodies*. Galileo spent much time attempting to experimentally support his mathematical convictions, with his work on the acceleration of balls on an inclined surface serving as a notable example. Failing to succeed fully in this attempt, Galileo hesitates to draw the same sort of ambitious conclusions that Descartes will soon present.

Descartes's solution, stemming from his account of God and the proper rectification of appearance, is to describe motion divorced entirely from the secondary peculiarities of any given body. In this way, the question of motion is detached from the question of appearance, as well as from the question of time; the essence of Cartesian motion lies in a spatiality which is instantaneously and analytically geometrical. Bodies in their essence are participants in this special form of spatiality, but as such they are essentially atemporal. Descartes does not accept the "authority of the real," but rather authorizes the reality of things based upon the prescriptive power of his God of infinite productivity. In this sense, the world *must* be infinite for Descartes. It is the edict of *ens infinitum* onto the world as a whole, an edict so powerful that it even turns back upon the very source of the rectification:

> Galileo wondered: what are in fact the processes of nature? Descartes asks: how *must* it be constituted and how *must* it act? Galileo, physicist, as much, if not more than, geometer, remained with the fact; he bowed to the real. Descartes, mathematician above all else, refuses to recognize the fact. As Galileo tells us that it is not his concern to know *if* God might have been able to create an infinite world; it is enough to know that he did not *in fact* make it so. Descartes, on the contrary, explains to us that God *could not* have not made it infinite, simply because finite space is an absurdity.[11]

In short, Koyré would say that it *is* Descartes's concern to know if and what God could create, because the Cartesian scientific project is predicated on the coherent power of the "creative ought." The binding together of pure mind and pure matter (i.e., extension and motion) springs from this immense moral power, this claim of the new science's divinely and naturally sanctioned territorial rights.

Doubt stands as the chief constructive force of the Cartesian project; its action of stripping away doxic mind and doxic matter only appears destructive. Descartes's commitment to the practice of methodical doubt stems from his faith that the emergence of pure doubt will in fact be the immediate anticipation of the double appearance of pure mind and pure space. This faith is grounded in his vision of the active moral power of

Pure Mind to create its resonant offspring in the world. Pure doubt can be understood as yet another embodiment of this active power of Pure Mind, one closely akin to pure motion and pure space. Indeed, pure doubt is not doubt at all, any more than pure materiality is composed of atoms and empty space. The harnessing of doubt announces the possibility of a science firmly grounded in the true state of substance. The realization of doubt's essentially affirmative core represents the positive form which will guarantee the power and legitimacy of the new Cartesian science.

The metaphysical dwelling place of Descartes's new science had to be built from the ground up. The materials from the destruction of the traditional scientific structure may be of use, but they must be cleansed. This metaphor is used with deadly seriousness by Descartes. Space—as both the physical and metaphysical dwelling place—must be swept clean. It must be, at least in its essence, sterilized of what does not properly belong in it. The well-rounded place of appearance must give way to the rectified space of clear and distinct motion. The Aristotelian notion of categories was always couched in terms of a cosmological schema, and Galilean physics conceded that one could at best find approximations of geometrical precision in the study of falling bodies. However, in the Cartesian structure the "mathesical" impulse defines both the category and the world in which things appear.[12] The basic mathematical project of modern science, which in turn gives rise to mathematical physics in the narrower sense, erupts with the Cartesian inspiration regarding the premier status of motion, not moving bodies.

The way is prepared for this new status of motion by the realignment and redefinition of mind and matter. Only once the intimate resonating structures of pure mind and pure matter have been secured can the new science go about the business of dealing with more straightforward scientific issues such as pure motion. In short, the new space must be given its spiritual and physical texture before the new science can actually begin to enjoy its promised advances. This is the lesson which Descartes believes Galileo had not learned and Aristotle could not possibly understand.

Descartes's sterilization of space is mathematical first and foremost, because it operates on the basis of the imperative of a proper proportion between what one sees and what one should see. His appeal to the infinite power and perfection of God in the face of an indefinite extended world, of a universe which holds so much promise for certain truth at the same time that it threatens to undermine this promise with its images and illusions, is a direct reflection of his vision of the necessity of a proper space, a space which is at once intellectual and physical. To get a better sense of the importance of this productively ambiguous space, a closer examination of Descartes's new concept of motion is crucial. For in the genetic development of this new motion one finds the direct and simultaneous mingling of mind and body in both their pure and doxic forms.

The Technical Truth of Rightful Motion and Mind

All facets of Cartesian science depend on the primacy of the new space which acts as both their point of origin and their stage of operations. All forms of Cartesian truth emerge in the midst of this proper space, because Descartes makes it clear that in its purest form this strange space is the backdrop for the presentation of divinely authorized action, that is, motion in its essential form. Only against the backdrop of this most proper space do extended things forthrightly concede the priority of what Descartes half-jokingly, half-seriously refers to as "right motion," *mouvements droits*, rectilinear motion:

> According to this Rule [of right motion], we have to say that God alone is the Author of all motions that there are in the world in so far as they are, and in as far as they are right; but that it is the diverse dispositions of matter that makes them irregular and curved, just as the Theologians teach us that God is also the Author of all our actions insofar as they are, and insofar as they have any goodness, but that it is the diverse dispositions of our will that may render them vicious.[13]

Indeed, what Descartes is claiming in so many words, that all motions and all actions in the world are initiated according to the rightfulness of divine intent, sounds like a position the venerable theologians of *La Flèche* might have espoused. The physical and spiritual realms (or in more Cartesian terms, the extensive and the cogitative realms) are siblings; they share a common source of rightfulness and a common source of deprivation.

In Descartes's rewriting of this older theological position, motion and human motion (action) suffer from the same fundamental tendency toward aberration. In this revision, Descartes borrows the notion of the privation or the perversion of the inner will and applies it to all truth, external as well as internal. Further, like his medieval forebears, the stakes of this quest for the true nature of matter and motion are very high indeed; the apprehension of the proper space in which all forms of truth emerge is not simply a concern for Descartes the physicist, but also for Descartes the metaphysician and ethicist. His principle of "right motion" seeks to show that the perversion of motion directly mirrors the perversion of intention, because both stem from a privation of essentially rectilinear or rectitudinal forms. Truth is only secured (and for Descartes the only authentic truth is secured truth) when this privative analogy of matter and mind is brought fully to light and then rectified.

Descartes's conviction concerning the universal adequacy of quasi-mathematical truth stems from his recognition that the world can be understood most completely by the human mind in terms of a technical precision. The commitment to technical precision which characterizes Descartes's hyperplatonism is not an arbitrary product of epistemology, but rather indicates an epistemological mutation which springs from far-reaching changes in how the world is seen:

> The dissolution of the Cosmos means the destruction of the idea of a hierarchically ordered finite world structure, of the idea of a qualitatively and ontologically differentiated world, and its replacement by that of an open, indefinite and even infinite universe, united and governed by the same universal laws. . . . It is in this new Universe, in this new world of a geometry made real, that the laws of classical physics are valid and find their application.[14]

In Koyré's terms, Descartes's methodology represents a decisive shift away from the world of the *à peu près*, the approximate and qualitative everyday world, to a precise world.[15] This shift corresponds to the dissolution of the cosmos and its replacement by a mathematizable universe of pure motion and pure space, because it is only by way of such a replacement that one can claim that the logic of mathematical and technical precision has universal scope.

Galileo's difficulties in reconciling these two worlds coincides to a significant extent with his difficulties in reconciling his drive to demonstrate the universal application of mathematics in physics with his recognition of the undeniably qualitative aspect of everyday experience. If Plato and Aristotle represent the two poles of his struggle, it is Plato and Aristotle seen through the eyes of an individual who already has experienced the shift from the primacy of the world of the "more or less" to the world of precision. Galileo's only partial success in demonstrating the "victory of Plato over Aristotle,"[16] of securing the role of the sovereign science for the mathematical study of nature, stems from his inability to put to rest once and for all the qualitative appearance which things throw up to us in everyday perception.

Unlike Galileo, Descartes believes direct perception can hardly be trusted in matters concerning the rightful truth of motion, since it depends so essentially on the existence, not of pure substance, but of a mixed or hybrid substance, the conjunction of doxic mind and matter.

The truth which springs from such hybrid substance is mixed as well; it offers up error as much as it does certainty. Descartes's solution to the problem of securing a truth which is pure and unmixed follows a line similar to his solution to the Galilean dilemma concerning the mathematical treatment of moving bodies: it is not perceptual truth, a mixture of certainty and error, that we seek but the pure truth which precedes such perversion. Descartes claims the difficulties of Galileo, the physicist, stem as much from Galileo's incomplete understanding of this fundamental perversion of truth as from problems of a more directly scientific nature:

> without having considered the first causes of nature, he simply seeks the reasons for some particular effects, and in this way he builds without foundations. However, it is because his fashion of philosophizing is much closer to the truth that one can more easily recognize his faults. Just as one can better tell when those who sometimes follow the right path have lost their way than those who never get on it.[17]

Descartes criticizes Galileo's mathematical approach to the question of physical motion, not because he finds fault with the Italian's mathematical commitments, but because this commitment lacks the proper metaphysical foundations necessary to guarantee its success. For Descartes, securing the foundations for the new science begins and ends with a recognition of the common rectitude that characterizes all truth. Chief among these necessary foundations are those forms of truth inherent in motion of both the physical and mental varieties. From the Cartesian point of view, the limitations of Galileo's mathematical science are largely self-imposed; Galilean science lacks the scientific will needed to realize a science of truly universal scope.

It is precisely Galileo's efforts to tolerate in an ad hoc fashion the conflicting strains of the Aristotelian and Platonic traditions (that is, to reconcile as best he could the obscurity and imprecision of the everyday with the rigor of the mathematizable realm) of which Descartes is so critical. Descartes cannot abide this sort of collusion, and he finds it absurd to even attempt such a reconciliation. He objects to the imaginary experiments in which such Galilean attempts are expressed, not out of some simple exegetical faithfulness to Plato, Archimedes, or Pythagoras, but because he knows that the path of the new scientific project lies in a very different direction from such experimental collusion of imagination and perception. In short, Galilean science suffers from a lack of understanding of what right mind and right motion are. From the Cartesian point of view, even the great Galileo is mired in the "wrong-mindedness" that inevitably accompanies an appeal to the mores and tenets of the scientific tradition.

For Descartes, it is not simply a question of making the decision at which Galileo balked, of choosing Plato over Aristotle. More than this, Descartes recognizes that a decision even more radical than any suggested by Plato concerning the proper authoritative source for the new science must be made: what is needed is a space more effective than the realm of ideal forms, a motion more rational than the perfect temporal orbits of the *Timaeus*, a mind more clear and more operational than *noesis*. In a sense, Descartes calls for a form of Platonism even purer than that of Plato. Mixed forms of knowledge, even Plato's "right opinion," would require stringent purification to merit in any way the Cartesian label of rectitudinal truth. Cartesian science appeals to a primacy of ideas well beyond that announced by Plato, because the former appeals to a notion of rectitudinal truth and epistemological precision at which the latter only hints. A perfect science—this is the vision that lies behind the Cartesian quest for right space, right mind, and right motion:

> Perfect: that which negates the desire for or the addition of anything more; as soon as such a science recognizes this, then it exhausts its object. For the understanding, as a result, the materiality of each particular thing amounts to nothing more than that which its idea manifests to the mind deductively. With regard to extension, involving an infinity of things, it contains nothing so distant, so complex, so particular, nor so hidden that this science could not expose it. Everything is knowable, totally; nothing less will do. For such a science it is not necessary, any more than it is for the geometers, to observe or to experiment. A completely simple and continuous chain of deductions suffices; the mind's inventory delivers the infinity of the world to us.[18]

Unlike Plato's science, Descartes's perfect science allows him to look at the sun and see it for what it is, an idea-object that depends more on the mind than the mind depends upon it. The term "ideal" takes on a new meaning with Descartes, now having less to do with some unattainable, but inspiring, goal than it does with a force whose time has come. The new science is perfect, because it engenders the emergent application of the rightful ideals of space, motion, and mind in the name of their separate as well as mutual realizations.

Like Plato, Descartes believes that the everyday world is an image of an ideal realm. And following Plato, Descartes believes that the essence of the everyday world came into existence through a craftlike process. However, Descartes goes further than Plato in his metaphor of construction or production, for he understands the world to resemble not so much a Greek temple which reflects magnificent architectural understanding as a machine of such precision and complexity that only the most remarkable form of analytical comprehension could possibly grasp it. Descartes's efforts are not driven by the epistemological virtues of harmony and beauty that framed Plato's project, but rather by the principles of clarity and complexity. In the *Republic*, Plato seeks to show the merits of a city-state based on the double harmony of individual and law; in the *Discourse*, Descartes claims that the best city would have only one architect (and one engineer), leaving the question of its actual composition for a later date.[19]

Descartes makes it clear that this machine of the world does not yet exist, except in the ideas and ambitions of the right mind and will. It is this "not yet" that represents a crucial difference between the Platonic and Cartesian approaches. For Plato, the development of the capacity to perceive higher forms of truth leads to a greater apprehension of true reality, of what is. However, the Cartesian version of such development (of mental capabilities) exists for the express purpose of analyzing and rebuilding not only the outer world, but the realm of mind as well. Put differently, the crux of Descartes's project comes down to this: the way is prepared for the machine of the world by the discovery of another nascent machine, the mind qua *res cogitans*. After all, Plato's temple exists in order to be prayed to, admired, or contemplated; the reasons for developing the powers of *noesis* begin and end with the promise of increased apprehension of the forms which drive the world. Descartes's machines are mutually generative: the development of the essential powers of the mind leads to a clearer vision of what the world's rightful nature should be. The inner rectitude always heralds the rightful possibility of the outer rectitude; the movement of Descartes's new science always involves this double measure of inner purification and outer restructuring.

The truth of bodies, of extended substance, depends upon the establishment of a properly precise space as their very shape and outline; such a space cannot be essentially perceivable, because it exceeds the level of precision and rectitude which the sensible realm can contain or possess. Such rightful precision must spring from another more subtle source, one which can serve as the constant metaphysical reference for the material or rather extended realm. Materially or extensively speaking, this source, which Descartes identifies with clarity as opposed to obscurity, with a certain knowledge rather than a wavering knowledge, comes from nowhere, from the power of an infinite but proper productivity which guarantees the truth of bodies only to the extent that they faithfully reflect their introjective ideas. The truth of bodies is not material, since this rectitudinal power renders every material thing radically contingent to the extent that the structures of thinking and material appearance form a ratio which must ultimately equal one. Physical truth must embody this ratio as best it can, even if it means the presentation of an initially confused form. In fact, it is this confused nature of physical truth that serves as a clue leading to its own rectification.

The Cartesian ability to neutralize the doxic aspect of perception, to render it secondary, lies at the heart of Descartes's insight into the true nature of motion and his solution to the Galilean dilemma. Overtly, Descartes claims that this authority of the precise over the apparent stems directly from God, from the *ens infinitum et creans*, but as Koyré and many others have pointed out, the profundity of this claim is only made clear in examining what sort of things this "sovereign being" *must* bring into existence. The Cartesian God's productive world-forming power is not only infinite, but infinitely true, and as such the true world must be, in its essence, the *right* world, the world of rectitude and precision.

Both right mind and right motion find their common source and guarantee in this rectilinear measure that exceeds the "more or less" of the everyday world and everyday thinking. The tremendous effort required to discover this new measure is partly revealed if one understands that Koyré's statements bearing on the destruction of the cosmos do not refer simply to the external world, but also to the upheaval of the mental world as well. It is, in fact, this intellectual and spiritual upheaval that serves as the catalyst for what is much more than an internal scientific debate:

> The dissolution of the Cosmos—I repeat what I have already said: this seems to me to be the most profound revolution achieved or suffered by the human mind since the invention of the Cosmos by the Greeks. . . . [The founders of modern science did not have] to criticize and to combat certain faulty theories, and to correct or to replace them by better ones. They had to do something quite different. They had to destroy one world and to replace it by another. They had to reshape the framework of our intellect itself, to restate and to reform its concepts, to evolve a new approach to Being, a new concept of knowledge, a new concept of science—and even to replace a pretty natural approach, that of common sense, by another which is not natural at all.[20]

It is upon the successful development of a new measure of mind that the viability of the new science stands or falls. The destruction of the old world is a call for a new world, a call which is answered by the discovery of a new mental world as much as by the discovery of a new world of nature.

With Descartes, modern science recognizes that its conquest is not of one world, but two.

Another space, a new ground, must be found on which the right and wrong, the true and the false, the actual and the manifest, can be correctly and exhaustibly charted. The discovery of such a space requires the implementation of not only a new method, but also a new mind. The "more or less" of the old world was tolerated because of a corresponding "more or less" of the old mind. Now the clearly improper nature of such imprecision of thought opens the way for a new world, because proper mind, right thought, is staking claim to a new territory. Between and beyond the wavering of this "more and less" stands the gauge which allows the resolution, even dissolution, of the age-old quandaries generated by the play of natural appearance. The new space, the new motion, the new science, all begin and end against the backdrop of another new space, that of mind.

The Measure of Mental Space and the Rectification of Natural Appearance

For Descartes, the space and motion that form the core of the new science entails a new and radical measure, one which aims at a rectification of natural appearance. Only with the accomplishment of such a rectification will the essence of extended substance as analytically geometrical, that is, as thoroughly measurable, be made undeniably and indubitably clear. It is in the name of this new measure that Descartes lectures Henry More on the latter's foolish suggestion that "all matter must be sensible."[21] If all matter were sensible, that is, if matter in its essence were sensible and thus were subject to the variegations and obscurities of appearance, on what would one stake one's claim to a new science and certainty? Only with the discovery of an unwavering measure which stems the tide of wavering appearance, which pierces the illusion of the primacy of sensible matter, atoms, and bodies, can the mind come to resemble its infinite precedent, pure, unmixed *res cogitans infinitum*. Again, for Descartes (and I would maintain for the sake of the emergence of early modern science) a decision must be made regarding the dangerous aberrance of appearance, an Archimedean point must be secured to neutralize the illusory ravages of *doxa*, so that a new form of knowledge is to be established.

However, such a radical measure can only be sustained if a thoroughgoing redefinition of the fundamental parameters has occurred. Thus, as Gaston Bachelard writes, "All precise measure is a prepared measure."[22]

A preparation is necessary for the measurement of space, a preparation which has to do with the redefining of space and which requires an elimination or at least a reduction of various qualitative aspects of space and the bodies which inhabit it. The qualitative space of Koyré's world of the *à peu près* does not lend itself to precise measurement, but rather to a reconciliation of theoretical thought and everyday appearance. Therefore, a new space, one prepared solely for the installation of rectitude and measurement, must replace this old standard. This new space cannot grant primacy to the perceptual and the natural, but rather it must subordinate them to an unwavering mental principle: only things which can be rightfully measured will be real, all others being merely apparent, that is, false.

A space must be prepared to receive this new form of reality. However, as part of its redefinition, such a space cannot in any way color the objects which reside within it. In fact, to say that objects "reside" in space is to speak improperly according to Descartes: space is no longer to be understood as a receptacle which holds things, but rather as the demarcation of each extended thing itself and its relative position to other objects. Void space, then, makes no sense, because it is only in the existence of objects, or at least in the existence of their geometrical essence, that space itself exists. Thus, the space which Descartes posits as real space has no existence independent of extended substance nor does it have any actual qualitative existence. The space for which Descartes prepares the way is a space which lends nothing to the objects with which it coexists, except the verification of their quasi-mathematical nature. And yet, space must have a distinct and nonphysical nature of its own; it must be comprehensible in itself.

How does Descartes prepare the space which engenders this new rectitudinally ordered form of natural appearance and perception? The basic stages of this preparation are fairly straightforward, although the actual claims and appeals are not. First, he appeals to the infinite productivity of God. Second, he shows how the human mind fulfills its divine essence most fully when it asserts its unwavering nature through methodical doubt. Third, on the basis of God's infinite productivity and the clarity of mind made possible by God, Descartes calls for a discernment of the precise and right nature of physical phenomena. Space is the ideal (i.e., analytically geometrical) shape which God grants to the proto-automata that comprise nature. Descartes discovers the true "syntax" of the medieval Book of Nature in this metaphysical and mathematical space which does away with the exigencies of everyday appearance by establishing a new form of measurement and organization: "This syntax of the world deduced from metaphysics permits us, then, to gather, organize, group, and order the graphism of matter into a coherent and intelligible totality of signs. Concerning the world, it is in fact a book. However, if this book is written in a language whose syntax we recognize, we ignore its vocabulary all the same."[23] Indeed, from the time of *The World*, Descartes is preoccupied with the dream of deciphering the unknown code of the medieval Book of Nature. As Grimaldi suggests, Descartes wants to convert the rich encyclopedia of the natural world into a terse grammatical text which reproduces the even more precise Book of Spirit (now the Book of Mind) in the most exact terms possible. This is the Cartesian project par excellence: to reduce the vocabulary of experience to its basic syntactical forms, to neutralize *doxa* by positing its wavering aspect, its dynamic richness, as false and its unwavering aspect as true.

However, Descartes's project of decipherment is in reality a rewriting of nature. From the Cartesian point of view, the only proper way to decode nature is to rewrite it. The protracted encyclopedic study of the analogous connections between spirit and nature is all fine and good, but the true analogies can be uncovered only if one understands that what is most essential is the spiritual priorities at play. In short, the order of material nature, its meaning as a "coherent and intelligible totality of signs," is extrinsic to nature itself. Unless one grasps the nonnatural core of nature, one cannot realistically hope to find this essential order or meaning. The Cartesian science of nature breaks the codes of material nature by relegating natural codes to a secondary status. By redefining the intrinsic structures of nature as forms dependent on other extrinsic forms, those of spirit, Descartes establishes a new space, a new field of play, for science.

In order to ground this new extended space of natural science securely, however, another realm must also be rewritten: the true essence of the book of spirit must also be deciphered, that is, must also be rewritten. One must purify the mind, *l'esprit*, of its transient ideas in order to determine the purest form of mental space. Once its purity has been established, mental space provides the vestibule which allows nature to appear "on its own terms." This is the crucial move in the development of Descartes's new science. Given the secondary status that the Cartesian project allocates to material nature, only by way of this reprocessing and securing of the realm of spirit can the new science claim its ultimate legitimacy. The rendering of spirit as a pure mental space sets the stage for the thorough purification of the physical realm via its redefinition as *res extensa*; it is a process of double redefinition, with the spiritual phase taking logical precedence.

For the Cartesian project, mental space solves the problem of the tenuous analogy of the books of spirit and nature by showing the logical priority of the one over the other. Only a pure intellectual space can be both intelligible in itself and yet serve to allow things to appear without influence. The measure of mental space is the purest and most elegant of all possible measures. It is the solution to the Galilean puzzle, for one is actually being more faithful to the phenomena themselves if one focuses on the space in which these phenomena arise and play themselves out rather than on the apparent entities and events. In fact, to be most faithful to natural phenomena now requires that one look beyond the qualitative vagaries to the essence of the field in which they occur.

The primacy of mental space also figures intimately in the increasing antagonistic exchanges between Descartes and More. Initially, More found in Cartesian science a new way of expressing his theories concerning the permeation of sensible matter by spiritual forms. He was not exactly mistaken to read Descartes's writings as supportive of such theories. Descartes's initial letters did not reject More's ideas outright, and even his last responses never expressed a wholesale rejection of these theories. More was in error, however, in believing that Cartesian spirit was the same as the older notion of spirit which he himself embraced. What he did not understand, in part because Descartes never put it in so many words, is that the success of the Cartesian scientific project hinged more on the purification of the mental realm than it did on a redefinition (i.e., rectification) of the sensible plane.

The Cartesian measure of space which engenders the possibility of recognizing the firm truths of nature must necessarily suppress the tendency to perceive the vagaries common to everyday experience on their own terms. It must deny the apparent in order to certify the true. However, to accomplish this double movement of denial and certification it must first establish a new measure, a new meaning, for the apparent and the true. The Cartesian solution to the problem which confronts Galileo, how to reconcile the everyday, the phenomenal, and the mathematical language which should by rights speak of the precise essence of Nature, is based on a basic perceptual mutation. Descartes sees a new world with new eyes, both springing from a very old dream seen in a new light. Descartes shares in the old Platonic dream of a world in which purity of mind is rewarded with a purity of insight into the truth of nature. However, Descartes realizes what his Platonic forebears did not and perhaps could not: to fulfill this dream it is not only the mind which must be purified but also the world itself. The rectification of appearance is a double movement, a rectification of the mind's appearance to itself as well as a rectification of the world which appears before it.

In the first three chapters, I have argued that if the early modern scientific decision concerning a new measure is to be better fathomed, then one must examine carefully the diverse preparations for this measure, a measure which is also itself a preparation for others to come. However, the Cartesian measure is by no means the final or sole manifest form which early modern science will take, and for this reason I now turn to another tradition which contributes to the emergence of early modern science, a tradition whose ambiguous doctrines concerning perception and appearance, science and nature, loom in the background of the puzzling question which Henry More puts to Descartes, the question concerning the limits of sensibility. In Francis Bacon's vision of the new science, perception is not the problem but the solution. It is not the denial of bodies but the affirmation of their inborn powers that will lead to unprecedented human power and knowledge.

MODERN SCIENCE AS TECHNICAL INTERVENTION: BACON'S PROMETHEAN MEASURE

4

Mythical Truth, The Weak Tradition, and the Power of Scientific Hope

In the estimation of Koyré (and many others before and after him), Bacon is not, properly speaking, one of the founders of early modern science. Koyré maintains this distinction largely because of Bacon's general disregard for the role of mathematics in the new science, but also because of his naive experimentalist faith. However, Koyré does not go so far as to exclude Bacon from early modern science altogether, for he identifies Bacon as "the *buccinator*, the announcer, of modern science."[1] Yet, while it might be unreasonable to situate Bacon squarely in the movement of modern science, Bacon stands as an extremely crucial figure with regard to the modern scientific decisions concerning the respective status of nature and perception. In Bacon's work one finds both the announcement of a new form of scientific perception that distances itself as much as possible from those that precede it. However, unlike many of the "true moderns," Bacon seeks to establish his singular new science by way of an extensive, though ambiguous, analysis of the scientific tradition, an analysis that provides a essentially pejorative backdrop for the new science's development.

What is it about modern science that Bacon announces? What is his specific contribution to this new set of visions and practices? Koyré is quite correct to point out that Bacon does not share (and probably would not even understand) the Cartesian conviction that the new science must be essentially mathematical in its approach and outlook. And if an unshakable commitment to the mathematicization of the physical realm is the singular hallmark of the modern scientific attitude, then it would be difficult to see how Bacon could very well be its authentic announcer. Something else must be afoot in modern science if Bacon is in fact its announcer, a fundamental scientific or philosophical concern which does not depend upon a mathematico-physical conviction per se, but which might ultimately make such a conviction useful or even necessary. In other words, there must be an impulse as essential (or even more essential) in the grounds of modern science than the simple recognition of the importance of mathematics, an impulse which may contribute quietly but significantly to the scientific projects of Descartes or Galileo as well.

In general terms, Bacon's role in modern science involves his call for a new way of seeing the world, that is, his vision of new possibilities beyond those foreseen by the tradition. The new science which he announces is ultimately a science of creation and intervention. As a result of this new science new things will be created as certain elemental truths of matter and experience are uncovered. One of the most coherent reasons for excluding Bacon from the modern scientific fold involves what appears to be a basic adherence to the renaissance conception of the arts as the more general category into which both technology and science fall. Bacon does seek to develop a new method or art of discovery which would engender both scientific progress and technical breakthroughs, but whether he conflates science and technology in this effort is not clear. Bacon sees the development of the method essential to the accomplishment of his new science as depending on the recovery of certain basic natural and experiential truths. This recovery of truth will entail a new understanding of the relation of the technical and natural realms, but this new understanding will be a propaedeutic to the new science rather than its result.[2]

However, through his call for a *scientia activa et operativa*, Bacon announces what he does not, and perhaps cannot, entirely anticipate. In this way Bacon may be seen as excluded from modern science at the same time that he prepares the way for its arrival; excluded and yet included because the future science (the science of a potent future) is to take a form which—at one and the same time—will resemble his compelling vision of it and yet be utterly alien to it. In examining Bacon's ambiguous inclusion in and exclusion from early modern science, one can see the crucial manner in which he anticipates the new relationship between technological and theological commitments that is to become the very hallmark of the new science. One must also ask to what extent the Baconian exploration of this relationship influences the basic form that the relationship between scientific perception and the proper object of this new perception will take in the modern scientific view of things.

Bacon's criticism of the tradition for its conflation of religion and science stems from his specific notion of revealed theology, and it would be a grave mistake to believe that Bacon is calling for a complete separation of religious and scientific concerns. In fact, Bacon's notion of natural science is directly linked with his fundamental division of philosophy into three forms, Divine, Natural, and Human. In order to understand the proper realm and pursuits of natural philosophy one must also understand the limits of natural theology or divine philosophy, as is clear from numerous passages in his work, including the *Advancement of Learning*: "And as concerning Divine philosophy or Natural Theology, it is that knowledge or rudiment of knowledge concerning God which may be obtained by the contemplation of his creatures. . . . For as all works do shew forth the power and skill of the workman, and not his image; so it is of the works of God; which do shew the omnipotency and wisdom of the maker, but not his image."[3] Thus, as Bacon goes on to point out, it is a grave error to believe that the world is made in the image of God. The natural philosopher would do well to remember that it is not the world which is made in the image of God, but only humanity. The proper realm of natural science is the study of the works of God, that is, the study of the production of all the creatures which fill the space of the world.

The Baconian belief in a sort of primordial truth is not unrelated to the theological element found in Descartes's effort to ground truth in something besides appearance. Bacon is, after all, suggesting a constitutional theory of perception and truth which, albeit ambiguously, anticipates that offered by Descartes, while at the same time diverging from it dramatically. Descartes also begins by making a radical distinction between religious and scientific knowledge. He emphasizes time and again that certain knowledge of nature is guaranteed by both the existence and the infinite productivity of God, yet without telling us much if anything about God. Further, the distinction between *res cogitans* and *res extensa*, with the human being straddling this distinction, can be read as a restatement of the subject matter of Bacon's three forms of philosophy, two pure forms (divine and natural) and a hybrid third form (human).

However, the materialist naturalism embraced by Bacon poses serious problems for a science like that of Descartes. Hints at the extent of such difficulties are to be found in the arguments between More and Descartes concerning the corporeality of space and the dynamic, even living, nature of atomic matter. The harsh Cartesian duality of mind and matter, the former "alive" and the latter inert, is fundamentally incompatible with Bacon's (and More's) neo-Democritean atomism. Just as the conflict between More and Descartes moves constantly between the realms of theology and physics, the conflict between Bacon and Descartes goes far beyond the straightforward dispute between naturalism and antinaturalism.

Thus, it seems crucial to define the nature of the relation between the scientific and theological impulses at play in Bacon as clearly as possible in order to understand the ramifications of these respective constitutional theories of perception for the structure of the new science. The strongest tie between the Baconian and Cartesian views of science (and the way in which Bacon is therefore most modern) may be said to involve the impact of their respective theological/philosophical commitments on their visions of science. In my view, Bacon announces modern science because he sets the stage for it *theologically*. Further, I seek to show how Bacon's theological view (through its coalescence with the mathematical commitments of Descartes) provides an indispensable ground for Newtonian physics as the first accomplishment of modern science.

Mythical Truth and the Purity of First Naturalism

Bacon studies the past in order to find hidden remnants of truth that demonstrate the perpetual revealing power of the light of nature. He does so in order to show that human perception has always been (by its very essence) open to a truth that is neither exactly eternal nor perishable. That is, he seeks to ground a form of truth which has a nontraditional form of certainty. Chief among the ancient instances which he examines as evidence of perception's nascent power are Greek and Biblical myths and certain pre-Socratic writings. As both Fulton Anderson and Paoli Rossi have tried to show, many scholars and philosophers have misinterpreted Bacon's studies of mythical knowledge by assuming they are inconsequential to his views of science. This is indeed "among the strangest phenomena in the history of philosophical exegesis," when one considers the constant reference to science in Bacon's mythical studies.[4] This oversight may be, to some extent, understandable when one takes into account Bacon's own ambiguous position with regard to mythical knowledge, for he seems torn between a glorious, almost prelapsarian past, and a future which promises the establishment of a science and a civilization never before possible. However, Bacon is always concerned first and foremost with what science will come to achieve, and his faith in the revealing power of an ancient, pristine, and uncumbered perception stems from the as yet unfulfilled promises of scientific achievement.

Undoubtedly, Bacon's exclusion from the circle of the new science has much to do with his lengthy studies of ancient myths and fables. As Paoli Rossi points out, Bacon dedicated at least five of his thirty-nine works to the question of "a hidden wisdom in classical myths and fables."[5] Since, in the past, many scholars have sought to deny any connection between this sort of question and the advent of modern science, and since myth finds its way into much of Bacon's discussion of his own scientific vision, Bacon is relegated to the realm of premodern science. However, as Rossi and Fulton Anderson have maintained, one must read Bacon's science alongside his reflections on ancient myth, for one finds in these reflections an important view of Baconian science.

Bacon's attitude toward ancient myth and fable undergoes considerable alteration between 1590 and 1620. His early writings tend to use myth as ammunition for his polemical attacks on traditional science, many of which he chose not to publish. However, the accompanying discussions of ancient myths reappear in later, less polemical, writings, either to support his own scientific project or as independent essays. In *De Sapienta Veterum*, the most extensive of these more mature accounts, Bacon offers interpretive essays of more than thirty myths. The first lines of his preface tell of the immense difficulty encountered in such interpretative efforts:

> The most ancient times (except what is preserved of them in the scriptures) are buried in oblivion and silence: to that science succeeded the fables of the poets: to those fables the written records which have come down to us. Thus between the hidden depths of antiquity and the days of tradition and evidence that followed there is drawn a veil, as it were, of fables, which come in and occupy the middle region that separates what has perished from what survives.[6]

Myth and fable are the mediating veil between the great knowledge which has been lost and the tradition that remains. They speak allegorically of ancient times because their stature still persist even when lost. The tradition cannot even aspire to reach these heights, instead tending to deny or denigrate the remarkable truth that serves as the obscured source of the tradition itself.

As Rossi points out, this attitude of mourning over the lost harmony of the ancient pagan and Christian worlds and their "unhistorical immediacy," their living presence, is a common motif of the Renaissance.[7] However, Bacon is not simply mourning a lost wisdom. First and foremost, he seeks to show that the germ of a new science can be found in the allegorical presentation of a materialist naturalism which appears in ancient myths such as Proteus, Saturn, and Cupid. Bacon uses these myths to support his reading of Democritean philosophy as well as his contention that the new science must turn its back on the unproductive biases of the intervening tradition. In short, Bacon follows in a long line of Renaissance writers who use ancient allegory and myth, but he differs from almost all of these writers because he studies them in order to formulate a new scientific outlook that stresses the importance of arduous research prior to the augmentation of human power over nature. In other words, although many other writers of his time (and the preceding generation), working out of the schools of natural magic and alchemy, appeal to ancient figures, Bacon makes it clear that more than the pristine perception of the ancients and the desire for power are required for his science. One must develop a method which makes the arduous research efforts necessary to the new science bearable by emulating, or rather expanding upon, the perceptual lucidity of the earliest naturalists.

Bacon's relation to the philosophical tradition is significantly ambiguous. On the one hand, he holds the pre-Socratics in relative esteem. According to him, their straightforward naturalistic philosophies represent a more appropriate form of philosophical pursuit than those of the thinkers who immediately follow them. Bacon's nostalgia concerning the lost wisdom of the ancient mythmakers is matched by his faith in the simple naturalistic clarity of pre-Socratic vision: "they represented the type of serious, unassuming questioner of nature, unencumbered by the characteristic 'pomposity' of Greek philosophy in general. They heralded the 'chaste, holy and legal wedlock with nature' that Bacon dreamt of substituting for Platonic 'evasions' and Aristotelian 'formalism.' "[8] Thus, these early naturalists enjoyed a perceptual freedom stemming from their historical position. They were not ensnared by the intellectual tradition that begins in full force with Plato and Aristotle. The clarity of vision of these first naturalists is also a clarity of mind and a clarity of relation to nature. For Bacon, the situation of these naturalists is a model to be emulated, because they were afforded an experiential and observational situation unparalleled in purity and lack of obstruction.

Bacon sees the purity of this early Greek naturalism as an aim implicitly linked to his own call for a wholesale reconstruction of science. This naturalistic purity is a basic insight for Bacon, and one needs to trace out some of the lines or trends that he sees at play in this naturalism in order to grasp his general scientific project. Bacon finds in it some fundamental tenets for his own materialist naturalism. Chief among the virtues of this general naturalism, Bacon identifies the notion of the "universal frame of nature," as well as the mysterious essence of matter, the atom, "the original and unique force that constitutes and fashions all things . . . it being, next to God, the cause of all causes—itself without cause."[9] Thus, Bacon discovers in the myths of Pan and Cupid a sort of concordance for the Democritean philosophical text, both emerging from an age of discovery whose integrity has been shattered, but whose powerful insights continue to shine as so many fragmentary beacons of light.[10]

However, following Rossi and many others, it is important to point out that Bacon does not seek a return to some lost state of knowledge. If he believes in such knowledge, it is only because he is even more convinced that we moderns have equal, if not superior, access to it.[11] Anticipating Descartes, Bacon maintains that "[t]ruth must be discovered by the light of nature, not recovered from the darkness of the past."[12] Further, like Descartes, Bacon takes these ancient examples as evidence of the fact that the light of nature is so potent, it even had convicting power for primitive and pagan minds such as Democritus and Heraclitus. Unlike Descartes, Bacon does not consider the powers of human perception to be fundamentally at fault; the larger source of error is found in the interpretations into which perceived things and experience are forced to reside. In other words, it is the excessive and unnatural interpretations of Plato and Aristotle, and their followers—not their perceptual flaws—which Bacon wishes to isolate as ideas which are acceptable as oddities, but dangerous as traditions and authorities.[13]

The Source of Improper Perception: The Platonic and Aristotelian Denials of Naturalism

Feyerabend discusses Bacon's view of perception in terms of the question of "natural interpretation."[14] By this term, Feyerabend means the activities of perceiving something and thinking about it that are virtually inseparable, because sensory facts involve "ideological components, older views which have vanished from sight."[15] Further, these more or less hidden components of perception are dubious in large part because of "their age and obscure origin."[16] Feyerabend points to Bacon as an example of the extreme position that labels the undue exaggeration of the importance of the mental aspect of this perceptual complex generally pejorative; such exaggeration is a dangerous impediment to something like pure perception. He is, of course, not entirely fair to Bacon (as Feyerabend himself concedes), because Bacon is all too aware of the intimate connection between perception and interpretation. I would say instead that Bacon seeks most of all to strip away those interpretational aspects which tend to systematize or legislate perception by way of constraining it.

On the other hand, Bacon holds in high regard those forms of interpretation which facilitate or encourage perception. Thus, what Bacon wishes to deny is not natural, but what might be termed "unnatural" interpretation.[17] Indeed, the difference between these two interpretive forms has much to do with what Bacon sees as the crucial difference between the mythical and the more straightforwardly philosophical forms of Greek thinking.

For Bacon, something is lost with the rise of classical Greek philosophy. A kind of purity or legitimacy of questioning and perception gives way to the arrogance of certain ways of thinking about things. In Plato (and it is clear that Bacon believes Plato, more than anyone, should be held responsible for the intellectual self-indulgence endemic to Greek philosophy) this philosophical perversion manifests itself in a confusion of the natural and the mystical, while in Aristotle it appears as a desire to place in metaphysics what belongs to, and is found in, physics.[18] Bacon finds that most received knowledge suffers from the impurities of traditional philosophical thinking, and thus his project represents an effort at recovering something like the lost perceptual purity of the early Greek naturalists.

Of course, Bacon is criticizing the Platonism and Aristotelianism of his own time as much as the classic texts of Plato and Aristotle which were available.[19] Thus, when he takes Plato to task for the confusion of mysticism and naturalism, he is pointing as much if not more to the magical naturalism of hermeticism and alchemistry only loosely inspired by Plato (and Pythagoras) as to Plato's own writings. From the Baconian perspective, this magical naturalism is representative of the fundamentally erroneous tendencies of the tradition: the avoidance by mentalistic "evasion" of the difficult and methodical work necessary to fully discover the workings of nature engendered. The distance between his own science and the tradition's account of science is as vast for Bacon as the almost two thousand years of evasive philosophizing which Plato's work inspires. In other words, Bacon identifies the course of Platonism as a widening path of divergence from the perceptually engendered truth enjoyed by the early naturalists. He sees his own project as the instrument by which a scientific and metaphysical "course correction" can be accomplished. His project seeks to close the vast abyss opened by the tradition by returning to and building upon the basic truth of early Greek naturalism.

Bacon acknowledges the accomplishments of Plato are worthy of honor, though not emulation; instead, the new science must follow a path radically different from the one established by Platonist science. In short, the Platonist leaps of thought are remarkable for their theoretical force, but less than laudatory if one's aim is to grasp nature. Whereas the pre-Socratics "submitted their minds to the nature of things," Plato "made over the world to thought."[20] Thus, Plato serves as the straw man for Bacon's attack on all mentalistic attempts to find a shortcut to the secrets and mysteries of nature. Bacon understands Plato as the ancestor of the magical naturalism of his own time, because of this "making over," this veritable mortgaging, of the world to thought. It makes little difference to Bacon whether the one is couched within a rigorously intellectualist framework while the other is based on a "poetic vagueness" and belief in magic.[21] Both are guilty of the same essential and self-imposed blindness and deafness to nature.[22]

In all its forms, ancient and recent, Platonism suffers from a theoretical blockage that denies it access to a necessary feature of true science, the play of actual forms of material nature. Much of what will serve as Bacon's instrument for identifying obstacles to the new science, his theory of idols, stems from his critical examination of the chief tendency of Platonism: for each of the true forms of nature, Platonism substitutes an idol, an ersatz form, which allows, even compels, it to consider its science *finished*. Thus, Baconian science sets itself to work at the very moment Platonic science declares itself finished, the moment at which the active contemplation of nature ought to commence. In order to recover or recapture this moment, Bacon's science must begin by peeling away the tradition's substitutions from the natural form.[23] As Bacon makes evident, this preparatory stage of elimination is an arduous process which demands not only a keen eye, but also a deep understanding of the substitutive techniques or practices of the Platonic tradition. Only a new enlightened form of naturalism can, in Bacon's eyes, both offset the sophisticated techniques of Platonism and establish a nonsubstitutive methodology. Such a methodology must combine the theoretical prowess of Platonism with the empirical faith of the early naturalists.

Bacon's criticism of Aristotle is not, perhaps, as ubiquitous in his work as his criticism of Plato, but it is a recurrent subject nonetheless. In his criticism of Aristotle, he homes in on the same shortcoming concerning the suppression of a naturalist understanding that forms the center of his criticism of Platonism. The *New Organon*, Bacon's last completed major work, offers a logical and philosophical frame on which to hang a much more productive and useful science than that engendered by the original *Organon*. Again, as with Plato, Bacon lauds the intellectual acumen of Aristotle; he grants quite easily the sharpness of his definitions, the breadth of his categories, and the eloquence of his explanations. However, for all this ability, Aristotle debilitated the possibility of future scientific development by his rash formalism, and because he sets a tone for almost two thousand years to come he is more guilty than any who come after: "he did not consult experience, as he should have done, for the purpose of framing his decisions and axioms, but having first determined the question according to his will, he then resorts to experience, and bending her into conformity with his placets, leads her about like a captive in a procession. So that even on this count he is more guilty than his modern followers, the schoolmen, who have abandoned experience altogether."[24] For Bacon, experience, that is, perceptual experience, must lead the way to the captivity of Nature, rather than by attempting an Aristotelian capture of experience by means of a conception of nature which precedes and therefore distorts observation.

The extreme nature of Bacon's criticism of Aristotle must, like that he aims at Plato, be couched in terms of his attack on the Aristotelianism of his own era. After all, the case can be made that Aristotle, perhaps more than any other philosopher, follows the guidance of perception. Bacon at times even seems to concede this point, acknowledging it by his frequent citation of Aristotle's observations of plants, animals, and human action.[25] Nonetheless, he goes on to write that Aristotle is at least guilty of spawning a very long tradition that suffers from a pervasive perceptual ignorance, that is, Scholasticism. To understand the reasons that move Bacon to reject Aristotle so vigorously, when in fact one might think the Baconian project has a great deal in common with the empirically committed project of Aristotle, one must examine Bacon's attempt to completely rework Aristotle's philosophical and scientific frameworks.

The *New Organon* represents the most comprehensive and mature expression of the Baconian effort to rewrite Aristotelian science. It further demonstrates the sincerity and seriousness of Bacon's belief in the superiority of pre-Platonic *and* pre-Aristotelian naturalism. Bacon in fact lays more blame at the feet of the Aristotelians than the Platonists when it comes to the specific issue of naturalistic truth, because the tradition stemming from Aristotle claims to be more sensitive to the presence of natural forms and essentially committed to the development of science grounded in experience. In other words, the Platonists may have ignored the naturalistic nature of truth, but Aristotle "corrupted natural philosophy by his logic";[26] the Platonists may have overlooked natural experience in their idealistic reveries, but Aristotle "did not consult experience, as he should have done, for the purpose of framing his decisions and axioms, but having first determined the question according to his will, he then resorts to experience, and bending her in conformity with his placets, leads her about like a captive in a procession."[27] The normative quality of Bacon's criticism (the "should have done") stems from what he sees as the self-professed commitment to natural philosophy of Aristotle (and his followers). Indeed, Bacon's aim is to reestablish the naturalism that should by definition be part and parcel of natural philosophy. The *New Organon* is thus both new and very old, because it is inspired by a form of truth that was discovered long before the first *Organon* was written.

Bacon's goal is to restore the naturalism inherent in science to its rightful place. Such a restoration demands an almost total rearrangement of the organization of traditional science. He replaces the tripartite structure of productive, practical, and theoretical sciences with a more straightforward dualistic schema in which the first and the third (the productive and theoretical sciences) constitute the realm of physics, while the second is the proper realm of revealed theology. Within this restructuring of the scientific domain mathematics becomes even more of an auxiliary science than it had been for Aristotle, and metaphysics, to the extent that it has legitimacy, lays out the general principles or the universal frame of nature.[28]

Bacon's establishment of a single science and a single theology (the latter serving as the proper domain of ethics and politics) stems from a single basic insight: human existence has two aspects, one natural and the other divine. Bacon sets up a science and a theology that mirror one another, and it is only by taking this mirroring of theology by science seriously that we can understand Bacon's attitude to all possible forms of human knowledge. For Bacon, knowledge always has a double meaning, at once theological and natural, and thus science is always accompanied by its theological twin. As Bacon understands it, Aristotle's philosophy (and, perhaps even more ironically, the philosophy of Scholastic Aristotelianism) does not sufficiently grasp this mirroring phenomenon that is fundamental to effective human knowledge. In other words, the tradition of Aristotle fails to grasp the meaning of this intimate and basic dualism and thus commits the fundamental and fateful error of "substituting Nature for God."[29] As Bacon sees it, the immensity of this error and its impact on the tradition cannot be overstated. By collapsing or denying this double aspect of knowing, Aristotle and his followers not only tread perilously close to hermeticism, but, more importantly in terms of the project of science, they close off any consistent future development of naturalistic and productive science:

> Aristotle is more to be blamed than Plato, seeing that he left out the fountain of final causes, namely God . . . and took in final causes themselves rather as the lover of logic than of theology. And I say this, not because those final causes are not true and worthy to be inquired in metaphysical speculations; but because their excursions and irruptions into the limits of physical causes has bred a waste and solitude in that track. For otherwise, if they be but kept within their proper bounds, men are extremely deceived if they think there is any enmity or repugnancy at all between the two.[30]

For Bacon, the way to a new and promising science is opened up *again* if we recognize the essential resonance between the double nature of human existence and human knowledge. To put it differently, unlike the old *Organon*, the *New Organon* will reflect its organic source and its organizer, the apparatus by which it comes to be and the architect of this primordial apparatus.

Thus, Bacon's major objection to the Aristotelian schema is that it does not allow, let alone encourage, the kind of pluralistic and time-enriched research which makes science a progressive, as opposed to traditionalist, enterprise. There is too much emphasis on the accomplishments of one individual and therefore too much faith in the path that this individual lays out. The promise of Baconian science lies in its appeal to the research of many, the denial of the dictatorial power of the tradition, and the recognition of the essential propriety of his theological naturalism. Aristotle is therefore criticized more for being the symbolic negation of these crucial tenets than for his own crimes against the futurity of science. Like Plato before him, Aristotle's guilt involves a dimming of the light of nature by the means of an artificial system that disorganized the realm which the early naturalists had found so remarkably well ordered.

The Deep Past of Natural Truth: Beyond and before Traditional Science

The intimate relation of a deep mythical truth and the scientific promise of the future results from Bacon's commitment to the idea that the light of nature which has shed a steady illumination on things has only been rarely and all too briefly met by a scientific gaze which is steady in its own right. The mythical truth laid out by certain pre-Platonic investigators is a sign pointing to what might be accomplished by a committed methodical science. Such mythical truth also offers hints of a human power as yet unrealized. For Bacon, the fact that the tradition is so fraught with error and bad judgment stems less from the experiential and perceptual frailty of those who built this tradition than from the proliferation of various forms of intellectual sophistication. Indeed, the tradition can be seen as a response to, or a flight, from the dense obscurities rife in natural truth and appearance. In comparison to the obscurantism springing from the suppression of direct naturalistic inquiry by the formalistic or abstract tradition, any error on the part of the pre-Platonic naturalist, any experiential disorientation due to the simple fact that the world was so new, so vivid and strange, is negligible. What is both remarkable and encouraging to Bacon is the fact that the early naturalists possessed a rudimentary but nonetheless clear vision of the world's frame and the entities which inhabit that frame.

Bacon takes mythical knowledge seriously insofar as he finds hidden within these stories certain crucial insights into nature. Myths present the light of nature allegorically filtered into a perceivable form accessible by these early peoples. In fact, Bacon maintains that the experience of these truths precedes their being actually understood:

> when the inventions and conclusions of human reason (even those that are now trite and vulgar) were as yet new and strange, the world was full of all kinds of fables, and enigmas, and parables, and similitudes; and these were used not as a device for shadowing and concealing the meaning, but as a method of making it understood; the understandings of men being then rude and impatient of all subtleties that did not address themselves to the sense,—indeed scarcely capable of them.[31]

In this manner, Bacon lauds these early questioners for their ability to perceive *through myth* what was as yet unfathomable to them directly through the intellect. In other words, though lacking any consistent theoretical framework, the early naturalist possessed the experiential structures which are just as, if not more, essential to Baconian natural science than a highly developed theoretical system.[32] The myth and the fable are veils which allow a vague understanding of what cannot yet be seen in total clarity, veils that evoke a resemblance between the unknown and the familiar. As such, this early mythical science can be seen as a positive forerunner of the new science. The theoretical advances of the new sciences must build on, and not bury, this mythical form of natural truth.

Thus, for Bacon, it is not an impaired perceptual ability that restricts the extent to which the ancients could see things as they really are. Nor is it precisely their lack of intellectual prowess or subtlety which denies them direct and full-blown experience of the light of nature. In fact, Bacon claims that the pre-Socratics perceived and understood—grasped with both their senses and their minds—the nature of things much more clearly than their more systematic descendants: "And therefore the natural philosophy of Democritus and some others, who did not suppose a mind or reason in the frame of things, but attributed to *the form thereof able to maintain itself to infinite essays or proofs of nature*, which they term *fortune*, seemeth to me (as far as I can judge by the recital and fragments which remain unto us) in particularities of physical causes more real and better enquired than that of Aristotle and Plato."[33]

Bacon stands ready and willing to accuse the Aristotelian and Platonic traditions of obscurantist crimes. They represent not a deeper understanding or appreciation of the nature of things building upon the work of the mythmaking naturalists, but rather a deviation from those earliest mythical insights. Rather than attempting to grasp the meaning of the veil that myth placed between the light of nature and the human mind and senses, these traditions blocked the view with their systems and their theories. They erected a screen upon which they projected their own image rather than pursuing the image of nature.[34] In this manner, the very thing that Bacon found most worthy of recovery in the ancients has been virtually emasculated by the two great philosophical schools. The purity of those early questions had granted the pre-Socratics insights into the workings of nature. The sophistications of the Platonic and Aristotelian movements—exemplified by their emphasis on the absolute distinction between form and matter—represents for Bacon a denial of what is most true in ancient wisdom: a certain sort of mythically delivered naturalistic truth.

It is Bacon's commitment to a rediscovery of the light of nature that grounds his comparative readings of the myths of Pan and Cupid and Democritus's naturalist philosophy, readings which appear in numerous texts. He is convinced that only by returning to a form and method of understanding which grants the natural reality of matter (a reality which is, in a crucial sense, distinct and independent from the theological force which originally brought it forth) can science begin to reach its promised fulfillment. In this effort, Bacon believes one must take a cue from the ancients, who "saw matter—represented by Cupid—as possessing a form and positive qualities, not a formless abstraction, which is how Plato and Aristotle came to see it."[35] Material nature is not an idea, a theory, or a philosophical schema for Bacon; it is the primordial and atomic stuff, "a true being having matter, form, dimension, place, resistance, appetite, motion and emancipation."[36]

It is this dynamic "atomistic" nature that inspires the sufficiently faithful observer, the one who can put aside (or preceded and therefore was never exposed to) the formalism and abstractions of the tradition. The light of nature shines forth in the writings of early Greek thinkers and the most ancient mythmakers because they possessed a sensitivity to what appeared before them and a poetically naturalistic talent to express something of the richness and depth of natural appearance. In order to regain something akin to this naturalistic sensitivity Bacon believes he must turn his attention more to these mythical and fabulous stories than to the great philosophical towers, Plato and Aristotle, and their respective followers, in his efforts to found the new science. Indeed, the two-thousand-year-old path trod by those who blindly and faithfully follow the tradition has led to a philosophy which is "more fabulous than the poets."[37]

Traditional science has confused science and theology; it has become consumed with "the spirit of systems and the cult of words" which Bacon thinks led to the sterility of ancient Greek civilization.[38] Indeed, such biases render the very reading of the more mythical or poetic pre-Platonic thinkers quite problematic, because they too sometimes gave into the urge to devise and promulgate first principles rather than steadfastly examine the emergent truths offered by nature. Bacon maintains that despite this faltering on the part of traditional science, the light of nature shines forth in the most ancient of these myths, and that this very same light of nature shines before the individual who devoutly seeks to read its wonders. What guarantees this identity of the light of nature is the most ancient truth of all, that of the frame of the world itself. Further, this oldest truth holds out a special promise for the new science, a promise which involves the advantages of those who are not most ancient but rather most modern:

> For the old age of the world is to be accounted the true antiquity; and this is the attribute of our own times, not that earlier age of the world in which the ancients lived; and which, though in respect of us it was the elder, yet in respect of the world it was the younger. And truly as we look for greater knowledge of human things and a riper judgement in the old man than in the young, because of his experience and of the number and variety of the things which he has seen and heard and thought of; so in like manner from our age, *if we but knew its own strength and chose to essay and exert it,* much more might fairly be expected than from the ancient times, inasmuch as it is a more advanced age of the world, and stocked with infinite experiments and observations.[39]

The oldest of truths, the light of nature, places the fledgling modern science in the position of rightful seniority. Bacon is convinced that this oldest truth in a sense inverts the normal conception of history, rendering the moderns the most wise and mature, and thus placing Bacon and his contemporaries in a position to take command of nature in ways never before imagined. For Bacon, the best evidence of the coming of the "New Atlantis" is the great body of experimental and observational knowledge that awaits incorporation by a new science, one which is motivated by the proper vision of the new scientific mission and guided by the proper vision of nature. This science has been prepared a time and place to arise: first, because the frame of nature, the world itself, is revealing its form in an unprecedented series of discoveries; and second, because modern humanity seems better equipped than any preceding epoch to answer a fundamental theological challenge, to fully master the natural realm. Bacon's historical inversion is not an inversion at all, but rather a reversion to what should have been. The challenge and promise of the human race depends upon its possessing the will to uncover the secrets of nature; for Bacon, the time has come for this new scientific will to appear.

To take up this challenge and this promise requires a rewriting of science, an appropriation of the past for the sake of the future, and a faith in the special position of modern humanity. All of this is possible not in terms of a complete dismissal of the radical past, but by further appropriating the veiled truth that still shines out of it. This truth is not that which the tradition preaches, the truth of ideal forms and formal principles, of syllogisms and scholastic texts, but rather the truth which shines in the material world when it is released from its formalist and abstractionist bonds: the light of nature is right before our eyes if we would but open them. Only in the rediscovery of this natural light and the true frame of the world do we begin to gain an unprecedented power and control over nature, a power so great that ancient figures could only express its unrealized possibility in mythical terms.

The Theological Virtue of Hope and the Proper Future of the New Science

Like Descartes, and perhaps even more vigorously, Bacon calls for the overthrow of the dominant, Aristotelian science. He seeks to replace the threefold medieval scientific divisions—theoretical, practical and productive—by a more straightforward structure. In Bacon's view, all science is essentially physics; the so-called practical sciences—that is, ethics and politics—being the responsibility and privilege of revealed theology. Baconian science, that is, physics, represents the general discipline through which the human potential for mastery of nature and acquisition of power is to be realized. This emergent mastery and power is a function of Bacon's belief that the present epoch will be even more successful than either the Greek or the Roman ones, because more than either of the other two, it marks the watershed of geographical and technical discovery. However, this potentially revolutionary form of human power depends upon theological sanction: God grants to the third and final epoch of human greatness, the modern period, the opportunity to rediscover its own human essence through scientific discovery. Bacon has no qualms in citing scripture to support this claim:

> Now in divine operations even the smallest beginnings lead of a certainty to their end. And as it was said of spiritual things, "The kingdom of God

cometh not with observation," so is it in all the greater works of Divine Providence; everything glides so smoothly and noiselessly, and the work is fairly going on before men are aware that it has begun. Nor should the prophecy of Daniel be forgotten touching the last ages of the world: "Many shall go to and fro, and knowledge shall be increased"; clearly intimating that the thorough passage of the world (which now by so many distant voyages seems to be accomplished, or in the course of being accomplished), and the advancement of the sciences, are destined by fate, that is, by Divine Providence, to meet in the same age.[40]

The modern epoch is the "oldest" epoch, because it will virtually close the circle of history by fulfilling the divine promise of an unexcelled human power over nature that was made at the beginning of time. Thus, a theological imperative is at work in the founding of the new science; it includes an imperative which makes discovery a multidimensional event which will assist in the accomplishment of God's plan for humanity.

This special theological framing of science has much to do with Bacon's thoroughly ambiguous attitude toward the tradition. The Baconian sense of history (epitomized by his reading of the history of science) receives its essential shape from his understanding of the relationship between revealed theology and science. He fiercely believes in the notion that the realm most appropriate for scientific investigation has been available to human awareness from the beginning and that some ancient discoveries still have great significance. At the same time he finds it extremely doubtful that the systematic work of the traditional giants— Aristotle and Plato—can be of much help in the advancement of the new science. As we have seen, it is only the more obscure, less systematic accounts of even more ancient thinking that hold for Bacon anything like the viable seeds of scientific truth, for they "more silently and severely and simply—that is, with less affectation and parade—betook themselves to the inquisition of truth."[41] Though pagans they may have been, these ancients share in the theological pageant which Bacon portrays by this almost devout naturalistic science. Indeed, they prepare the way for the modern fulfillment of science as the practice by which humanity will possess full title to nature.

What these devout naturalists lack, in Bacon's view, is a catalyst to propel them beyond the limits of their old world and their "suburban excursions." The catalyst that they lack is precisely the "stock of experience" provided by the recent appearance of the true age of discovery, technical, historical, and geographical, an age which represents the threshold and the watershed for the development of human potential.[42] Only with the appearance of new possibilities, only with the emergence of a new world (in every sense of the term), will the blind habits of tradition science finally be left behind. This breaking open of the Old World is not an arbitrary event, nor can it be accounted for strictly in terms of natural science, but rather it arises historically on the basis of a principle with a distinctly theological edge, a principle which Bacon calls "Hope":

> But by far the greatest obstacle to the progress of science and to the understanding of new tasks and provinces therein is found in this—that men despair and think things impossible. . . . And therefore it is fit that I publish and set forth those conjectures of mine which make hope in this matter reasonable, just as Columbus did, before that wonderful voyage of this across the Atlantic, when he gave the reasons for his conviction that new lands and continents might be discovered besides those which were known before; which reasons, though rejected at first, were afterwards made good by experience, and were the causes and beginnings of great events.[43]

This principle of hope is cited some sixty times in the *New Organon*, forming the dominant focus of the last thirty-five aphorisms of Book One.[44] It serves as one of the basic elements in Bacon's effort to formulate a means to leave behind the old world of false, hubric knowledge, the cavern of experience dominated by idols. These idols of false gods and false appearances can only be eliminated through a process of discovery that opens ups the immense vistas of a new world. The metaphor of America alludes to this new world of the new science, a space in which almost everything is possible, especially the rectification of the tradition which has embroiled itself in a seemingly inescapable realm of error and blindness.

In his essay "L'espérance dans la science," Michèle le Doeuff characterizes the Baconian notion of hope as "an epistemo-theological virtue, capable of guaranteeing the passage to the wholly new, or to another world . . . the great world of the things themselves."[45] Hope serves then as a crucial force in Bacon's effort to fulfill the power and responsibility of science. To accomplish this mission the new science must shed the doubts and limitation of traditional science, turning its back on both the obstacles that have plagued tradition epistemologies and the traditional epistemologies themselves. Hope represents the new science's crucial ability to leap beyond the realm of traditional science, beyond the limited inductive realm to a realm in which painstaking empirical studies will finally pay off.

For Bacon, the escape from the world of idols, the world of the tradition, is sanctioned by the special relationship between God and humanity, a relation which renders the future a space of hope and always new possibilities. The human will (and hope engendered through discovery) is God's gift. By it, humanity (through collaboration) is empowered to emulate God's singular power to produce the infinite multiplicity of nature with the world's unifying frame. Bacon's new science is the accomplishment of possibilities of this emulative will, because it is guided both by the frame and the phenomena of nature. The power that corresponds to this will is the power to re-create in proper homage to God: not to *improve* on God's creation, but rather to *prove* its richness and *rightfulness* by new creation and invention.

Ultimately, myth plays a crucial part not only in Bacon's study of early naturalism and the shortcomings of past science, but also in his vision of the new science. Perhaps nowhere is this mythical impulse of Baconian science more strikingly seen than in the *New Atlantis*. He tells us that this myth will give hope to the new scientist. When all is dark and the light of nature has yet to appear, the myth will serve to light the way. The New Atlantis, however, will not simply restore the greatness of the past, but rather will show the way for a future that promises more than can be revealed by what has come before. Bacon's scientific force of hope pushes beyond what is immediately and definitely possible to what at first appears only mythical: a new world in which the human will coincides with human power. This coincidence is the fulfillment of the most ancient prophecy and the most modern science; it is the site in which revealed theology and revealed science show themselves to be two sides of the same project of human power.

5

The Question of Technical Creation and the Second Nature of Baconian Science

B acon's Hope is not mere hope, but rather a projective attitude which sets the tone for his scientific work. His reading of traditional science and ancient naturalism is not based on scholarly desire but rather stems from an overarching commitment to the (re)gaining of human power over nature. The futural drive of Baconian Hope and his almost constant preoccupation with the traditional and mythical past are two poles of one project: to discover the fundamental components of nature which will lead to an unparalleled level of power for humanity.

This quest for and unprecedented acquisition of power is not based solely on the principle of utility, but rather stems more directly and essentially from the emulative structures of Bacon's theological vision. Because of this vision, the preliminary development of Bacon's massive scientific project involves not only a new notion of material nature, but a clearer idea of the human essence as well. Indeed, Bacon calls for an explicitation of the anthropological mission and a new notion of matter in almost the same breath, for "seeing that every natural action depends on things infinitely small, or at least too small to strike the sense, no one can hope to govern or change nature until he has duly comprehended and observed them."[1] Bacon's efforts to push beyond traditional natural philosophy toward the new science necessarily mean a reassessment of the essential tasks of human life and a redefinition of history. Both the nature of nature and the nature of the human must be reexamined, because the "roads to human power and to human knowledge lie close together and are nearly the same."[2] In short, and using a not entirely irrelevant image, Bacon claims that one must better understand the worker *as well as* that upon which the worker works.

In the Image of the Unmade Maker: The Place of Homo Faber

The theological horizon against which Bacon's reconstruction of the sciences is set involves a peculiar notion of the past, specifically, of a past that waits to serve as modern science's own proper, though confused, origins. Implicit within this proprietary claim is a belief in something like a prelapsarian age. However, it is important to notice that Bacon never talks about such a pristine period naively, nor does he ever call for a wholesale return to such a moment in human history. Rather, something more profound is at play in Bacon's concern with origins. The Great Instauration is the call for revolution not only in science and technology, but also in anthropology. This call is made in the name of a reaffirmation of the proper role of the human as that special creature which stands both within and outside the realm of nature.[3]

Bacon's reconstruction of the sciences is framed by his understanding of the proper status of this unique creature and its relation *both* to its creator and to what resides in creation. The fundamental scheme which lies at the root of Bacon's vision of the new science is his modification of the tripartite order, divinity-humanity-nature. According to Bacon, traditional science has collapsed this order, placing human life in either the realm of nature or the divine depending on its focus at the time. Bacon's rewriting of the tradition seeks to reinstate the third term, the human order. Bacon understands the collapse of this third term to represent a crucial moment in human history, a moment which may have consequences even more severe than those incurred as a result of the First Fall:

> We copy the sin of our first parents while we suffer it. They wished to be like God, but their posterity wish to be even greater. For we create worlds, we direct and domineer over nature, we will have it that all things *are* as in our folly we think they should be, not as seems fittest to the Divine wisdom, or as they are found to be in fact; but we clearly impress the stamp of our own image on the creatures and works of God, instead of carefully examining and recognizing in them the stamp of the Creator himself. Wherefore our domination over creatures is a second time forfeited, not undeservedly; and whereas after the fall of man some power over the resistance of creatures was still left to him—the power of subduing and managing them by true and solid arts—yet this too, through our insolence, and because we desire to be like God and follow the dictates of our own reason, we in great part lose.[4]

Even in the midst of his condemnation of this self-imposed double impotence of human knowledge and power, one can see the traces of Baconian

Hope. At each point where Bacon eulogizes what has been lost, he also sees the promise of recovery. Indeed, it is the double Fall which has made this Hope and recovery possible.[5] However, while the first Fall, from paradise, is a primeval cleft, the second Fall is historically engendered and therefore futurally remediable.

Bacon's claim, then, is that we must rethink and reorder anthropology for the sake of the new science. In other words, the rediscovery of who we are is a propadeutic to our rediscovery of what we should be doing with Nature. Bacon reads the tradition as a collapse of the properly tripartite structure of human knowledge, a collapse which has blurred the essential qualities of each of the three forms. Therefore, it seems to him that a vital component of the new science must involve a clearer anthropological vision as well as a deeper recognition of our essential relations with God and Nature.

In the name of this proper anthropological mission, Bacon believes he can criticize the Humanists and Alchemists, the Scholastics, and Plato and Aristotle in one fell swoop, the first two for seeking to abrogate the laws of nature by false magical powers, the Scholastics for maintaining the strict resemblance of the divine and the natural, and the last two for denying humanity and divinity respectively. In every case the crime is the same: the denial of the human order is also the denial of the true orders of God and Nature.

Moreover, it is the peculiarly Baconian appeal to a rehabilitation of this three-term ontological structure, Divinity-Humanity-Nature, which distinguishes him from the Renaissance movements which had such an obvious influence upon him, the humanist and alchemical traditions. As Rossi points out, Bacon's negativity toward Platonism stems in large part from his rejection of the humanist idols of "verbosity, slothfulness, and the desire to please."[6] Just as he had attempted to do with the ancient tradition, Bacon seeks to rewrite humanism. Baconian humanism appeals to the theological right and responsibility of humanity to work toward the transformation of nature as the fundamental motive for a deeper understanding of nature, rather than striving in the direction of some Platonic *eros* or *eidos*. The humanists suffer from the same basic malady as their role models, Plato and Plotinus: they mistakenly believe that the essence of human life lies in the development of a contemplative mind wrongly divorced from action. According to Bacon, they see human existence and nature in terms of a single ideal, the purity of intellectual soul, and compress all phenomena—divine, human, and natural—within the limits of this singular though prorated stuff of the world (e.g., Plotinus's "World Soul").

The Renaissance tradition of alchemy or natural magic stands at the other extreme of the same fundamental error. Bacon's own notion of the innate human power of transformation is reminiscent of the image of the magi, at least superficially. Quite clearly, Bacon does believe in magic, but this true magic, like everything else the tradition hands to us, must be refurbished. In *De Augmentis Scientiarum*, he lays out his views on magic: "But I must here stipulate that magic, which has long been used in a bad sense, be again restored to its ancient and honorable meaning . . . as the science which applies the knowledge of hidden forms to the production of wonderful operations; and by uniting (as they say) actives with passives, displays the wonderful works of nature."[7] The desire on the part of some scholars to conflate the alchemist notion of *magus* with Bacon's idea of human power must be tempered by Bacon's strong condemnation of natural magic. As with all of his readings of various components of the tradition, one must acknowledge that Bacon is offering a rereading, an appropriation of certain movements, texts, or schools of thought, including those of alchemy and natural magic. Therefore, if the claim is made that Bacon holds with the idea that the magus is an accurate and essential depiction of human potential, one must also qualify this claim by pointing out that the Baconian magus practices *technical magic* not natural magic, the latter having "but few discoveries to show, and those trifling and imposture-like."[8] On the other hand, the technical magus recognizes that an entire world cries to be investigated, a world that will yield its secrets to the questioner who possesses a clear sense of inventive purpose.

Like humanism, the alchemical tradition eliminates the third ontological term, humanity, both by asserting that the magician possesses supernatural powers and also by claiming that nature is predominantly animistic. Bacon actually has fewer qualms about the basic aims of the alchemical tradition than he does the more mainstream Neoplatonist tradition, feeling compelled to "rationalize and make respectable a tradition which was heavily suspected by its opponents, by the Aristotelians of the schools and by the humanists of the rhetorical tradition."[9] Bacon fiercely criticizes alchemists such as Paracelsus for occluding the essential tripartite structure of truth—humanity, divinity, and nature—by their false magic, truths which are necessary to the emergence and development of the new science. In so doing, they have brought about the aforementioned second Fall: "By mixing the divine with the natural, the profane with the sacred, heresies with mythology, you have corrupted, O you sacrilegious impostor, both human and religious truth. The light of nature, whose holy name is ever on your lips, you have not merely hidden, like the Sophists, but extinguished. They deserted experience, but you betrayed it."[10] In short, the primary offence of Paracelsus and the practitioners of natural magic stems from the fact that they enjoyed an unusually intimate proximity to natural truth without discovering, but instead denying, its proper structure.

Bacon clearly considers this "second Fall" more egregious than the first. The penalty for this second offence is impotence, loss of power. Bacon makes it clear that although the promise of power remains, we had fooled ourselves into believing in our impotence that we are like God. The road to true human power can only be entered by recognizing the depths of error to which human life has fallen. Only once the idolic forms have been at least provisionally identified and proper correctives employed to counteract the "historical indolence of man," can the quest for true power begin anew. What makes Paracelsus and natural magic so culpable is the fact that their quest for power and knowledge over nature was impeded chiefly by their own presuppositions and their excessive appeal to past greatness rather than to the promise of a rightful, though as yet uncharted, future: "Bacon sees the satisfaction of the human appetite for knowledge with the achievements of the ancient world as a result not of conscious self-restriction in view of supposed limit-settings but rather of an illusionary underestimation of one's own powers and means, which at the same time can be described as an overestimation of what has been achieved."[11]

Thus, Bacon's call for a new anthropological vision is clearly linked to the need for a new theological framework. His effort to correct the multiple errors of traditional science and natural magic centers upon an new emphasis on the relation between God and the creature that most resembles him, the human. Bacon forges an intimate connection between this theological frame and the essential role of a properly established science in the fulfillment of the human capacity for power and knowledge: "But if the matter be truly considered, natural philosophy is, after the word of God, at once the surest medicine against superstition and the most approved nourishment for faith, and therefore she is rightly given to religion as her most faithful handmaiden, since the one displays the will of God, the other His power."[12] For Bacon, human understanding of God's Will can never be more than limited at best. However, God's Power is consistently and overtly manifest *if* one has the aid of this "*surest medicine*" *of natural philosophy*. In other words, human access to God's Will is narrow, while the scientifically directed potential for discovering the structures and implications of God's Power have no such limits. Indeed, Bacon sees the new science as the helpmate of a clearer, more coherent theological vision, the discovery of nature providing a clearer, though never transparent, picture of the Divine Will and Plan.

In conjunction with the theological display of God's Will, one sees the trajectory, according to Bacon, of the technical and science-inspiring power of God. Collective human will and power, when properly coordinated, combine to emulate the productive force of God. The proper future of humanity lies precisely in the direction of bringing its divine image, its own potential for power, to the fore. The new science will be both the expression of this potential and the catalyst that enhances the speed and overtness of its appearance. In short, Bacon claims that true scientific discovery (and technical invention) recapitulate the power of the *Deus Faber*, the productive force of ex nihilo Creation. The proof of this emulative relation between divine creative power and the prospective power of the new science lies in the promise that the latter, like the former before it, will transform the world:

> Again, discoveries are as it were new creations, and imitations of God's works, as the poet well sang:
>
>> To man's frail race great Athens long ago
>> First gave the seed whence waving harvests
>>> grow,
>> and *recreated* all our life below.
>
> And it appears worthy of remark in Solomon that, though mighty in empire and in gold, in the magnificence of his works, his court, his household, and his fleet, in the luster of his name and the worship of mankind, yet he took none of these to glory in, but pronounced that "The glory of God is to conceal a thing; the glory of the king to search it out."[13]

It is as a special variety of *Homo faber* that modern humanity will fulfill its role as the creative creature, the one who is made in the image of the Unmade Maker.[14] Bacon sees the essential human feature to be the capacity to emulate the creative power of the Maker. Natural philosophy in its proper form, the new science, will be the full embodiment of this emulative power of creation and production; it will be the restorative or curative path for the reordering of human understanding, both of the world and of itself.

This innate human power of recreation found only haphazard expression in all but the most infrequent periods of human history, most notably the early Greek and Roman epochs. According to Bacon, the greatest general hindrance to the development of this essence of power stems from the fact that "the author lays the weakness of his art to the charge of nature: whatever his art cannot attain he sets down on the authority of the same art to be in nature impossible."[15] Thus, Baconian science seeks to establish an universal art or methodology of discovery which denies absolute impossibility at the same time that it acknowledges the virtually unlimited possibilities of the human will to power.

This is not to say that Bacon is committed to the development of new technologies for their own sake. Lisa Jardine is correct to challenge the notion that "technological advance is the main goal of Baconian science."[16] Following Rossi, Jardine stresses the inseparability of truth and work for Bacon, which implies that technology is more a by-product than the chief goal of Bacon's project.[17] However, the fact that technological progress is but a secondary objective of Baconian science does not mean that contemplative truth, at least in its traditional form, is its main goal. Bacon seems to be developing a new form of truth which is at once theoretical and technological, both in its objectives and its internal structures. Thus, to characterize Bacon's science as aiming chiefly at contemplative truth is no more to the point than claiming that Bacon is the "father of modern technology." Bacon seeks to break down such distinctions in order to reveal both the reality of the things themselves and the proper work that science should be about: "things as they really are, considered not from the viewpoint of appearance but from that of existence, not in relation to man but in relation to the universe, offer conjointly truth and utility."[18] Indeed, presented in this form, Bacon's scientific call involves a discovery of the technological face of nature that is already at play prior to human comprehension.

The double gift of knowledge and power is in fact one and the same talent, and science should reflect this coincidence. Bacon's new science reasserts the existence of the third general term, humanity, in the tripartite structure of reality, defining and situating it as the double of the productive power of *Deus Faber*. Science will fulfill this potential emulation by revealing the correlation between this double human talent (knowledge and power) and the theologically legitimated power of doubling Nature. Through a recognition of the inventive essence of human life, its rightful and open-ended goal of transforming nature, Bacon believes science will step out of its troubled past and into a proper future of true growth and discovery.

Second Phusis and the Proper Reproduction of Nature

Bacon's account of the rightful power of the new science is accompanied by another issue, for just as the human corner of the ontological triangle must be rethought and recast, so must the corner known as nature. On the basis of Bacon's theological and naturalist edicts, the reinterpretation of nature (that is, of "the things themselves") forms a crucial part of the Baconian effort to implement the appropriate power of scientific truth. Only by a rediscovery of the basic structures of natural phenomena, both in their singular and their universal aspects, can science begin to fulfill its role as the avenue for the full development of the essential human power of reproduction. Indeed, Bacon's project remains a hodgepodge of contradictory commitments until one recognizes just how intimately his projects to rewrite the philosophy of nature and to develop a powerfully productive science are interwoven. In an important sense, they are one and the same project, the former serving as a propadeutic for the latter. Only by a radical restoration of the true elements and structures of nature can the new science begin to approach its rightful degree of power over nature.

The importance of this recasting of nature for Bacon's vision of the new science can be seen most strikingly in Bacon's conception of natural history, and it is this notion that stands as Bacon's most direct and lasting legacy to the moderns, though it is also the aspect of his work which lays him open to the most criticism. The ambiguous nature of this Baconian legacy stems from the fact that Bacon conceives of natural and technical entities as essentially the same, though he is adamant that this sameness is not be taken as either an idealization or an abstraction. In other words, Bacon would agree with Descartes's statement that there is no difference "between machines made by artisans and the various bodies that nature alone can fashion," but not in order to support the Cartesian claim that the essence of matter is quasi-mathematical.[19] Rather, Bacon's conflation of nature and art stems from a naturalistic conviction that all matter lends itself to an as yet undetermined re-creation, to a further creation engendered by human technical power. Thus, rather than invoking a normative force which imposes some quasi-mathematical structure on natural things, Bacon posits the accommodating tendency of natural things. Both views share a commitment to a manipulative science, but, where the Cartesian form is essentially mechanistic, the Baconian version sees science as naturalistic from beginning to end.

Bacon's notion of natural history also offers additional evidence of the theological impulse which guides his views on science and nature, and which, though in a transformed manner, draws the rough but crucial outline for the modern vision of things—natural and artificial. Ultimately, Bacon's conception of natural history—which is not only concerned with natural things in the everyday sense—foreshadows a dramatic shift in the way in which the Aristotelian distinction between the realms of *phusis* and *techne* is thought. This radical reconsideration of the relation of the natural and the technical will come to stand as one of the fundamental features

of early modern science. As Jean-Claude Margolin puts it, Bacon's "abolition of the frontiers which separate the orders of nature and the technical
in Aristotle" is "the very heart of Baconian philosophy," and "one must
take the creation of *new* natures in the literal sense of the term."[20]

In his conception of the relation of *phusis* and *techne* (as set forth in
the *Physics*), Aristotle maintains at least one crucial difference between
them: as "physical" entities, things possess within themselves the source
(*arche*) of their emergence, whereas technical items are produced by a
source which is not essentially their own. As Aristotle states, "Again a
human is generated from a human, but a bed is not generated from
a bed."[21] Aristotle does not impose this as a radical or strict distinction, but
he does assert a steady difference in the ways natural beings as opposed
to artificial things come to appear, a critical difference which springs
from the rich Aristotelian concept of *kinesis*. By this distinction, Aristotle
underlines the difference between natural appearance and technical production, the latter, but not the former, being synonymous with "making"
for Aristotle. In other words, the essential Aristotelian difference between
natural things and those produced by *techne* stems from the fact that the
latter make their appearance through the intermediary of human mind
and hand.

While *phusis* may be thought of as a process analogous to the
technical phenomenon of production, such analogies fail to capture the
"self-production" essential to natural appearance.[22] Aristotle was himself
aware of the tendency to conflate the two forms of production, since it
is implicit not only in Plato's notion of the Demiurge, but also in the
general Greek recognition that culture remakes whatever natural beings
it incorporates into itself.[23]

This notion of a fundamental frontier of self-production distin-
guishing the realm of nature from technically produced entities entails
certain assumptions on Aristotle's part, chief among these a view of
nature as self-originating (*phusis* qua *genesis*) and wholly accountable for
its existence within the structural horizon of its own appearance. Thus,
Aristotle's notion of nature as *phusis* differs fundamentally from Bacon's,
precisely because of the enormous field that the former entails, a field
which includes "the shape of man" among the many shapes of growing
things.[24] For Bacon, on the other hand, the realm of nature will be a
more limited, albeit still seminal, territory, a territory whose richness
is due as much to its plasticity, its almost willing acceptance of human
efforts to appropriate and transform it, as to the fact that it gives rise to
spontaneous growth.[25]

While Aristotle's conception of nature springs from a basic perceptual faith in the coherent indigenous grounds of natural structures and

appearance, this faith involves a form of naturalism crucially different from Bacon's own naturalistic commitments. The sources of this difference lie at the heart of Bacon's decisions regarding the essence of a theologically endorsed and technically engendered human power and knowledge that depends crucially on the essential sameness of naturally and humanly generated entities. Of course, the fact the one of the major signposts of the tradition, Aristotle, should so direly misunderstand the proper relation of nature and technology hardly surprises Bacon. It is simply another crucial error of which we must divest ourselves in the name of the new science: "And I am the more induced to set down the History of the Arts as a species of Natural History, because an opinion has long been prevalent, that art is something different from nature, and things artificial different from things natural. . . . Whereas men ought to be surely persuaded . . . that the artificial does not differ from the natural in form or essence, but only in the efficient."[26] The "efficient," the productive agent, may be some divinely ingrained natural code or it may be the human hand, mind, and will. To entertain any other essential difference between natural things and technical items is tantamount to replacing God by Nature, a typical Aristotelian sleight of hand, and therefore to do grave damage to the special theological privileges of human power.[27]

The understanding of nature delineated in Aristotle's *Physics*, as well as the philosophical framework developed in his *Metaphysics* and *Ethics*, represents much of the tradition which Bacon seeks to rewrite as well as appropriate. Bacon understands nature to have three possible forms: free-moving, impeded, or artificially transformed. In accordance with his view of the sameness of natural and technical things, he makes it clear that these three forms are not strict categories, but rather subject to infiltration, each by the others. That is, nature in its technical form and nature in its natural form intermingle and influence each other. Nonetheless, when seen in the light of his claim that "the human race seeks to recover its right over nature"[28] (a claim which takes the form of a recurrent legislative metaphor), the transformative aspect becomes the dominant pole.

The trajectory of Bacon's restructuring of the Aristotelian *phusis/techne* relation seems clear: where Aristotle had allowed the possibility of the accidental convergence of a *technikon*, an other-made thing, and its source (e.g., the doctor curing him or herself), Bacon suggests something wholly different. He begins with the premise that *all* things are created or made. This is not a simple recital of an old religious precept, but rather the elucidation of a new metaphysical ground for understanding nature and science. God's power should be revealed by natural philosophy, and imitated by the arts and by Baconian physics. That is, the power of the *ens creans* shines forth in the careful observation of its creation, and by such observation a human simulation of this creative movement is empowered and incited.

Bacon's effacement of the art-nature distinction is not simply a means to encourage the development of some crude industrial power, but rather an effort to make room for a new form of certain knowledge. His move is not unlike that attempted by Descartes: to guarantee that human understanding can eventually enjoy something like total control over phenomena, the phenomena themselves must be reconstructed.[29] Granted that the Cartesian effort in this regard will involve an expansion of the geometrical onto all of nature, while Bacon's effort is not essentially mathematical, in both cases it is only by effacing the frontier between that which occurs prior to human imposition and that which is born from the human hand that human understanding approaches the certainty which both Bacon and Descartes claim is its innate privilege and responsibility.

Further, this collapsing of the natural and technical realms into a single space over which science holds sway represents a theme shared by the different strains of modern science, the one dominantly mathematical and the other not. Thus, not only Descartes and Bacon, but also others including Mersenne, Hobbes, and Gassendi, will invoke the image of a single constructed (and reconstructible) worldly stuff: "Nature no longer appeared as a context of forms and essences in which 'qualities' inhere, but of phenomena which are quantitatively measurable. It was declared that there were no 'hierarchies' in nature and the world no longer appeared as constructed for man or to the measure of man. All phenomena, like all the component parts of a machine, were declared to have the same value."[30] The scientific project of calculability, of pure mathematical description, depends no less than the more crudely mechanistic project upon this conception of nature as essentially technical, both in its structure and genesis. Bacon's praise of the old atomism of Democritus is, in fact, a recognition of the fundamental technicity of nature. However, Bacon's own views on material nature are considerably more subtle and importantly nonmechanistic.

Insofar as Bacon's natural and experimental history represents an attempt to recount the generations and pretergenerations of this productive knowledge/power—as well as that of its mimetic offspring, human invention and technique—the collapse of the distinction between the natural and the technical is imminent. The freedom of natural things which Bacon cites is a largely deficient freedom, one which must be uncovered, clarified, and reshaped by experiment just as surely as these things were originally called into existence by God; miracles of divinely produced nature stimulate miracles of humanly produced nature: "But by rare and extraordinary works of nature the understanding is excited and raised to the investigation and discovery of forms capable of including them, so also is this done by excellent and wonderful works of art, and that in a much greater degree, because the method of creating and constructing such miracles of art is in most cases plain, whereas in the miracles of nature it is generally obscure."[31] Nature becomes truly free only once it has been "translated" by technical and scientific work. What was not "free," in the sense of being purely unrestrained, then becomes "free," in the sense of being opened up to new manifestations and new possibilities of existence. The new science frees nature, because it broaches the releasing power of operative nature, that is, nature coaxed and manipulated by truly operant knowledge.

Thus, Bacon seeks to dispense with, or at least subjugate, the difficult and troublesome notion of built-in *archai* which somehow distinguishes natural things from the things of *techne*. From the Baconian point of view, Aristotle's subtlety has turned out to be a source of discouragement rather than encouragement for the advent of the new science. Where Aristotle has depicted nature and art as uneven realms separated by a frontier, the former vast and the latter more limited, Bacon will invert the differential of size and significance. He continues to maintain that "it is nature which governs everything," but the nature of nature must be seen as on the way to becoming technical. Bacon's second *phusis* calls for a realignment of the fundamental understanding of nature, an understanding which must trace out the productive lines present in all phenomena. Indeed, the difference in *who* does the producing is almost as important an issue as the fundamental fact of production itself. What is most essential, most proper to all things, their similitude, lies not in the fact that they are natural or human-made, but that they have all been produced and can be reproduced.

Only when Bacon's project to substantially erode the frontier that divides the natural and technical realms has been taken seriously enough, does the famous statement at the opening of the *New Organon*, "Nature to be commanded must be obeyed," cease to be merely apocryphal and become the shorthand for the method for the new science. Indeed, there are two natures contained within this terse statement: the one to be commanded has not yet arrived on the scene *because* the one to be obeyed has been forgotten. The Baconian rediscovery of "nature obeyed" involves the effacement of the extreme division between humanly and divinely produced items. The emergence of "nature commanded" depends upon the success of the preparatory project of effacement.[32]

Bacon's Appeal to the Ancient Atom:
The Convergence of the Theoretical and the Technical

Bacon's vision of science depends on a reordering of certain basic theological and natural positions which he appropriates from the tradition. This reordering pivots around his conception of the human essence as a transformative and inventive power. Bacon's God assigns more to human undertaking than the contemplative understanding of what the world should be like. First and foremost, Bacon takes the God-given mission of human life to involve the normative production of new realities and the invention of new techniques for the shaping and discovery of these realities. Thus, the advent of Bacon's great scientific reconstruction begins not with a Cartesian-like demand for the total clarity of all that is real and true, but rather with an attitude which tolerates, even embraces, the possibility of reality and truth that is only partially visible to us at the present moment. The fine line that divides natural and technical entities, the Baconian view of natural things as "awaiting" their productive and technical reproduction or reappearance, is the frontier between somnolent truth and truth awakened.[33] Indeed, the chief power of Baconian science lies in what it has yet to unearth, bring to light, or create, and therefore will take its cue to some extent from the truth which is hidden naturally beneath the richness of natural phenomena (and artificially behind the indolence of the human spirit):

> For Bacon, the great world hide-and-seek of the hidden God of late-medieval nominalism, which Descartes intensified into the suspicion of the universal deception of a *Dieu trompeur* [deceiving God] and sought to break through by grounding all certainty on absolute subjectivity, has exactly the innocence of a game laid out with the goal of eventual discovery and solution and free of any suggestion of jealousy of man's insight into the secret of the creation.[34]

Indeed, Blumenberg is understating the relation between creation and discovery, since, as we have seen, Bacon calls for a second nature which will mirror and extend original nature. Just as the human spirit, concentrated in the new science, is a reflection of Divine Spirit, so human works will reflect and thus do honor to Divine Works.

This view of the essentially ameliorative role of science with regard to nature shows that Bacon's call for the separation of religion and science is not so much a demand for a complete divorcing of the two but instead for a proper ordering or relation of two intimate and mutually supportive movements. Without being self-contradictory, one can say that Baconian science is imminently theological, because science seeks to emulate the creative power of God presented to us constantly by the natural phenomena that permeate our experience. When these phenomena are explained in religious rather than naturalistic terms, such as in the case of the Pythagoreans or their latter-day disciples, the alchemists, the Neoplatonists, and so forth, the proper relationship of religion and science suffers, or as Bacon puts it, the problematic issue of God's Will is confused with our natural knowledge of God's Power. The foremost imperative of Baconian science springs from an ever greater expansion of this knowledge of God's Power in order that we might emulate it in human terms.

In his quest for historical support for his new science, Bacon feels compelled to look beyond the tradition and its misreadings of the relation of religion, nature, and science. His considerable interpretation of Democritean physics represents a major effort to muster this kind of historical precedent for his work, an effort that involves Bacon in the movements to rehabilitate ancient atomism. The appeal to pre-Platonic atomistic theories offers Bacon a precedent which is at once naturalistic and nonformalistic. That is, ancient atomistic views serve to sweep away much of the metaphysical and theoretical blockage that Bacon claims impedes true scientific progress. As Graham Rees states, Bacon is less committed to atomism than he is to dislodging the confounding and counterproductive view of nature (and its companion theology) central to traditional science: "For Bacon, the atomists outshone Plato and Aristotle in both physics and virtue. . . . Not only were matter and motion better than act and potency, proximate causes were better than final ones. Bacon did not hesitate to invoke the example of the atomists in order to sanction the summary expulsion of final causes from the field of natural philosophical enquiry."[35] Thus, according to Rees, one of Bacon's chief motives in appealing to atomism involves his effort to expose the tradition's scientific vices and theological excesses.[36]

However, this effort to reveal the tradition's obfuscating and counterproductive elements is not the central aim of Bacon's project, so much as a maneuver to clear the way for the vast reordering on which the new science depends. As Rees's analysis shows, Bacon's relationship to atomism is a very complex one. He not only claims that Bacon is not an atomist, that Bacon uses atomism largely as an heuristic tool, but goes so far as to claim that Bacon is, in a very important sense, anti-atomistic. Rees stakes this claim of Bacon's anti-atomism to the large number of passages in which Bacon rejects the concept of the void that is central to classical atomistic theory. In other words, Rees argues that the Democritean atomism which most scholars claim had such an overwhelming influence on Bacon's scientific views is not "swallowed whole," but rather only in pieces, and in order to further a theory of matter that Bacon believes will ultimately outstrip atomism entirely.[37]

Rees seeks to show that the "pieces" of atomism which Bacon takes up are to be fitted into a theory of matter distinctly different from atomism. Bacon's theory of matter reflects his recognition of the subtlety of nature. As a result his theory diverges widely from most atomistic doctrines, because he stresses the play of spirits, rather the existence of a void, within material bodies. At the same time, one must stress the basic differences between the physical views of Bacon and Henry More, for the latter shows little or no concern to develop a consistent material theory, while the work of the former can only succeed with the development of a fully operational chemical theory of matter.

More's major concern, in the fairly typical manner of the Cambridge Platonist, is to show how the action of spirit upon matter is not only allowed, but even required by the principles of reason.[38] Thus, while Bacon would not object to the general notion of a "Spirit of Nature" that influences all natural bodies, his theory of matter sought "a measure of unity and theoretical integrity which joined together the celestial and the terrestrial realms in an articulated system embracing plant and planet, material soul and star, the processes of growth and decay, the movements of the heavens and the oceans and, in principle, practically everything in the natural order."[39] In short, where More is content with providing enough concrete evidence to support his metaphysical commitments, Bacon seeks an account of matter that renders nature at once knowable and accessible.[40]

Baconian physical theory involves a conception of matter that is considerably more dynamic than that offered in the typical atomistic conception. Most historians of science concerned with this aspect of Bacon's work have tended to separate the aspects of Bacon's views on matter that seem straightforwardly atomistic from his suggestions concerning a more dynamic, even spiritual, form of matter.[41] Rees takes Bacon's interest in atomism to be less naive and more critical; he sees Bacon as in fact looking for yet another historical precedent to support his own theory of matter and his general scientific project:

> Bacon thus evidently saw atomism as the one ancient philosophy which foreshadowed and therefore sanctioned the idea of subtlety enshrined in the pneumatic theory of matter. . . . Bacon therefore found in atomism a means of conferring the authority of antiquity (authority doubtless greater if related to the wisdom of the ancients) upon the notion of subtlety . . . he found in atomism a means of showing his readers what sort of thing subtlety was.[42]

The demonstration of matter's complexity, its subtlety, by an appeal to ancient atomism is not the culmination of Bacon's theory of matter, but rather only an initial stage. Ultimately, Bacon seeks to reveal the true dynamic of material nature that stems from its particulate aspect (as well as its overarching frame). Bacon sees this uncovering of the true subtlety of pneumatic matter as a crucial moment in the development of the new science, because only once this natural subtlety has been identified can it be matched by a new subtlety of the human mind and hand.

Rees's work on Bacon's supposed atomism begins and ends with the assumption that Baconian matter theory involved more than a syncretic effort that slapped arcane Renaissance alchemical theories together with more current and viable scientific concepts. Instead, Rees claims that Bacon was seeking to elaborate a material theory that could be reconciled with his overall speculative philosophy. In other words, following Rees (and to some extent Rossi, Deleule, Margolin, and certain others), it is not unreasonable, perhaps in fact more reasonable, to read Bacon's scientific work as part of an overall cosmological scheme that is more original than syncretic, more influential than arcane.[43] To put it in Bacon's own terms, the frame of nature and the material spirits which play within this frame are the metaphysical and physical keys to the new science. Only by better grasping the relation between the frame and stuff of nature will science move beyond its empty conjecture and into the realm of productive truth. Seen in this way, Bacon is not antitheoretical as long as scientific theory has been consistently informed and guided by a naturalism that recognizes the order and play of the frame and matter of nature.

The general aim and mood of Bacon's project clearly falls within the arena of modern science. That is, he seeks a new level of scientific legitimacy and power by recovering the natural realm as a massive source of experimental knowledge. However, the specific manner in which Bacon attempts to realize this aim and solidify this mood as the new scientific norm has almost always been viewed suspiciously, particularly because of his appeal to the Paracelsian tradition. In short, the appeal to the ancient atom, to a simple, largely inert, particle, at play in a void, places Bacon within the circle of early modern science. However, the appeal to a material form that is not inert, that possesses what Bacon unabashedly calls "spirit," throws him back outside this circle.

The ordinary atom allows for a mechanically coherent, if all too simple, material theory, one which supposedly neither involves nor requires a vast metaphysical story to support it. Bacon's theory of pneumatic matter, on the other hand, can only be sustained by the concomitant development of a theological and theoretical frame. Bacon's use of the myths of Pan, Cupid, Coeleus, and the like, his not always critical mention of

Paracelsian notions, and his skepticism concerning the work of scientists like Gilbert and Galileo are seen as recidivist maneuvers, rather than movements which are significant if not entirely direct influences on the emergence of the new scientific view of the world.

Baconian science, then, apparently springs from a sort of "philosophical schizophrenia."[44] Portrayed as somehow straddling two worlds, one old and worn-out, the other pregnant with immense possibilities, Bacon cannot make up his mind. This at least implicit portrayal is naive, for Bacon has not only made up his own mind (and fiercely in favor of the new world), but he also shapes how the new science will be taken up by those who are yet to come. Behind the overt recidivism lies the struggle to rewrite how science will be done and why it will be done. Bacon's efforts to show that the new science must stand on a new foundation, one built on the legitimate convergence of new theological, technical, and theoretical priorities, remains the central force and movement in all subsequent efforts.

The new scientific institution conceived by Bacon exists for the express purpose of expanding the creative and inventive power of human life. One has only to study the first five aphorisms of the *New Organon* to understand how deep this theological guideline runs in his vision of science. The coincidence of human knowledge and human power of which Bacon writes in the third aphorism, the unwavering position that Nature is the proper ground for all human endeavor cited in the first and forth, and the promise of true technology (and the disappointment engendered by false technology) mentioned in the second and fifth are woven together to form the basic texture of his divinely inspired science of power. Through this naturalistic and technical science, humanity will reassert itself as theologically and theoretically distinct from Nature and God. Thus, for example, the God of Descartes and his geometricized world would be unthinkable for Bacon, largely because the structure of such a world would seem a grave limitation of the power which Bacon attributes to God *and humanity.*

The New Authority of Technical Intervention: From "Natural History" to "Experimental Nature"

In Bacon's estimation, the power of human perception is not responsible for the shortcomings of the sciences, at least not in itself. We have already seen this in a consideration of Bacon's essentially affirmative attitude toward pre-Socratic thinkers. Rather, Bacon maintains that perception, when augmented by various technical "helps" and guided by the proper theological outlook, is the true and revelatory medium for progress in the sciences:

> To the immediate and proper perception of the sense, therefore, I do not give much weight, but I contrive that the office of the sense shall be only to judge of the experiment, and that the experiment itself shall judge of the thing. And thus I conceive that I perform the office of a true priest of the sense (from which all knowledge in nature must be sought, unless men mean to go mad) and a not unskillful interpreter of its oracles; and that while others only profess to uphold and cultivate the sense, I do so in fact. Such then are the provisions I make for finding the genuine light of nature and kindling and bringing it to bear.[1]

As "true priest of the sense," Bacon situates himself in the scientific office which his alliance of theology and technology (i.e., the primacy of technical nature) seeks to create. Only by means of this proper "cultivation" or augmentation of perception will the new science acquire its legitimately immense degree of power. To pursue the metaphor, one can depict Bacon's cultivation of natural perception as preparing the fertile grounds on which the new science will thrive and prosper.

Bacon's rewriting of the relation between natural and technical entities in conjunction with his new theory of matter lies at the heart of this preparative effort. Indeed, the trajectory of Bacon's general project, the total reformation of all knowledge for the sake of a new level of human power, makes this rewriting of the natural realm (and the cultural realm) vitally necessary. To put it in terms which places Bacon's project dangerously close to that of the natural magician, only with the realignment of the interplay of the material and spiritual realms can power and knowledge find reconciliation in their native bond.

And yet at the same time that Bacon's allusion to the "priest of the sense" seems to invoke the image of the magus, it is crucial to see that Bacon calls for a priest of the *sense* and not of the spirit. Although greatly obscured by the various idols of the mind, sense perception is for Bacon an unfailing constant which links the experience of the earliest of the Greek mythmakers and that of the contemporary scientist. In short, perception is the immediate capacity which represents a permanent structure that defies historical obfuscation, but also puts us in contact with the deep past. Further, the science which Bacon envisions will not improve perception so much as disentangle it from certain tradition-engendered limitations.

Bacon's "scientific priest" is, then, not quite the modernized magus that Yates and others suggest, for Baconian science aspires to the difficult, laborious discipline of a science that will transform both mind and matter. Bacon is centrally concerned with the status of spirit, seeking to shift the emphasis from "mock spirit" to the true spirit, the latter caught up within and giving form and meaning to matter. As a result, the Baconian key to this disentanglement of perception and empowering of science lies in a restructuring of the relation of the things of nature and the things of art. The Great Instauration, perhaps the most overtly ambitious project in the history of science and philosophy, centers on the restoration of a naturalist perception that can recognize and exploit the basic truth that the active nature of matter is naturally attuned to the active essence of human technico-scientific enterprise.

According to the Baconian vision, this global restoration will be achieved through the proper alliance of nature and experiment. If Bacon finds the results of past and contemporary experimentation disappointing, he does not find fault with the aims of the research, so much as with the commitments of the researchers. Thus, Bacon feels free to criticize the experimental conclusions of Galileo and Gilbert almost in the same breath as he lauds the goals of Paracelsus and Tilesius. This is not such a shockingly misguided act if one acknowledges that Bacon's call for a technically supplemented naturalist perception is not only the means (and perhaps the end) of his Great Instauration, but is in an indirect manner the essential project of early modern science as a whole. Indeed, despite the indisputable difference between the Baconian anticipation and the authentic modern project of science, what is required in both is a wholesale conversion of what is at play in nature, in science, and in history. By paying attention to certain structures and commitments of the Baconian precedent, we may find traces of the more subtle and systemic conversion that lies at the heart of early modern science proper.

Bacon's Technical Magic: Beyond the False Power of Hermeticism

For Bacon, a most properly human, divinely inspired power is revealed through the play of creation and second creation, of natural production strengthened and enhanced by technical production. Both the divine and the divinely inspired productive forms render what was formerly invisible visible; all truly productive forms of power involve the appearance of something new. All of these are basic tenets of Baconian science, whether expressed outright or not. Collectively, these tenets demonstrate that Bacon embraces a notion of truth as perceptual revelation that is not found, at least not manifestly, in Descartes.[2] That is, where Descartes writes of a *lumen naturale* that strikes directly and essentially the human mind, Bacon appeals to a natural light which aims at more than the intellect. The Cartesian form has a single proper essence (i.e., the mathematical) and a single proper target (i.e., mental substance in its purest form), while the Baconian version of the natural light bathes the entire field of human perception with a supremely productive power that beckons us toward a perhaps more limited, but nonetheless vast, field of potential human productivity. Bacon's version of the natural light could be called more "natural," both because Bacon makes it clear that it is indigenous to the frame and composition of nature *and* because he sees it serving as a constantly active mnemonic force reminding the human spirit of its own nascent productive power.[3]

For Bacon, the truth lodged deep in nature by the productive power of God reveals that other power that can and should augment or upgrade it, the productive power of human science and technology. What had been lost for most of the history of western science is the understanding of the basic similarity between the primordial productive power embodied in nature and this other productive power which is the essence and proper future of humanity. Bacon dwells upon this fundamental sameness of the two productive powers, in his reading of the myth of Prometheus, as well as in his reading of the prelapsarian and Adamite myths:

> The meaning of the allegory [of the Promethean theft of fire from the gods] is, that the accusation and arraignment by men both of their own nature and of art, proceeds from an excellent condition of mind and issues in good; whereas the contrary is hated by the gods and unlucky. For they who extravagantly extol human nature as it is and the arts as received; who spend themselves in admiration of what they already possess, and hold up as perfect the sciences which are professed and cultivated; are wanting, first in reverence to the divine nature, with the perfection of which they almost presume to compare, and next in usefulness towards man. . . . They on the other hand who arraign and accuse nature and the arts, and abound with complainings are not only more modest . . . but are also stimulated perpetually to fresh industry and new discoveries.[4]

As we have seen, original sin becomes the sin of forgetting that the sameness of divine and human power is a promise but not yet a fact. This promise of sameness is futural and has been rekindled in the human mind by the emergence of the modern age of discovery, particularly technical discovery. In short, the natural light which Prometheus once offered, and which Adam once enjoyed, has reappeared with the emergence of a technical light which, albeit crudely, resonates with its primordial parent. For Bacon, the "accusation and arraignment of nature" portrayed by the Promethean myth represents the emergence of ancient techniques; the new Promethean initiatives must be just as ambitious.

As Frances Yates, Rossi, and others have shown, Bacon's notion of natural light owes a debt to certain hermeticist and Platonist trends of his time. However, this tradition's appeal to the plasticity of nature and the Plotinian notion of a Logos buried in nature is transformed by Bacon in terms of his demand for the careful separation of theology and science. As Ernst Cassirer points out, Bacon "releases the province of religion in order the better to safeguard the dominion of natural cognitive powers within the province of experience and knowledge. . . . But to the Cambridge men this release itself cannot but appear as an actual surrender [and] to sever the bond between God and man."[5] Bacon's use of the language of the Cambridge Platonists is accompanied by new understanding of the nature of natural light. Ultimately, Bacon is not a hermeticist or a Platonist, because he is committed to the full naturalization of the natural light. Such a naturalization can be seen clearly in the fact that he appeals to the early naturalists as much as to the experimentalism and Platonism of his own time.[6]

Bacon's early scathing polemics against the ignorance of natural magic vilifies its impotence more than its hubris, its unproductiveness rather than its ambition. What the natural magicians suffer from most, for Bacon, is a belief that one can coax nature to give up its hidden truth by the manipulation of symbols or the mixture of a few crude substances, when in fact the power needed to bring natural truth out of concealment must closely and faithfully resemble the productive force of nature itself. Thus, Bacon lauds the exceptional members of the experimentalist tradition (e.g., Roger Bacon) for their efforts by the "subtle applications of mechanics, to extend the range of discoveries."[7] The technical magic to which Bacon appeals embraces the spirit of such attempts at discovery, but challenges the impoverished view which the alchemist and the hermeticist share concerning the essence and form of the new human power. In short, Bacon finds no fault with their aspirations but only with their technical clumsiness or outright mechanical ignorance; they lack an understanding of the essential resemblance of natural appearance and technically induced discovery.

Bacon grasps the generally transformative power that the new science can have, because he is not a hermeticist or a believer in natural magic, unless by this one means that he believes in the power of technical and scientific intervention. Bacon's "hermeticism" is predicated on the power and promise of technical intervention. New species can be brought into existence through such experimental intervention, and in this belief he will ultimately be joined by most of the Royal Society. The metaphor of the New Atlantis is, for Bacon as well as the Society, a metaphor to be taken seriously, for by it they express a certain faith in the real and effective human power to rewrite nature. Further, while Bacon retains a trace of the hermetic initiate, he makes it clear that the circle of scientific investigators is a large one, including both "mystery-men" (experimentalists) and miners.[8]

For Bacon, the only bona fide natural magic is technical magic. He finds traces, but only traces, of this truth in the works of some of the more sincere practitioners of alchemistry and hermeticism. They all suffer from the crucial inability to recognize the fundamental resemblance of natural and technical appearance, an inability which stems from their overeager efforts to transform nature by preemptory manipulations. Bacon's rejection of the overt metaphysical tenets of these traditions (e.g., the notions of microcosm and macrocosm, symbolic manipulations, etc.) is accompanied by a rewriting of their fundamental appeal to power in terms of a new natural magic, one which emphasizes the vital role of a new technical vision:

> By this *practical* assimilation of a humano-technical scheme and a natural process, Bacon restores the value of rational efficacy to magical practices. The proximity established between these three terms—*generatio, superinductio, incisio*—or the verbs to which these operations correspond, reveal the experimental link which exists between *creation* and *fabrication*. There is no nature, given once and for all, where humanity must content oneself with piercing arcane aspects, but rather the created or produced *natures* by its technological initiative; in this way, the [Baconian term], novelty, or "new nature" is justified.[9]

Just as there is a fine line between natural and technical entities, there is also a intimate relation between the natural power of "generation" and the technical power of "incision." Indeed, the only difference between these powers may ultimately be the logical priority of the former over the latter; in all other ways they are similar. The new nature of technical entities follows in the wake of the always already operant precedent of natural beings. What the new science must undertake is a sort of surgical procedure (i.e., *incisio*) to reveal this kinship of the powers of natural and technical generation. Contrary to the hermetic "cover-up," the project of the new science according to Bacon is the opening up of nature to its as yet only nascent possibilities.

Concealment and discovery, creation and re-creation: these are the essential and overarching elements of the Baconian view of the familial play of nature and science. The new science and its new way of seeing and acting must stem more deeply and consistently from the revelatory play of these same elements. For Bacon, this is what all science, ancient, medieval, renaissance, and modern, has striven and will strive toward. All forms of past science have each in their own way, however, lost their way in this search. The new science will succeed where they have failed, because its chief mission, its specific self-defined goal, embodies most directly this play of nature and second nature. Each of the preceding forms of science has in its own way tried to supply the "missing pieces," but only modern science has at its disposal the power and perspective necessary to restore them all to their true significance. In other words, they are all true in part, but false in comparison to the emergent science, which promises an unparalleled power upon completion.

Technical inventions are one of the keys to the new science for Bacon because they potentially embody this subtle surgical power of in(ter)ventive discovery. Bacon is quick to recognize the transformative properties of new devices, such as the telescope, the microscope, and the astrolabe, properties and principles that serve as the constant, if virtually invisible, theme of early modern science. Such technical "aids to the immediate actions of the senses" Bacon will call "Instances of the Door or Gate," for through them new things are revealed to the diligent.[10] Thus, Bacon is quick to honor Galileo for his technical discoveries, though more critical of what he takes as the latter's hasty theoretical conclusions, that is, what Bacon views as the disappointing unproductiveness of Galileo's work. In Bacon's view, the in(ter)ventive power of the telescope still remains largely untapped despite Galileo's efforts, or rather because those efforts preclude the fuller power of discovery that the telescope enables. The "gateway" is, at it were, opened only to be shut much too abruptly by theoretical commitments that are in spirit antagonistic to interventive tendencies of the new science. In short, Galileo is laboring under very old prejudices of traditional science, blinded by the idols of traditional scientific theories that are devoid of the sort of revealing power that must ground the new science according to Bacon.

In Bacon's naming of the new technical instruments as a "gateway" or "doorway" phenomenon, the experimental vision crucial to modern science emerges, for the invisible and intangible are no longer inaccessible, in short, are no longer necessarily invisible and intangible. The creation of new devices will render up new phenomena to the senses. In this way, Bacon offers an anticipatory solution to the problem which Descartes will put to More almost thirty years later: to detect and measure bodies that are too small or moving too quickly for the unaided senses one must improve the senses technically. If this measurement is not yet possible, Bacon believes it only a question of time and hope, and the persistent effort of technical intervention.[11] Rather than the later Cartesian solution which demands the recognition of the primacy of intellectual apprehension, Bacon sees the answer to lie in the technical upgrading of both natural entities and experimental perception. In fact, though Bacon does not anticipate Descartes's blatant claim that intellectual perception has primacy over naturalistic perception, this Cartesian claim can be at least partially fitted within the Baconian call for the technical upgrading of natural phenomena insofar as Bacon is appealing to what is not yet visible and may never be visible to the natural eye.

Thus, accompanying the Baconian claim that technical devices will serve as perceptual aids runs another, perhaps more central, technical theme: one is not simply extending or augmenting the power of the senses, one is also transforming what is to be perceived. Induction by itself, even technically supplemented induction (*superinductio*), cannot achieve the ambitious goals of Baconian science. The power of induction must carry with it the power to draw out the nascent forms of nature, to transform what already offers itself for re-creation. This double and interactive power of technical re-creation and technical vision resolves the otherwise ambiguous statement that opens the *New Organon*, "Nature to be commanded must be obeyed." Baconian technology may embody the alchemical dream of recapturing the essential human right to transform nature and thereby to transform itself, but it also anticipates something very much like the Cartesian ambition to rework the perceptual and natural realms in terms of an as yet merely nascent structure.[12] From this perspective, Bacon's vision of the new science as the general project by which this technically engendered right of interventive discovery can be best accomplished stands as a companion to the Cartesian vision; it is a second and decidedly modern vision of the new science.

Like his alchemical and hermetic forebears Bacon grasps the theological significance of the scientific will to transform, as well as the importance of erasing the limits which currently restrict human power and discovery. However, unlike these predecessors, he recognizes that this transformative essence will not be reclaimed through simple desire for power, but rather through a method and a theory of matter which will give this essence a body or a living form, namely, interventive science. Not only is a new set of technical commitments making its appearance here, but a new theoretical order as well. Given the global implications of Bacon's overall scientific project, it is little wonder that his naturalistic "true priest of the sense" bears a distinct resemblance to the magus he hopes to render antiquated. It is, however, much more remarkable that Bacon's scientific vision is a direct and not wholly inferior anticipation of the Cartesian science that is so often depicted as utterly alien to it. Bacon's "true priest of the sense" symbolizes not only the new science's need for guidance and faith in its commitment to the uncovering of the truth of nature, but also the promise that through such faith the light of nature can be "brought to bear." The temple of nature in which the scientific ambitions of this "true priest of the sense" will be achieved is a technical temple.

The New Theoretical Authority of Bacon's Technical History

Like the whole of his scientific project, Bacon's "experimental and natural history" is dedicated to the regathering of the Promethean force which belonged to humanity from the beginning. However, the Baconian call is not a call to return to the state of Adamite nature, but rather the aforementioned recognition that the modern period has its own innate promise of greatness.[13] Whitehead points to the prophetic nature of Bacon's Promethean attitude in *Science and the Modern World*: "The greatest invention of the nineteenth century was the invention of the method of invention. . . . The prophecy of Francis Bacon has now been fulfilled; and man, who at times dreamt of himself as a little lower than the angels, has submitted to become the minister of nature. It still remains to be seen whether the same actor can play both parts."[14] The establishment of the possibility of this double role of human life is heralded by Bacon's double notion of science and technology. Whitehead suggests that this double nature of human life, part naturalist experience and part divine knowledge, finds reconciliation and fulfillment in the development of inventive or technological science. In other words, Bacon's scientific project can be seen fundamentally as an attempt to show human understanding and power the way to its rightful level of efficacy by a demonstration of the power of perception or observation. His ambition to be the "true priest of the sense" and "minister of nature," as well as his emphasis of the central importance of compilation of natural and experimental histories, are clear indications of the depth of his faith in the power and promise of technically enriched perceptual experience.

To put it differently, and yet to say the same thing, Bacon's notion of "natural history" depends upon his conception of human life as Promethean. For Bacon, what we can most properly see is revealed to us as a result of our propensity for power and for knowledge, these two residing most intimately in but one area, that which Bacon calls "works." In his call for a philosophy of invention (rather than of cultivation), the truth of perception lies in seeing what awaits transformation, in "grasping appearance" in every sense of the phrase. In short, Bacon's vision of the new science is a radically appropriative one which stems directly from the quasi-cosmological status of humanity that he embraces.

If Bacon's science is not, in the Cartesian sense, theoretical, this is not to say that it is merely a crude empiricism. The Baconian commitment to an interventive science of discovery precludes this all too simple and easy dismissal. Indeed, the question of whether the new science sketched out by Bacon is, in some important sense, theoretical may lead to a better sense of how this science actually figures in the formation of subsequent modern science. Rather than posing Baconian science as a theoretical rival of the Cartesian form, it is a question of uncovering the way in which the theoretical stance of early modern science, including its Newtonian moment, depends on a set of commitments that are as much technological (and theological) as directly theoretical. If this ambiguously derived theoretical science is indebted to Bacon's project, then this debt may be seen best in an analysis of his work on the question of natural and experimental history.

The third part of the Great Instauration, the panoramic collection of natural and experimental histories that Bacon began but never finished, was the crucial juncture in Bacon's scientific project. This claim is supported by the fact that Bacon devoted the last few years of his life to certain exemplary efforts in natural and experimental history. Bacon explains the source of this devotion in the *Parasceve*, making it clear that only with the development of these histories will "progress worthy of the human race" be made. Just a few lines further on, Bacon is even more emphatic and optimistic in his assessment of the central importance of these histories: "let such a history be once provided and well set forth, and let there be added to it such auxiliary and light-giving experiments as in the very course of interpretation will present themselves or will have to be found out; and the investigation of nature and all sciences will be the work of a few years. . . . [I]n this way, and in this way only, can the foundations of a true and active philosophy be established."[15] Much like Descartes in the *Discourse*, Bacon expresses great optimism concerning the relatively brief period of work that might be necessary for the completion of the new science. Bacon also more than anticipates Descartes's solicitation of others to undertake experiments and studies to supplement his own.[16] Both appeal to the productive promise of a scientific community in the name of expediting the crucial work necessary for the fulfillment of the new science.

However, unlike Descartes's request that other researchers send him their experimental results to confirm his own theoretical claims, Bacon sees natural and experimental histories as more than the means to accumulate data to support or deny theoretical stances; rather they represent an intermediate step in the emergence of active science. As Rees puts it, the histories serve two distinct purposes for Bacon: to "assemble cosmological material and [to] put the principles of his natural-historical programme into practice."[17] Rees goes so far as to argue that Bacon had already developed a general cosmology but chose not to present it in thorough form in publication, the *Thema Coeli* alone offering a "thumbnail sketch" of Bacon's basic cosmological commitments.

Indeed, Bacon was convinced that his vision of a modified cosmos would be encouraged by the great number of encyclopedic histories he was working so hard to finish before his death. Bacon's theoretical commitments differ from those of Descartes, because of their almost naked cosmological tendencies. Yet, the former represent what might be termed a less precise, more tolerant, form of theoretical bias. What some have called Bacon's crude empiricism involves not so much a scientific vision devoid of theoretical commitments as a theoretical structure that seeks to embrace natural entities by introducing them into new relations, his "natural-historical programme." This theoretical frame represents the intertwining of Bacon's theological and technological notions into a system that simultaneously expresses his cosmological vision and his scientific hopes.

By disregarding this linkage of the theological and technical commitments of early modern science Bacon is left in the dubious position of "good empiricist, bad scientist." Without sufficient recognition of the way in which Bacon calls for this linkage, and the various ways in which subsequent modern scientific thinkers respond to this call, one is left with the impression that Baconian science is without any legitimate theoretical underpinnings. In fact, without a proper understanding of the importantly theoretical aspect of Bacon's scientific commitments something fundamental to the emergence of early modern science remains hidden, though active.[18]

This strangely theoretical science of Bacon makes what may be its most overt appearance if one compares or cross-examines Bacon's discussion of the new theories of Galileo and Gilbert and his assessment of new technical devices, particularly the telescope. Here one finds Bacon appealing to both the past and the future, to the legitimate tradition and the as yet unseen technical and scientific possibilities, in his criticism of the groundbreaking scientific practice of his own time. In particular, Bacon's disappointment that the telescope did not engender more progress than it did is triggered in large part by his own "personal prevision of the kind of world picture which [he] thought might emerge from the proper implementation of the method with which his name is most closely associated."[19] In other words, Bacon's theoretical hopes and ambitions led him to believe that once discovered, "Instances of the Gate" such as the telescope would lead to a dramatic, even transformative, moment of scientific progress.

Bacon's criticism of the research of Gilbert is almost identical to that leveled against the work of Galileo, for "after he had employed himself most laboriously in the study and observation of the loadstone, [he] proceeded *at once* to construct an entire system in accordance with his favorite subject."[20] The similarity of Bacon's criticism of these two scientists, both generally held in higher esteem than Bacon by most historians of science, is instructive.[21] In both cases, Bacon expresses his appreciation of their experimentalist commitments, while faulting them for their impatient leaps to the construction of theories and systems.

Of course, Bacon's criticism of the theoretical preoccupations of both figures stems much more from his own theoretical and cosmological commitments than from some naive notion of experimentalism.

The claim that Baconian science has no essential theoretical guidance, a claim that Bacon's own writings have justified when interpreted along certain lines, is not opposed simply by his thematic appeal to the technical future. In fact, this appeal to technical novelty is itself based on a schema that is even more central to the Baconian vision of the new science. It is not technical devices alone, or even most essentially, that will bring the new science to fruition, but rather a new theoretical authority driven by a fundamental Baconian principle: the human essence, its very future, depends upon its ability to emulate divine power and creation more and more effectively. The new science must embody this principle in its instruments and its institutions. As Blumenberg puts it, Bacon is committed to a "politomorphic" conception of the world, a conception that grasps both nature and human nature to be the manifestation of a sort of primordial "global politics" in which divine law decrees and implements natural structures and substance:

> What lies open and what remains hidden, what results in good and evil, is determined by this quasi-political state. Commandment and law, which were promulgated over nature verbally and are carried out according to the word, also have the word as their appropriate medium of knowledge. The determined antithesis of this position is constituted by the metaphysics of the mathematization of natural science. It proceeds from the impossibility in principle of secrecy in nature and things withheld from knowledge, to the extent that mathematical regularities are *implemented* in nature.[22]

Here one can clearly see the distance between Bacon and Descartes, as well as the source of much of Bacon's skepticism concerning the Galilean scientific project. Descartes will reproach Galileo for not insulating his mathematical physics from the deceptive force of natural appearance, while Bacon is concerned that such insulation has gone too far already. This mathematically willful ignorance of nature has inhibited what should have been a much more rapid rate of scientific and technical discovery. It is not a question of theoretical knowledge versus empirical knowledge, but rather of two theoretical sciences whose respective forms of certainty both spring from the faithful manifestation of divine law and word. However, for one this manifestation is essentially mathematical, while for the other it is a much richer and more rhetorically powerful lawfulness which shapes the world and guides the science to be.

For Bacon, the key to the new science is the detection and productive reproduction of these "politomorphic" natural laws. The great civil constitutions had to be written and read before they could implemented; the new science must first learn the constitution of the state of nature before it can interpret it properly.[23] Indeed, the new science can only exercise its "political rights" over nature once it understands its multi-dimensional lawfulness. This preliminary reconstruction of the natural laws is the task Bacon appointed for himself in the *Parasceve*: natural history will produce the "legal archives" of nature in which the scientist will find precedents for further development of science. Here humanity will find its right to subjugate nature, as yet only provisionally achieved, to be already theoretically (i.e., constitutionally) sanctioned.

Seen in the light of this "politomorphic conception," natural history represents not the end but rather the beginning of Bacon's active science. In fact, to pursue the legal metaphor, natural history by itself only makes explicit the already operant constitution. The implementation of this active science is the province of the technical history that is the precedent built on and yet already moving beyond natural history. The previously mentioned appeal to past and future, to the rightful tradition and to the unforeseen but promising possibilities of future science, is embodied in the move from natural to technical history, from what has always been to what should be. Bacon does not move beyond his "politomorphic" stance in this ambitious effort, but rather seeks to fulfill the legal course of nature, or as Bacon puts it, "by the help and ministry of man a new face of bodies, another universe or theater of things, comes into view."[24] This "new face of bodies" makes its appearance on the stage engendered by this technical history, this "mechanical or experimental history."

Bacon's theoretical commitments, then, are at once traditional and radical in form. What Bacon takes from the past is a lawfulness that is deemed older than all science, a lawfulness which is, therefore, seen better or more clearly in the naturalism of Democritus than in later, more sophisticated scientific efforts. This primordial lawfulness serves as a sort of theoretical background of Baconian science, and one that helps to explain Bacon's promotion of a pneumatic theory of matter and his adherence to a modified cosmos. The theoretical foreground of Baconian science is not the technical discoveries themselves, but what they harken. They herald a new epoch of human knowledge and power. The actual theoretical impetus is not technical devices, but rather the new way of seeing and saying the world that encourages the appearance of such devices. Bacon's science embodies theoretical commitments that revolve around the promotion and development of this new scientific language.[25] Natural history will exhaustively lay down the existing grammar and syntax of nature so that the technical histories to come, accompanied by their facilitating devices, can make nature what it should be: a realm fit for the total exercise of human knowledge and power. In short, the constitution of new entities always appeals to an already operant constitution based on natural forms tabulated within the rubric of the natural histories: technical histories are preceded by natural histories which in turn rightfully lead to their own self-exceeding by these *new* histories. The span between natural histories and the new technical histories is the space in which Bacon's theoretical science finds its ground. In this space, entities can be redefined and thus transformed; in short, they are given a new theoretical abode.

On the Way to Mathesical Science: The Revealing Power of Technical History

From the Baconian point of view, new advances in science, and technology, are never made without precedents. As a great legal mind, Bacon knew the importance of studying precedents no matter how obscure their origins may be. And yet Bacon does not adhere to the past for its own sake; his appropriation of the tradition, of past science and past myth, is highly selective. When examined carefully this selectiveness reveals the sketch of a science that cannot be confused with any of the predecessors from which it borrows. Instead, what emerges is a vision of science that in an very important manner anticipates the Cartesian form about to appear on the horizon.

Descartes's concern with establishing the "constancy of mind" is not overtly shared by Bacon. In fact, Bacon ridicules the tradition for bemoaning the wavering which confronts the mind in the play of nature. In this regard, it is hard to see how two figures could be more distant. However, Bacon's notion of the normative production of second nature, of technical nature, reveals a fundamental bond between the Baconian and Cartesian scientific visions, because the net effect of technically produced nature is the reduction of the wavering of natural appearance by a technical upgrading of nature. For Bacon, constant and firm experience is established by a methodical emendation of natural history by technical history.

At the same time, if Bacon does not fit entirely within the rubric of early modern science, it is because he believes in something like a modified cosmos, a global qualitative order which can be reworked but only by following the principles embodied in that order. Consequently, his understanding of the "who" and the "what" of science is dramatically different from that of Descartes. In the Baconian view, science is not mathematical, but in a strange sense, mythical: mythical insofar as there is a difficult decision to be made. For Descartes, such decisions are already made: what can be properly perceived by science is both measurable and correct. For Bacon, as he states in "Sphinx or Science," "there is necessity for present action, choice, and decision."[26] Like the Sphynx, the riddles of the natural realm must be solved rhetorically. Mathematical treatment can only have a productive effect once these fundamental difficulties have been at least provisionally deciphered.[27] What is needed most immediately is not a new logistic or a new mathematical style, but rather a new language for enunciating the forces and structures of nature. This new language will not simply facilitate the conversion of nature, but is itself this conversion.

At least a sketch of this conversion project is found in Bacon's program of natural and technical histories. It is supported by the new scientific language under development in the *New Organon* and *De Augmentis*, but it is the histories that will provide the most significant traces of this most natural grammar, as well as indications of how this grammar can best lead to full fruition and implementation of the new scientific power. The histories are divided into two sorts, natural and experimental, according to which of these missions they most directly serve: the natural histories help explain (via hints of the natural grammar) why the technical histories are, or at least promise to be, highly effective. The new scientific language, then, will open the way for the power that expresses the actual aims of the new science.

In themselves, Bacon's natural histories do not represent a radically new idea. However, as with his use of Paracelsian terms and notions, Bacon takes up this venerable medieval schema for very new reasons. Indeed, natural histories are in a basic sense as old as naturalistic thought itself, since naturalism appeals to the innate structures and principles of natural phenomena for its truth. The natural histories are not an end in themselves (for by themselves they prove very little), but rather only the beginning for Bacon. It is only in the light of the technical histories, in the light of nature's power to offer itself up for transformation, that natural history has its most essential meaning for Bacon's new science.

Like Galileo, and perhaps for importantly similar reasons, Bacon reaches an impasse in this quest for a new language of science. How can one go further than the Baconian call for new entities which would better reveal the workings of nature by surpassing them? Galileo understood the crucial importance of discovering the mathematical language that should underlay nature, and yet he also understood what Bacon sees so clearly: the task of science is to take nature as it is so that it can be understood on its own terms. Bacon goes further than Galileo, though less mathematically. He sees that such knowledge of nature is only gained by and for the control of nature. If the new science turns out to be faithful to this double-sided project, the control/understanding of nature, then it is hard to fault Bacon's logic.[28]

It might still be claimed that this kind of thinking is a relic of the traditions of hermeticism and natural magic and that this attitude, as much as his mathematical oversights, prohibits Bacon's membership in early modern science. However, the intimate connection between these two issues also tell us something else which is perhaps more significant: what keeps Bacon from seeing what Descartes sees so clearly—the need to start from a radically new and clean foundation—is Bacon's conviction that much of what the sciences need in order to be rejuvenated has been here all along. The exclusion of Bacon from the ranks of modern science is warranted to the extent that he does not see just how powerful this human inventiveness, this capacity for technical recreation, which he himself proclaims will indeed become.[29]

The gap between Bacon and true modern science can perhaps be best seen in this issue of natural history. Despite his valorization of future science and future discoveries, Bacon still holds that the tradition, or at least the "pretradition," helps set the stage for the last great epoch of science and history. In this way, Bacon still maintains the basic importance of past scientific and naturalistic endeavors, no matter what the excesses or shortcomings of traditional science and philosophy. History (like nature) holds secrets, but these secrets are not maliciously withheld from us by history (and nature) so much as we have hidden them from ourselves. In other words, while much of Bacon's project involves the clearing away of the rubble of traditional science, history (Bacon's "river of time") is the source of the future science's promise.

Bacon's faith in the future of his science of technical history will take on new promise and new possibilities once the other faith he embraced, the faith in naturalistic experience, has been rewritten and re-created. Only when experience has undergone this re-creation will it too make its proper contribution to the emergence of the full power and knowledge of the new science. What remains to be done, however, cannot be done by Bacon, for it involves the elimination of a difference that is central to his vision of the new science, the productive difference between natural forms and historical precedents. That difference, embodied in the very term "natural history," will have no favored place in the new science of Descartes and the science that will supersede it: "For natural history to appear, it was not necessary for nature to become denser and more obscure, to multiply its mechanisms to the point of acquiring the opaque weight of a history that can only be retraced and described, without any possibility of measuring it, calculating it, or explaining it; it was necessary—and this is entirely the opposite—for History to become Natural."[30] What Bacon had preserved, even depended upon, namely, the depth of the tradition and the richness of the natural realm, will be leveled to a common denominator by Descartes. In the face of the new science, History and Nature will not be the allies they are for Bacon, but rather obstacles to the total apprehension of phenomena in general.

Ultimately, it does not matter whether we choose to classify Bacon as modern or premodern, baroque or Renaissance, for the fact is that his influence on modern science is undeniable. His name is invoked constantly by Boyle and Hooke, Newton and Leibniz, and if these references sometimes seem banal, the neo-Baconian impulse toward intervention and transformation which courses through all their scientific efforts is not. What Bacon gives first and foremost to those who follow him is the promise that what is imperceivable need not be so, that through new techniques and new discoveries science can come fully into its rightful power. It is to this promise of the as yet imperceivable Peirce seems to appeal in his celebration of the Baconian attitude:

> Now Lord Bacon, our great master, has said, that the *end* of science is the glory of God, and the use of man. If then, this is so, action is higher than reason, for it is its purpose. . . . So then our age shall end. . . . What sufficient motive is there for man, a being in whom the natural impulse is—first to sensation, then reasoning, then imagination, then desire, then action—to stop at reasoning, as he has been doing for the last 250 years? . . . Man must go on to use these powers and energies that have been given, in order that he may impress nature with his intellect, converse and not merely listen.[31]

Modern science in its first full accomplishment will embody this ambition retrospectively identified by Peirce, but not explicitly. Instead, what Peirce describes as the Baconian call for "action" will turn back on itself, taking on a fiercely theoretical guise at the very same moment that it seeks to achieve the active mission which Bacon championed. A new form of theoretical science will emerge, one which is both empirical and mathematical, but one which will redefine the nature of both these scientific traditions. The new science will be, at least when compared to Bacon's prospective definition of it, as much sphynx as science.

NEWTON'S PERCEPTUAL AUTHORITY AND THE DECISIVENESS OF TECHNICAL APPEARANCE

7

The Merger of the Corpuscular and the Mathematical: Newton's Empirical Science

I n the first section of this project, I have portrayed Descartes's effort to found a new science of Archimedean proportions in terms of a dream of rectifying the quotidian realm into a mathematically accessible and exploitable system. This project establishes the fundamental goal of modern science, a goal Descartes claims to have discovered through his examination of the weaknesses of traditional as well as Galilean science. Chief among the weaknesses of the former are the tendencies toward proliferating species of motion (beyond the right motion of locomotion) and species of inner charms, virtues, or forces. Chief among the weaknesses of the latter, though hardly through an effort of exegetical fairness, is Galileo's inability to grasp the essentially noncorporeal nature of physical bodies. Descartes grounds his new science on the double principle of nature as purely mechanical and thoroughly noncorporeal and thus "solves" the problem raised by the Galilean dilemma. Modern science becomes manifestly modern with Descartes.

However, early modern science does not culminate as a Cartesian but rather as a Newtonian project. In fact, since the actual culmination of early modern science labels itself a vociferously anti-Cartesian project, instead appealing to other traditions, including those symbolized by the ambiguous strains of Bacon's sometimes obscure conception of the new science. Chief among these strains is a resurrection of a corpuscular philosophy, one already found in Bacon's call for a new examination of Democritean science, as well as by the work of others such as Descartes's early admirer (and later critic) Henry More. Interestingly, while the atomic theories of Epicurus and Lucretius are often the target of harsh criticism because of the atheistic implications of their notions of atomic randomness, moderns such as Boyle and Newton rail more fiercely against the radical Cartesian division between mind and matter (e.g., its dependence upon the convoluted physical system of vortices to account for the apparent concretion of *res extensa* as bodies).[1] As a matter of fact, Newton sometimes gave Epicurus and Lucretius the benefit of the doubt concerning atheistic tendencies, while he stridently held Descartes responsible for every implication, theological as well as physical, of his philosophy and science.[2]

A distinct element of modern science, but one which is intimately related to the corpuscular conception of matter, involves the ongoing battle over the possibility (or impossibility) of attraction as a real force. Bacon, following in his own manner certain hermetic traditions, had suggested that bodies contained physical virtues or secondary qualities such as attraction and repulsion, virtues or qualities which belonged to the very essence of corporeal reality. Even natural philosophers, such as Boyle, who were completely committed to the ideal of a mechanical philosophy were tempted to invoke forces in violation of the Cartesian edict labeling any principle based on "action at a distance" irrational. Thus, the problem of attraction dramatically defines the lines of battle drawn in modern science after Descartes: on the one side, those, such as Leibniz and Huygens, who were certain that attraction could never be anything more than an occult quality which required God's repeatedly miraculous intervention in the most mundane of matters; on the other side, Boyle, Newton and others, who, following Bacon and More, were astounded by the audacious compulsion these "Cartesians" had to circumscribe God's ongoing concern with the world, very often at the price of bad science.[3]

Yet, despite the fury of these battles, both sides in some sense agreed upon the battlefield, and through these skirmishes a resolution occurs, one which establishes the vast new authority of modern science. Tying the neo-Baconians and the neo-Cartesians together is a common vision—in spite of numerous differences—that is, a synthetic vision which represents the culmination of a revolution, what Koyré calls "one of the profoundest, if not the most profound, revolutions of human thought since the invention of the Cosmos by Greek thought."[4] I would amend Koyré's statement by adding what he himself has shown again and again: the revolution was also the most profound perceptual mutation since the appearance of the Greek cosmos. Involving an uneasy alliance between the fundamental assumptions of the sciences of Descartes and Bacon, this mutation reaches its most pronounced state of synthesis and dissension in the milieu of their immediate—and sometimes resentful—descendants: Boyle, Huygens, Newton, Leibniz, and the rest. In this second generation of modern science the issues of natural appearance and divine presence take on a new and decisive form, a form that is the very ground upon which Newtonian science will come to stand.

Cartesian Mathesis vs. Cartesian Bodies

On what basis does Newton claim to have distanced himself from Descartes? Certainly, it cannot be his mathematical prowess, since the profound degree to which Descartes sets a precedent in this area is indisputable. In other words, it would be a mistake to read too literally the mathematical "improvement" which Newton signals he has made over Descartes in entitling his major work *Philosophiae Naturalis Principia Mathematica*.[5] Yet, a clue to the difference between the Cartesian and Newtonian views of science does lie in the Newtonian title, in that it refers to a natural philosophy, "natural" in a positively non-Cartesian sense. It is, in fact, a reference to the tradition which Bacon has a significant hand in establishing (or at least, in renewing), the tradition which maintains the primacy of corporeal nature.

Newton understands the difference between himself and Descartes by the fact that he does not distance nature (i.e., corporeal matter) from spirit in the Cartesian manner. On the contrary, Newton follows Bacon and Henry More in calling for a return to corporeal appearance, a return which attempts to undo the damage done by the Cartesian "atheism":

> All sound and true philosophy is founded on the appearance of things; and if these phenomena inevitably draw us, against our wills, to such principles as most clearly manifest to us the most excellent counsel and supreme dominion of the All-wise and Almighty Being, they are not therefore to be laid aside because some men may perhaps dislike them. These men may call them miracles or occult qualities, but names maliciously given ought not to be a disadvantage to the things themselves, unless these men will say at last that all philosophy ought to be founded in atheism.[6]

Newton's famous proclamation *Hypotheses non fingo* contains the germ of the position just quoted. He has no need to feign fabulous stories like those of Descartes, when he has the overwhelming evidence of the world before his eyes, or more properly, before his mind.[7] Newton's defensive reference to "these men" is, of course, directed at Leibniz, but it is precisely the central Cartesian principle that any appeal to nonmechanical factors represents an appeal to occult powers that Leibniz feels Newton is violating. Thus, Newton and Leibniz will take up in a new manner the old argument between More and Descartes concerning the structure and form of material nature.

And yet it is precisely this difference—between what Newton maintains can be learned from sense perception and what can be learned from mental perception—that makes Newton more Cartesian than he claims to be. For despite his appeal to a corporeal nature, Newton is neither the naive empiricist that Bacon was nor an innocent like More who was convinced that it was reasonable that spirit should entail the existence of ghosts as well as absolute space. Rather, Newton understands something which Bacon and More had, at best, barely glimpsed: there are things, or better, forces, in the natural world which are immaterial but natural all the same. In this difference between the material and immaterial aspects of the visible world lies the bond, as well as the chasm, between the Cartesian and Newtonian projects. In other words, Newton's call for a return to corporeal appearance is in fact a new appropriation of natural appearance, one which owes much to that appropriation undertaken—successfully or not—by Descartes.[8] As a result, Leibniz's criticism of Newton is, as we shall see, strangely both Cartesian and non-Cartesian in form.

In his demonstration of the perfection of God as *ens infinitum*, Descartes found it necessary to prove that the world was a coherent and rational system based on God's infinite commitment to the distinction of *res cogitans* and *res extensa*. For Descartes, this distinction provided a bold example of the priority which God gave to ideas, a priority which was unassailable even by the most radical, but consistent, doubt. In other words, the Cartesian distinction between thinking substance and extended substance was a direct and necessary derivation of the very processes by which God gave rise to the world. Thus, as I have shown in the first section of this project, Descartes was able to solve the Galilean dilemma concerning the nature of moving bodies, because he conceived of space and bodies in a manner radically different from that of Galileo. Descartes's projection of an ideal space provided the proper locus for bodies as real, that is, extended, things. I have termed this movement Descartes's "rectification of appearance," because by this projection he brought about a new conception of natural appearance in which the propriety of the ideal was dramatically and radically expressed.

Newton must have recourse to the primacy of corporeal nature for much the same reasons that Descartes felt compelled to appeal to the primacy of extended nature: Newton must solve the Cartesian dilemma. Central to the Cartesian conception of extended substance is the denigration of all philosophies which would posit that the primary nature of matter is corpuscular. By such denigration, Descartes cleared the way for the aforementioned "rectification," a solution which escaped Galileo and a feat which would have been unthinkable from the viewpoint of a Lucretian or even Democritean physics. Newton's anti-Cartesianism springs in part from a recognition of the serious, even insurmountable, difficulties in accounting for the structure of material things based solely upon the primacy of extension and motion (difficulties which forced Descartes to construct his convoluted theory of vortices). Instead, Newton poses a tripartite structure of the material world: space, motion, and matter. In rendering the elements of the visible world in this manner, Newton grants that God has introduced into existence certain hard, discrete particles which reside and move in space, but which are not altered by motion. At the same time, Newton apparently eradicates the Cartesian primacy of ideas, for he posits corporeal existence independent of, and even prior to, any reflection short of God's own.

Because of Newton's ambiguous relation to the Cartesian project, he can claim to be both against the physical theory of Descartes and for the mathesical project which Descartes expressly inaugurates. In Newton's view, it is not necessary, nor even reasonable, to embrace the crude Cartesian distinction between mind and "matter" in conjunction with the Cartesian commitment to the primacy of the mathematically intelligible. At the same time, Newton is, as Clarke tries repeatedly to point out to Leibniz, no crude materialist; Clarke even goes so far as to label the materialists the "great enemies of the mathematical principles of philosophy" and the subject of matter or bodies the "smallest and most inconsiderable part of the universe."[9] Such hyperbole is justified in the eyes of the Newtonian Clarke, since Leibniz continually harps on the question of corporeality to the exclusion of the more essential aspects of Newton's theory.

Leibniz, however, continues to push the point in his reply to Clarke's reply: "But I believe the author has no reason to add, that the mathematical principles of philosophy are opposite to those of the materialists. On the contrary, they are the same."[10] Leibniz sees beyond Clarke's (and Newton's) hyperbole and understands what Newton himself must grant: without its appeal to corporeal nature, Newtonian mathematical philosophy is not truly possible. That is, only on the basis of a quasi-atomic physical theory, as opposed to the nonmaterialist stance of Descartes, is Newton free to develop his notions of attraction, absolute space and time, and universal gravitation; he must have an ultimate bodily stuff to support all of these.

Leibniz claims that Newton's atomism goes even further, that in conjunction with his notion of space as *sensorium dei* Newton is postulating a notion of material nature which is much more atheistic in its tendencies than anything suggested by Descartes's philosophy. In short, Leibniz sees

Newton's atomist commitments as both a violation of Newton's own motto, *Hypotheses non fingo*, and a statement of God's caprice. Leibniz sees the claim for the existence of absolute particles as a limitation of the rational and creative power of God: "There are no ultimate small bodies; the smallest particles of matter are each like a world completely full of an infinity of creatures even smaller yet. This division unto infinity is alone compatible with the universal continuity that atomism violates."[11] For Leibniz, any rigid atomism calls into question the very continuity of material nature, for it posits a natural finality that only God is entitled to assert.

Newton seeks to release bodies from their Cartesian strictures by way of his notions of attraction and space and time (as divine sensoria). He wants nothing to do with the ideal reduction of matter to extended stuff, because Newton believes it is this denial of the corpuscular essence of nature that places Descartes in the awkward position of postulating vortices. However, Newton's apparent eradication of the Cartesian primacy of ideas, of Cartesian mathesis, is not undertaken solely for its own sake, but rather to clear the way for a new primacy of the intelligible. In short, Newton's project involves the development of a new mathesical structure, one which is compatible with a corpuscular philosophy because it can more fully account for it. In order to accomplish this he overturns certain key elements of Descartes's scientific project, but maintains, even enhances, the general Cartesian commitment to the primacy of ideas. Here again, Leibniz and Newton differ in which Cartesian elements or commitments they hold and which they dismiss.

Beyond Mechanical Forces: Newton's Platonic Appeal to the Principle of Attraction

The foregoing is not the entire Newtonian account of matter, and if it were, Newton would only be a sort of hybrid of Bacon and Descartes, suffering from the obscure vision of the former and the blinding clarity of the latter. Newton, in fact, brings about a synthesis of the Baconian and Cartesian traditions, a synthesis which transforms them into a single project. This transformation is defined by his struggle to demonstrate the existence of a physical force of attraction and to show the essential importance of a commitment to the notion of absolute space and time. Newton is ultimately obliged to posit the force of attraction, not as a constituent element of the material universe, like matter, motion, and space, but as a mathematical law. This law, however, represents for Newton the power of God's action, which transcends the material world it acts upon. Newtonian attraction is, if you will, the missing link in the Cartesian account of the extended world, but it is also a radically anti-Cartesian principle that flies in the face of Descartes's call for a thoroughgoing mechanistic explanation of the working of extended substance.

Yet, at the same time, Newtonian attraction is a mathematical law, written in a syntax inspired directly by the mathematical forms which Descartes (and Galileo) stressed time and again as the most proper form of articulation for the new physics. Ironically, Newton criticizes Descartes for not using mathematics enough, for not taking the mathematical project far enough. Such an accusation can only make sense—given the undeniable and radical commitment of Descartes to the establishment of a mathematical physics—if we recognize two significantly different conceptions of mathematics.[12] By this I mean to point out not so much the obvious differences between Descartes's analytic geometry and Newton's calculus, but rather how, in each case, an understanding of the nature of mathematics shapes (and is shaped by) the understanding of the essence of nature. In the case of Descartes, the geometrization of nature demands that all physical phenomena be, in the last and best analysis, clear and knowable. The very definition of Cartesian mathesis rests on a capacity to detect the efficient reasons behind the actions of extended substance. Thus, for Descartes, anything short of a thoroughgoing mechanistic approach, that is, an approach which can achieve a totally clear and distinct account of motion and extension, does not meet the exacting standards of his mathematical commitment.

While Newton does not absolutely deny the influence the Cartesian commitment had upon him, many of Newton's proponents maintained that the Englishman's mathematical conviction ran much deeper and was therefore more faithful than that of his French predecessor. Voltaire, a great proponent of the Newtonian project, states, "Geometry, which Descartes had, in a sense, created, was a good guide and would have shown him a safe path in physics. But at the end he abandoned this guide and delivered himself to the spirit of system. From then on his philosophy became nothing more than an ingenuous romance."[13] From the Newtonian perspective, the Cartesian emphasis on matter as extension—as opposed to a corpuscular conception of matter—has everything to do with a lack of commitment to the mathematical project. That is, if one is to describe, rather than prescribe, the motions of real bodies mathematically, then one must admit real bodies (and real space) as basic entities or elements. According to the Newtonians, because of his conflicting metaphysical commitments Descartes is not prepared to make such an admission.

The debate between Leibniz and Clarke (and Newton) once again sheds much light on the question at hand. Leibniz calls into question the ultimate motives and grounds for Newton's appeal to the invisible force of attraction. He does so on the basis of a commitment to rational clarity that goes beyond even that of Descartes. Leibniz sees the influence of certain alchemical conceptions in the Newtonian idea of attraction, conceptions which seek to legitimate scientifically the existence of occult qualities in nature. For Leibniz this is to erase the dividing line between the natural and the supernatural (i.e., the miraculous) as well as the difference between the rational and the irrational:

> Thus in the order of nature (setting miracles aside) God does not arbitrarily give these or those qualities indifferently to substances; he never gives them any but those which are natural to them, that is to say, those that can be derived from their nature as explicable modifications. Thus we can judge that matter does not naturally have the attraction mentioned above, and does not of itself move on a curved path, because it is not possible to conceive how this takes place, that is to say, it is not possible to explain it mechanically; whereas that which is natural should be capable of becoming distinctly conceivable, if we were admitted into the secret of things. This distinction between what is natural and explicable and what is inexplicable and miraculous removes all the difficulties; if we were to reject it, we would uphold something worse than occult qualities, and in doing so we would renounce philosophy and reason, and throw open refuges for ignorance and idleness through a hollow system, a system which admits not only that there are qualities we do not understand (of which there are only too many), but also that there are some qualities that even the greatest mind could not understand, even if God provided him with every possible advantage, that is qualities that would be either miraculous or without rhyme and reason. And it would indeed be without rhyme or reason that God should ordinarily perform miracles, so that this do-nothing hypothesis would equally destroy philosophy, which searches for reasons, and the divine wisdom, which provides them.[14]

For Leibniz, to imbue natural entities with the power of attraction is neither natural nor reasonable. And yet in the last few years of his life Leibniz will be hard-pressed to make these objections in the name of reason appear reasonable in the eyes of various supporters of the Newtonian principle of attraction.

What commitments place Leibniz and Newton (and Clarke) in the position of calling into question the philosophical, scientific, and theological integrity of the other side? Clearly, there must be two significantly distinct ideas of nature and science at play in this prolonged and very heated argument. For Newton and his colleagues, the Leibnizian objections represent a throwback to the scholastic arguments which in their view (and in much the same way that Bacon had put it before them) are counter to the progress of science, occluding rather than revealing, objecting rather than discovering. Newton himself is not above allying his position with that of common sense in this fight: "by the word bodies I will understand the bodies which float in [the ether], taking this name not in the sense of the modern metaphysicians, but in the sense of the common people and leaving it to the Metaphysicians to dispute where the Aether and bodies can be changed into one another."[15] Such language indicates that Newton was less stimulated than annoyed by Leibniz's objections, seeing him as yet one more relic of the philosophical tradition which Newton obviously finds of little value.

Interestingly, Leibniz uses the same sort of label on Newton with regard to the principle of attraction, suggesting that because of its instability as a concept it is "a chimerical thing, a scholastic occult quality."[16] Given Newton's claim, as Leibniz understands it, to have discovered a new species of physical factor which operates invisibly, intangibly, and nonmechanically, it should not be surprising that Leibniz recalls Henry More's notion of extension as somehow akin to God's external form, the notion which so annoyed Descartes. For Leibniz, this active force of attraction is a metaphysical rogue, diverging wildly from the legitimate principles which affect natural entities: visible, tangible, and more or less mechanical, efficient causes which are thoroughly accessible to the human mind, at least given sufficient time and proper care.

The crux of the dispute between Leibniz and Newton, in fact, directly involves More's notion of God's external manifestation in space and the mediating forces which stand in for God's direct action in the world. In the anonymous review of the second edition of Newton's *Principia* which appeared in the 1714 *Acta Eruditorum,* a review that Leibniz almost certainly wrote,[17] Newton's notion of attraction ("hypothesis of a gravitational cause") is considered to be a new version of the archaic idea that spirit pervades all bodies. Then the reviewer goes on to suggest parenthetically that this notion is "closely related to Henry More's 'hylarchical principle,' "[18] this principle representing the generic mediating force which God uses to act in the physical world. Thus, Leibniz saw Newton in much the same light in which Descartes came to see Henry More: guilty of violating fundamental metaphysical and theological divisions by rashly appealing to mysterious forces and principles in an effort to establish new theories.

Newton responded to this specific "accusation" by pointing out that "in the Newtonian metaphysics there was really no place for the 'hylarchical principle,' an entity mediating between God and the world. The Newtonian God did not need such a mediator: he acted himself."[19]

More than this, Newton counterattacked by pointing out the differences between the two views of natural philosophy:

> The one proceeds upon the Evidence arising from Experiments and Phaenomena . . . the other is taken up with Hypotheses . . . to be believed without Examination. The one for want of Experiments to decide the Question, doth not affirm whether the Cause of Gravity be Mechanical or not Mechanical: the other that it is a perpetual miracle if it be not Mechanical. . . . The one teaches that God (the God in whom we live and move and have our Being) is Omnipresent; but not as a Soul of the World: the other that he is not the Soul of the World, but INTELLIGENTIA SUPRAMUNDANA, an intelligence above the Bounds of the World; whence it follows that he cannot do any thing within the Bounds of the World, unless by an incredible Miracle. . . . But must the constant and universal Laws of Nature, if derived from the Power of God or the Action of a Cause not yet known to us, be called Miracles and occult Qualities, that is to say, *Wonders* and *Absurdities?*[20]

It is worth noting that Newton could almost as easily have been writing about the differences between the Newtonian and Cartesian approaches to natural philosophy. Yet, Newton's declaration is extremely revealing, for in it we see something of the struggle to break with the mechanical view to which Newton himself had so often appealed. Only when Newton is pressed by Leibniz to show how his system can be reconciled with the rigorous tenets of mechanical philosophy does Newton expressly call the basic tenets of this philosophy into question. Newton's break with this tradition forces him to look elsewhere for theoretical or better metaphysical grounds. In More (and others such as Joseph Raphson and Ralph Cudworth) he found a tradition (or traditions) which provided at least metaphorical support for this break.

From Leibniz's perspective, the implications of this Newtonian blurring of the natural qualities of entities and the supernatural forces which intervene at providential moments move far beyond the proper purview of science: "All the natural forces of bodies are subject to mechanical laws; and all the natural powers of spirits, are subject to moral laws. The former follow the order of efficient causes; and the latter follows the order of final causes. The former operate without liberty, like a watch; the latter operate with liberty, though they exactly agree with that machine, which another cause, free and superior, has adapted to them before-hand."[21] The Leibnizian stakes concerning the positing of a natural force of attraction extend beyond the realm of physical bodies. Such a position threatens the fundamental categorical differences which ground existence as such. Because it violates this essential difference between the realms of physics and ethics, of nonliberty and freedom, Leibniz feels compelled to term the Newtonian conception of attraction "occult." Insofar as it calls into question the framing difference between spirit and body, Newton's attraction also renders the grounds of rational science questionable.

Needless to say, Clarke's reply to Leibniz's fifth and final paper is at least as "forthright" as Leibniz's own. Clarke's reply repeats the same line of argument he had used previously. Once again Clarke accuses Leibniz of taking away God's (and human) freedom by his demand for a simple mechanistic system. Nor does Clarke find anything stunning about Leibniz's appeal to the principle of sufficient reason, especially since Clarke does not see why "the bare will of God is not sufficient reason for acting in this or the other particular manner."[22]

However, Newton's own reply to Leibniz's objections in Query 31 of the *Optics* is much more to the point. Once again the accusation of "occult quality" is thrown back at Leibniz, this time accompanied by an appeal to the tradition of Aristotelianism that Newton had so often rebuked:

> These [active] principles I consider not as occult qualities, supposed to result from the specific forms of things, but from the general laws of nature, by which the things themselves are formed. . . . For these are manifest qualities and their causes only are occult. And the Aristotelians gave the name of occult qualities not to manifest qualities, but to such qualities only as they supposed to lie hid in bodies, and to be the unknown causes of manifest effects: such would be the causes of gravity, and of magnetic and electric attractions, and of fermentations, if we should suppose that these forces or actions arose from qualities unknown to us, and incapable of being discovered and made manifest. Such occult qualities put a stop to the improvement of natural philosophy, and therefore of late years have been rejected.[23]

Newton is not subscribing to occult qualities per se, but neither does he show wholehearted commitment to mechanical explanations. In short, Newton sees a third possibility, one which Leibniz does not accept as a viable alternative: there are forces in nature that are more than mechanical; quasi-spiritual forces exist as well.

The Appearance of Attraction and Newton's Revealed Empiricism

Newton feels liberated from the rigidity of Cartesian and Leibnizian mechanics by his appeal to empirical truth, to the truth of the "things themselves," and therefore empowered to describe the nature of the physical universe even if this means admitting the existence of not exactly physical forces like attraction. This fundamental shift in scientific commitments, so evident in the remarkable dispute between Leibniz the natural philosopher and Newton the scientist, when seen in a certain light demonstrates that it is, in fact, Newton rather than Leibniz who continues the trajectory of Descartes's mathesical project. Indeed, Newtonian mathesis is not bound by the radical Cartesian need for accountability of reasons, but rather by the commitment to a universally applicable set of laws. The ultimate nature of these laws need not be clear or fully known, that is, their reasons need not be fully grasped, for us to take cognizance and advantage of their existence. Mathematics, in the Newtonian view, can reveal and render to us laws whose grounds are not necessarily known or knowable, because the Newtonian conception of mathematics involves a revelatory element which is not found so overtly in Descartes, a revelatory strain which bears a striking resemblance to many suggestive moments in the respective work of Bacon and More.

With Newton, the Cartesian effort to demonstrate the authority of certain forms of appearance over others, to show that there is or can be a proper perception, finds expansion and further accomplishment, but only at the same time that appearance and perception are reappropriated. Descartes's quest for the total rectification of appearance was untenable as it stood; he overshot the mark. However, the Cartesian effort, though extreme, establishes a precedent that is not lost on Newton. Where Descartes had decreed that one must be concerned with pure motion, not moving bodies, Newton declares, on the contrary, it is precisely bodies, hard, discrete, ultimate bodies, that the physicist should study. But the bodies of Newton are not pre-Cartesian, Newton is not "recovering" Galilean, Lucretian, or Epicurean bodies. Rather, Newtonian bodies are post-Cartesian, for where Descartes was only partially successful in bringing corporeality into the proximity of the pure field of mathematics, Newton recognizes that "mathematics itself has to be transformed. . . . Mathematical entities have to be, in some sense, brought nearer to physics, subjected to motion, and viewed not in their 'being' but in their 'becoming' or in their 'flux.' "[24] The transition from Cartesian bodies to Newtonian bodies is a transformative movement: Cartesian physics is overcome by neo-Cartesian metaphysics.

Leibniz's most significant concerns with the Newtonian system revolve around this "Cartesianism done one better." The Cartesian reduction of bodies to their analytic essence has been extended by the Newtonian investment of bodies with a new kind of mathematical quality. What Leibniz finds so objectionable in Newton has much to do with the manner in which Newtonian bodies come to be much more than corporeal entities. The fact that Newton's physical system requires such a formidable legitimizing discourse (i.e., the attractive force, divine sensoria, God as *Makom*, and so forth) is from Leibniz's point of view a bold indication of the extremely speculative nature of the Englishman's system. Leibniz's criticism aims at exposing these speculations directly, and thus he calls into question the Newtonian notions of corporeality and their underlying metaphysics simultaneously. As Leibniz sees it, Newton's concept of natural bodies and his principle of attraction do not bear rational scrutiny. That is, Leibniz cannot find the grounding principles which structure the Newtonian system as a coherent and consistent whole, and therefore he assumes the system to be scientifically as well as philosophically untenable.

One might reply that Leibniz's inability to understand the significance of Newton's project stems from his commitments to a more traditional philosophical understanding, that Leibniz is steeped too much in Aristotle to be able to participate constructively in the radical changes occurring in science at the end of the seventeenth century. Certainly it is true that Leibniz was much more committed to the truth of the philosophical tradition than was Newton who like Bacon and Descartes appropriated any figure that might seem useful, positively at one moment and critically the next. However, the fact is that both Newton and Leibniz's general philosophical outlooks represent radical departures from the tradition.[25] Thus, although the "directions" of these departures, as well as the respective appropriations of traditional metaphysics and science, are quite different, Leibniz's qualms about the Newtonian discourse do not represent merely an apologetic for the tradition.

Thus, it seems reasonable to take Leibniz's objections at more or less face value, to examine in specific terms what it is about Newton's notions of atomic nature and of the active forces which influence (inherently and externally) these bits of material nature, both separately and in aggregate form. As we have seen, Leibniz considers Newtonian atomism a rash theory that depicts material nature as inert and closed off. Such a theory places God in a position of having to intervene directly in the concourse of matter from time to time in order to correct or improve upon the existent situation. Leibniz is perplexed at Newton's response that such occasional divine intervention is part of the *natural* play of the physical world and should not, in any way, be considered miraculous.

In particular, with regard to the force of attraction posited by Newton, Leibniz finds himself again placed in the quasi-pastoral position of having to remind the Newtonians that such a theory suggests that invisible forces are at work as part of the natural world, forces that can only be called spiritual. In other words, God is once again inserted into the natural equation of the operations of matter in a fashion not unlike More or even certain alchemical thinkers. Once more Newton approves of Leibniz's general point, seeing it not as a severe criticism but rather as a recommendation for his system, because the appeal to God's direct intervention in the natural world is not a drawback of Newton's system but in some sense its hallmark.

If there is some key aspect of the Newtonian system that Leibniz could never comprehend it was precisely this recurrent notion of divine intervention as "natural." Of course, Leibniz's inability to follow this line of reasoning was a direct result of his own view that God's role in the workings of nature must be supremely rational. The Leibnizian commitment to mechanistic philosophy is not simply a restatement of Descartes's position, because Leibniz is committed to a qualitative richness and depth of nature, to the "depths in which aspects of things slumber," that the Cartesian system sought to suppress.[26] In fact, it is the neo-Cartesian "flatness" of Newton's atomistic view of material nature that Leibniz claims puts God in the ungodly position of fixing or enhancing the workings of nature from time to time. For Leibniz, Newton's notion of a "work-day God"[27] is a more vulgar expression of Descartes's view that God must not only create, but also constantly conserve what he has created. More significantly, Leibniz understands the key Newtonian tenets of atom, attraction, and absolute space and time as dependent upon a notion of material nature which itself requires periodic unnatural intervention to remain viable.[28]

What of Newton's claim regarding the intervening power of God in the natural world? Why does Newton feel obliged, even compelled, to make this claim? The debate over the actual relevance of Newton's theological outlook to his natural philosophy has grown increasing acute in the past fifty years as more and more of his unpublished manuscripts have been examined. Newton's own unpublished writings have called into question the once common attitude of philosophers of science like Stephen Toulmin that we "must restrain our very proper interest in historical questions" when trying to understand the "scientific function of Newton's distinctions," that is, we must strictly honor the integrity of the "internal history of science."[29] The recent flood of research would seem to reflect a growing realization that for Newton himself the issues of science and theology, as well as those of physics and metaphysics, were intimately intertwined. I believe this is a testament to the greatness of Newton the philosopher, though perhaps at the slight expense of the reputation of Newton the scientific genius.

Again, the nagging question arises: What is the fundamental differ-ence that separates Newton and Leibniz, that renders their disagreement so rabid in tone? In the midst of more than twenty years of debate over certain Newtonian (and Leibnizian) scientific notions the argument always returns to the subject of God. More specifically, it is the question of God's role in the workings of the natural world that recurs again and again. Newton sees it as undeniable that God's will and power are such that what he decides and does are by the very fact rational. Leibniz responds that such arbitrariness goes against the very spirit of a supreme rationality, since nature as divinely created has surely been given the capacity to change, even evolve, by its own natural power. Newton and the Newtonians consider this attitude to lead to an outrageous displacement of God as *Pankrator*, rendering him little more than an obsolete idol.

For Leibniz, God's will and power are coextensive with his wisdom: "A will without reason, would be the chance of the Epicureans. A God, who should act by such a will, would be a God only in name."[30] For Newton, God's will and power are the source of all knowledge, because everything that exists, the "things themselves," is intelligible by the sheer power of God. Newton has no qualms about appealing to invisible forces at play in the world, since such forces are revealed empirically to the careful and faithful observer. In short, the question of whether such forces fit into some overall metaphysical schema or not is less important than the undeniable fact that these forces are revealed to the observer.

The intelligibility of the natural world for Newton is qualified and guaranteed by the constant emanation of God's power into the world. He wants nothing to do with Leibniz's God whose Reason and Will cooperate so perfectly in bringing the world about that this world is the most perfect one, that is, the most rational and profound one, that could ever exist. Newton even grants that this world will be overturned at some later date, eventually replaced by some better order of things. How would such an apocalyptic shift take place? The answer is found in the same generic category of active force to which Newtonian attraction belongs: "Active principles are intimately connected with the causation of Divine agency. By virtue of God's concurrence with second causes what laws of nature sustain the physical order: 'Where natural causes are at hand God uses them as instruments of his work.' . . . But nature, according to Newton's interpretation of Providence, has been so conceived by God, that from time to time he will more directly intervene to reform it and replenish motion and activity."[31] Even should this natural world pass away, the one that replaced it would be structured by the same kinds of forces at play in this one.[32] It is Newton's "invisible realm" that is the natural extension of God, the "instruments of his work." These active, invisible principles embodied in the natural world are what make it truly real.

Ultimately, the Newtonian form of mathesis posits a new authority and propriety with regard to appearance and perception, strangely undercutting the Cartesian mathesis by extending its authority over the real. This new perceptual authority embodied in Newton's mathematical convictions can be seen in his manner of dealing with the issue concerning the existence and nature of the force of attraction. Several times he attempts to prove it as a physical force (by an appeal to the nature of the ether), and each time he is unsuccessful. Ultimately, he declares it to be a mathematical force and not a physical element like space, matter, and motion, and furthermore that, whether or not it can ever be fully accounted for, it is undeniable all the same. This mathematical, not physical, force of attraction which holds bodies together and makes planets revolve about stars need not be entirely understood to be of immense applications. Its immateriality does not preclude its consequences for material nature, but rather makes it all the more crucial as a law. As Newton's friend John Locke says, if it is perhaps a law that can never be fully understood by anyone other than the Creator himself, this is hardly a devastating criticism: "The gravitation of matter toward matter in ways inconceivable to me is not only a demonstration that God, when it seems to Him good, can put into bodies powers and modes of acting which are beyond what can be derived from our idea of body or explained by what we know of matter; but it is furthermore an incontestable instance that He has really done so."[33]

The decisive importance of the Newtonian mathematical vision regarding the issues of natural appearance and perception is dramatically revealed in the concept of attraction: what we see with our eyes demands the existence of what may never be seen, but must be mathematically granted. Only divine perception, that is, perception in the most proper sense, beholds the appearance of attraction; Newtonian mathesis is the admission and appropriation of the necessity of this invisibility, this quasi-occultation, which is unapologetically without clear reasons. Newton's appeal to God as the all-powerful fulcrum which balances the empirical and the mathematical, the corporeal and the spiritual, harkens back to the Gods of Bacon and Descartes, but in so doing, Newton brings about the emergence of a radical science which all but casts the Baconian and Cartesian sciences out of the modern world and into the obsolete tradition.

8

The Divine Propriety of Spirit and the Insufficient Space of Nature

Annon Spatium Universum, Sensorium est Entis Incorporei, Viventis, et Intelligentis; quod res Ipsas cernat et complectatur intimas, totasq; penitus et in se praesentes perspiciat; quarum id quidem, quod in Nobis sentit et cogitat, Imagines tantum in Cerebro contuetur?[1]

Leibniz rejected what he perceived as Newton's reification of the occult quality of attraction, or what seemed to him an attempt to insert a form of action-at-a-distance into mainstream natural philosophy. The Newtonian explanation that attraction was not a physical property of matter, but a mathematical force which expressed a universal and divine law, and therefore could in no way be construed as action-at-a-distance, did not mollify Leibniz in the least; a hyperphysical force is not a natural force. Newton's further argument that despite the fact that attraction could not be fully accounted for by contemporary physical theory and experimentation, attraction still represented a very useful notion because it accounted for something very real which was at play in the physical world, did nothing to alleviate Leibniz's concerns.

The related issue of absolute space, repeatedly explained as one of God's two sensoria by the Newtonians, was an even more questionable idea for Leibniz, since Newton was now positing not only an unprovable force, but also a quasi-divine spiritual entity to support his scientific position. Absolute space also provided a means of legitimizing speculative forces and structures such as attraction by acting as the infinite locus of attraction. In short, Leibniz saw Newtonian absolute space and time as an attempt to provide the infinite substrata for ensuring the continuity of physical phenomena; they were depicted as the universal physical law "incarnate." In his indirect and often heated correspondence with Newton's colleague, Samuel Clarke, Leibniz took up the issue of absolute space again and again. This controversy reveals the changing but still crucial role which God plays in the modern scientific understanding of natural appearance. Also, this theological mutation offers further evidence of the profound and decisive merger of Baconian and Cartesian movements. This shift in how the appearance of the divine is characterized bears intimately on the manner in which things, animate and inanimate, are seen and said to exist.

The Space of Spirit and the Standard of the Great Sensorium

By his belated addition of the "as it were" (*tanquam*) Newton makes it clear that the image of absolute space as God's sensorium he offers in his *Optics* is not to be taken literally.[2] At the same time, Newton's reference to the image of the sensoria at key junctures in his arguments indicates that it should not be taken as a merely poetic turn of phrase. It has been suggested that Newton's "real conviction" is much closer to the literal meaning of the image than simply its heuristic usefulness as a metaphor. This conviction is undoubtedly caught up with the Anglican and Latitudinarian tendencies of Newton's special form of natural religion, but it is difficult if not impossible to say which inspired the other more, his natural religion or his natural science.[3]

Granting Newton's religious reasons for repeated mention of the image, it also plays a major role in his efforts to distance himself from the dominant Cartesian notion of space. For Newton nothing remotely like Cartesian extension can ever account for the ubiquity of lawful motion, and, further, to attempt to account for it in Descartes's crude mechanistic way is to revert to something bordering on the bad materialism ascribed to Lucretius and his followers. Cartesian space, the space which is local and exists strictly in relation to extended objects, the space which Newton calls "place," is only secondary space. For Newton, primary space, primordial space, is the "disposition of being qua being"; it gives each thing its possibility of being somewhere, in other words, of existing.[4] Further, Newton considers Descartes's hesitance to label extension infinite because it might be identified with God an idle fear. Newtonian space is an infinite attribute of God's infinite perfection which gives evidence of God's power and intellect rather than representing a heretical challenge to God's greatness.

The critique of Cartesian space and the emergence of his own conception of space represent a very early double predilection for Newton.

Although well aware of the contribution mechanical philosophy has made to the formation of a rigorous scientific approach, Newton nonetheless is also cognizant of the limitations of a strict mechanical doctrine, be it that of Descartes or even Boyle. The limitations of such a scientific outlook are nowhere more damaging than in the investigation of the nature of space. Mechanical principles cannot ground a coherent natural philosophy, no matter how committed such a philosophy may be to the rational clarity of mechanical philosophy. Only something like spirit, that is, an immaterial structure, can serve to explain the first cause of all the phenomena with which we are constantly confronted.

> What is there in places almost empty of Matter, and whence is it that the Sun and Planets gravitate towards each other without dense Matter between them? . . . How do the Motions of the Body follow from the Will, and whence is the instinct in Animals? . . . And these things being rightly dispatch'd, does it not appear from Phaenomena that there is a Being incorporeal, living, intelligent, omnipresent, who in infinite Space, *as it were* in his Sensory, sees the things themselves intimately, and thoroughly perceives them, and comprehends them wholly by their immediate presence to himself?[5]

As Newton had suggested much earlier in his career, there must be a "motionless thing" to serve as a reference system for all things.[6] Space would be such a special unmoving thing, but only immovable because it is a space which God uses *like* a perceptual medium.

Despite the belated "as it were," the metaphor of space as *sensorium dei* stands as an essential and persistent image for Newton. It is God, and God alone, who sustains by His providence, the motions of planets and stars, animals and humans, for it is only by God's absolute perception and comprehension (and hence the necessity of God's presence) that true, lawful motion, real motion, occurs. Space as a direct emmanent effect of God's active presence ("an effect arising from the first existence of being")[7] cannot be accounted for strictly in terms of the locale, and the local motion, of bodies. Rather, it is this form of space which accounts for the places which bodies take up. This form of space cannot be identified, then, as belonging to the realm of extended things, for it gives this realm its coherence. It is a form which resides in the midst of material (i.e., extended) things without being determined by their positions. Such a form calls into question the strict Cartesian dichotomy between mind and extension: absolute space is a spirit-like stuff dwelling in the material world.

Small wonder Leibniz believed he perceived the "revival of the odd imaginations of Dr. Henry More" in Newton's divine sensoria.[8] The

Leibniz-Newton debate over absolute space can be read as a replay of
the argument of Descartes and More concerning More's suggestion that
the physical universe might be God's body. Newton does not follow
More in this claim, but his use of the notion of God as *Makom*, the
Cabalistic Place, the space in which "we live and move and have our
Being" is not unrelated.[9] Newton's use of the Hebrew term *Makom* was
not unprecedented; More (and later Joseph Raphson) had used it in
discussing space as a divine attribute of God:

> There are not less than twenty titles by which the Divine Numen is wont
> to be designated, and which perfectly fit this infinite internal place
> (*locus*) the existence of which in Nature we have demonstrated, omitting
> moreover that the very Divine Numen is called by the Cabbalists MAKOM,
> that is Place (*locus*). Indeed, it would be astonishing and a kind of Prodigy
> if a thing about which so much can be said proved to be a mere nothing.[10]

Thus, More's "infinite internal space" is not nothing, but neither is
it something in the sense that each thing has a particular and finite
place. More felt obliged to call this kind of space a spiritual effect, a
definition of space which contributed mightily to his growing dispute with
Descartes. Indeed, the remarkable "nothing" of which More writes is akin
to Newton's early conception of space as that special immovable thing
which makes the place, the somewhere, of all somethings possible. Thus,
Leibniz's comparison was not without textual support nor was it a strictly
questionable connection. And yet, the objections of Newton (and Clarke)
are fair to the extent that the tone and purpose of More's "spiritualization
of space" lacks the theoretical apparatus that Newton will develop.

Raphson was one of the first to attempt to develop the connection
between the respective work of More and Newton. He combined the two
in the development of what he termed "Real space," a space which was
described in a set of Newton-like axioms, corollaries, and propositions as
"the *innermost extended*", "pure act," "all-containing and all-penetrating,"
"actually infinite," "incorporeal," "immutable," "eternal," etc.[11] Raphson
goes on to posit that "Real space" is incomprehensible to us because it is
infinite both in source and manifestation. Inspired by Newton, Raphson
claims that despite this fact of incomprehensibility (and invisibility) we
can make "progress *in aeternum* of our knowledge both of the things
themselves and the perpetually geometrizing God" because "Real Space"
is an actual attribute of God.[12] He further amplifies Newton's own line of
reasoning by stating that it makes no sense to argue that "Real Space"
is ungrounded in reason, since the "infinite amplitude of extension

expresses the immense diffusion of being in the First Cause, or its infinite and truly interminable essence."[13] In other words, to argue that "Real Space" is not reasonable is to forget that what "Real Space" expresses is in fact that First Cause, the Ground, of all Reason.

Raphson's work cannot be seen as a faithful rendition (quasi-transcript) of Newton's work, in the way in which one assumes much of the work of Clarke and Richard Bentley to have been. However, Raphson's efforts to synthesize Newtonianism and the Platonism of his day (à la More), specifically with regard to the notion of absolute space, does show the proximity of these intellectual positions. The work of Raphson serves to demonstrate just how closely More's spiritual space and Newton's notion of space as divine sensorium converge. Further, it serves to show how Newton's notion represents a metaphysically more satisfying position, that is, a more mature version of More's spiritual space. Finally, in what is ultimately a project to reveal the divinity of space, Raphson reveals the most extreme result of what Newton is suggesting. The line between absolute space as an attribute of God and as God incarnate is a fine one indeed.

In an unpublished manuscript written some ten years before Raphson's book appeared, Newton shows just how close he is to the Platonism of his day: "Space is not compounded of aggregated parts since there is no least in it, no small [or] great or greatest. . . . In [each] of its points it is like itself and uniform nor does it [truly have parts] other than mathematical points, that is everywhere [infinite in number] and nothing in magnitude. For it is a single being, [most simple], and most perfect [in its] kind."[14] What Newton is suggesting here becomes a recurrent theme for him, a theme which may have led him to posit the absolute and infinite nature of space so fiercely: space is always both mathematically real and choric. The former commitment is an obviously legacy of Galileo and Descartes, while the latter notion, the choric quality of space, stems from the vision of space as filled with spirit, as *Chora/Makom*. Newton's commitment to this double quality of space places him ambiguously in the two camps of Platonism, the rational and the mystical, the Archimedean and the Pythagorean, the Cartesian and the Morean.[15]

More than this, and in an effort to establish the primacy of his system, Newton brings these two Platonic strains together in a new way. He seeks to establish the primacy of spirit not as strictly opposed to material substance as Descartes had done, but rather as permeating all things. This project of universal law, that whatever "necessarily exists, exists always and everywhere, since the law of necessity is the same in all places,"[16] will fulfill the Cartesian project for the rectification of appearance in a wholly new manner. To do this, Newton was obliged to posit both an adequate source of this permeating power as well as an infinitely consistent and continuous medium in which such a power could operate. The matrix of God as all-powerful Will and the sensoria of space and time as the emanations of this Will, as *effectus emanativus Dei*, provide the context necessary for this effort.

Thus, Newton undertakes to legitimate the project of universal law by establishing a theological and spatial precedent. The distinction between the metaphysics of spirit and the physics of space is difficult to discern at this level. Space is provisionally filled with spirit so that the chief danger inherent in the ancient atomism that Newton had appropriated, the danger of a space void of everything (matter and spirit), can be avoided. At the same time, Newton's project requires a mathematically real space, one which is homogenous and mathematically consistent, and therefore infinite. The metaphysico-theological support necessary to validate such a project is formidable: "For it can readily be seen that absolute space . . . is described as 'God's organ of sensation' precisely because physical infinity seemed to Newton to be in dire need of justification through union with the Deity, as his instrument. Space, if one may put it this way, tolerated the attribute of infinity only with difficulty because as an overwhelming empty space it was bound to give rise to metaphysical problems."[17]

With this claim of space as the divine emanate, Newton posits a new, more powerful, authority of the invisible; it is an authority which exceeds that of the Cartesian God, for the Newtonian form is more firmly rooted in "the things themselves." Space disposes things to be what they are by giving them a place, an essentially mathematical place to be sure, but a place nonetheless. By positing God as the direct source of space, Newton both challenges the traditional segregation of matter and spirit and solves the problem inherent in mechanistic natural philosophy: spirit does not give life to dead inert matter but rather embodies it, lives within it. By his sensorium of space, God acts in the world as the ground of all natural phenomena; "Space for Newton . . . is the eternal realm of God's presence and action—not only his *sensorium* but also, if one may say so, his *actorium*."[18]

Thus, Newton solves the problem of physical space, the bane of all mechanical philosophers, by grounding it in a spiritual space, a space which makes a legitimate place for all the rigors an informed mechanical philosophy demands. By a rigorous blurring of the timeworn distinction between spirit and matter, he empirically (and experimentally) grounds his scientific project in a way in which Descartes could not (and perhaps would not) have grounded his own science.

The Singularity of Sufficient Reason:
Leibniz's Denial of Newton's Spiritual Space

Newton is not falling back into a position precisely like that of More or even Raphson, for in his invocation of the primacy of spirit, spirit itself is transformed. He does, however, take up something akin to the Neoplatonist position: space is not strictly speaking dependent upon the proximity of things for its existence, but rather space is infinite insofar as it is a quasi-divine whole. For Newton, there is relative space (space as *partes extra partes*) and absolute space; without the former, the relationality of a particular group of things would be imperceivable, but without the latter, we would have no reference from which to perceive anything at all for nothing would exist.

Leibniz understands the shortcomings of Descartes's conception of space; he views Descartes's concept of extended matter as extreme. Nonetheless, Leibniz remains committed to the idea of a uniform space which is differentiated not by its own qualities but by the bodies which exist in this or that place:

> Space is something absolutely uniform; and, without the things placed in it, one point of space does not absolutely differ in any respect whatsoever from another point of space. Now from hence it follows, (supposing space to be something in itself, besides the order of bodies among themselves,) that 'tis impossible there should be a reason, why God, preserving the same situations of bodies among themselves, should have placed them in space after one certain particular manner, and not otherwise.[19]

For Leibniz, absolute space represents an unacceptable challenge to God's perfection, since the Newtonian idea of an infinite and whole space (as infinite sensorium) posits a pure, unqualified entity coeternal with God. This unqualified being of space, space void of everything but its source and its spatiality, has no reason for existence except the mere fact that it is possible. Thus, according to Leibniz, the Newtonians do not seem to grasp that nature is the incarnate principle of sufficient reason. For Leibniz, the source of the best of all possible worlds must be singular and unique; there cannot be two sources of sufficient reason, God and Absolute Space/Time.

Thus, Newton's new authority of the divine sensorium of absolute space is not without its challenges. Leibniz accuses Newton of having put God in the rather undivine position of tinker or clockmaker, or even worse of obliging God to stand forever as the world's monitor. Further, in response to the counteraccusation by Clarke that it is he, Leibniz, who has made God the clockmaker, and an adventitious one at that, Leibniz replies that he only referred to God in this manner to show the perfection of God's omniscience in anticipating every optimal possibility of the as yet uncreated world.

In fact, Leibniz's God is more of an artist than a craftsman when one looks at the whole of nature rather than examining the individual parts:

> The imperfection of our machines, which is the reason why they want to be mended, proceeds from this very thing, that they do not sufficiently depend upon the workman. And therefore the dependence of nature upon God, far from being the cause of such an imperfection, is rather the reason why there is no such imperfection in nature, because it depends so much upon an artist, who is too perfect to make a work that wants to be mended. . . . [E]very particular machine of nature, is, in some measure, liable to be disordered; but not the whole universe, which cannot diminish in perfection.[20]

We find a trace of the Greek cosmos here in the Leibnizian account of the natural world. Leibniz's God is the God of sufficient reason: He sees and projects the perfection of everything which comes to exist as nature, because of the infinite scope of his vision, power, and perfection. In the world fostered by this God of sufficient reason, first causes by themselves are never whole or true causes, for one can only find the causes, the grounds, or the reasons of a given entity by understanding both its context and its unfolding nature. Nor is infinite power by itself enough to account for the creation of the world, since it involves more than just the "bare production of every thing, [which] would indeed show the power of God; but it would not sufficiently show his *wisdom*."[21] Consequently, the world created by God will not only reflect the power of God but will also intrinsically embody the infinite and dynamic reason of the divine. The natural world will have its own internal grounds, requiring nothing for its continuance but the fact that God initiated it at the beginning of time. For Leibniz, this ability to embody sufficient reason in the core of each being, and thus to render each thing in some way distinct is overwhelming testament to the infinite power and knowledge of his artistic God.

Leibniz charges that the Newtonian God, who it is claimed is everywhere in the world via absolute space (and time), is not a God of sufficient reason, but rather a God of brute power who finds it necessary to intervene in the most common or everyday actions. Further, even with the insertion of the *tanquam* the image of the divine sensoria, as well as the suggestion that if we know how we are able to move our bodies, then "by like reasoning we should know how God can move [and create] bodies," seems to justify Leibniz's concern that he is in the presence of a new form of animism.[22] The power of the Newtonian God is a vital power, a brute force which thrusts beings into (and rips them out of) existence on the basis of blind ambition; such a God is power without reason, implying creation without grounds.

Undoubtedly, Leibniz did not have access to this most blatant statement of Newton regarding the almost animal nature of God's presence in the natural world. Yet, the statements which Newton, Clarke, and others publicly repeated (e.g., God is no mere *Intelligentia supramundana*, God as *Makom*, time and space as *sensoria dei*, and so forth) leads Leibniz to suspect that Newton's God is a virtual *animus mundi*. It seems to Leibniz that posing God as the source of space and time, both emanating out of him like aetherial fluids, is akin to the alchemist belief that they had direct spiritual access to the divine.[23] The old alchemical quest for power through direct induction of divine or spiritual forces shines through the Newtonian idea of absolute space. Thus, for Leibniz, the Newtonian charge that Cartesianism smacks of atheism represents a very effective, if indirect, form of self-criticism.

Again, the argument involves much more than a simple theological disagreement. What is at stake in all these exchanges, these charges and countercharges, concerning God and his emanative qualities goes to the heart of the fundamental modern decision regarding the status of space and the nature of the things which occupy it. Leibniz takes up, at least in a modified or improved way, the Cartesian (and, strangely enough, Aristotelian) stance that space is a function of the position of bodies. Leibniz does not agree with the Cartesian effort of total geometrical reduction of material entities, but he does grasp the importance of Descartes's objection to the conception of space void of bodies. Only by the presence of some kind of extended and/or material body does space have meaning; to posit a space radically independent of entities is to render it meaningless, without reason for existence or for coming into being: "Absolute space had for [Leibniz] precisely the characteristics that exclude a rational origin of reality; there are in it no meaningful differences of quantity and of place, so that there is an aggregate of rational undecidabilities."[24]

Absolute space, pure space, void of all characteristics except its spatiality, requires not only the support engendered by God's constant presence, but also desperately needs a more rational legitimation. Newton's claim that it finds legitimacy from the simple fact that it is an effect of God's all-powerful will does not satisfy Leibniz in the least. Nor does Leibniz take comfort in the notion that absolute space is not empty of everything, since it is a spirit-filled realm. In fact, Leibniz finds this perhaps the most troubling part of the Newtonian argument, since it leaves him to wonder if it is not "overthrowing our notion of things, to make God have parts, to make spirits have extension?"[25]

The idea that absolute space is not void but rather full of spirit, the idea that Leibniz rightly suspects links More and Newton to one another, stands as a crucial and recurring aspect of the debate concerning Newton's absolute space. Leibniz maintains that all this talk of absolute space as the choric domain, as "the place of all things,"[26] serves only to obscure, not clarify, the natural world. Further, to depict the natural world as a material realm permeated by spiritual space does not serve to explain natural structures, but rather subjugates their natural significance to some nonnatural and irrational principle. Leibniz identifies Newton's metaphysics of spirit as the driving force behind his notion of absolute space as divine sensorium, and thus concludes that such a notion cannot illuminate *this world . . .* the whole universe of material and immaterial creatures taken together" because it leaves out an entire side of the equation of creation.[27] That is, Newton's bias toward absolute space is a bias toward the spiritual and ideal, a bias which inevitably leads the natural world to be cast in an quasi-occult light.

The issues involved in this dispute are not limited to the relation of God to space and matter, but also call into question the possibility of a thoroughgoing human rationality. In other words, Newton's challenge of basic distinctions, such as those between matter and spirit, divine and natural phenomena, and so forth, renders that rational thought which believes itself grounded in a rational world structure problematic. One could say that Leibniz sees the Newtonian perspective as questioning the place of the human, and thus throwing open the question of whether human inquiry can ever gain consistent and reliable access to the fundamental structures of human life or those of the natural world.

The issue of absolute space, then, sparks accusations from both camps. Leibniz challenges the Newtonian notion as an effort to replace God with an invisible and unprovable "stand-in" that renders the world untrustworthy. Newton (and Clarke) accuse Leibniz of making God a dwarf, of seeking to second-guess the power of God by imposing on his creation a small-minded form of rationality which smacks of Aristotle. However, Newton's appeal to the invisible, and the Leibnizian reaction to it, bear on more than the respective piety of these thinkers. What is at play in the midst of the argument over absolute space is the propriety of the human mind, a propriety resembling that of its creator. For Newton, the will of the creator finds its reflection in the human will; God's will to establish a lawful universe out of chaos is mirrored in the human will to discover these laws in the things themselves. For Leibniz, such discovery is only possible as long as a dynamic but consistent order lies at the heart of the world. Such order is a result of the divine principle of sufficient reason which does not handcuff God, but rather is the fundamental evidence of the divine origins of the world. This principle guarantees the singularity of the natural world by establishing the permanence of the categories, structures, and divisions that have appeared, are now appearing, and have yet to appear. From the Newtonian perspective, there are other concerns, other commitments which exceed the meager limitations of the principle of sufficient reason, chief among them the power and propriety of the new science.

Leibniz's New Science: A Space Sufficient to Nature

Given the compelling force of Newtonian scientific thinking, Leibniz's sustained critique of its grounds is clearly based on a distinctly different vision of the new science. Leibniz's own conception of the new science of nature is both the reason and the cause for his ongoing battle with Newton and the Newtonians. We do not find simply rival forms of the new natural science here, for Leibniz objects as much if not more to the theological and moral implications of Newton's vision of nature as he does to the Newtonian concept of nature itself. Indeed, it is the Newtonian tendency to sever natural science from ethical science, to divorce questions concerning matter and bodies from questions concerning the rational structure of the world as a whole, that most troubles Leibniz.

Leibniz's criticism of Newtonianism has its source in his unrestricted commitment to philosophical inquiry. Whereas for Newton, philosophy has at best an important subordinate role in the investigation of nature, for Leibniz nature cannot be understood strictly by way of physical theories and mathematical laws. This is not to say that Leibniz objects, in principle, to the identification of natural laws, such as those pertaining to motion. However, he breaks away from the Newtonian and the Cartesian projects in denying that the basic laws of nature depend primarily upon merely mathematical or logical truths:

> God's supreme wisdom has led him, above all, to choose *laws of motion* that are best adjusted and most suitable [*les plus convenables*] with respect to abstract or metaphysical reasons. The same quantity or total and absolute force, or of action, is preserved, the same quantity of respective force, or of reaction; and finally, the same quantity of directive force. Furthermore,

action is always equal to reaction, and the whole effect is always equivalent to its full cause. And it is surprising that, by a consideration of *efficient causes* alone, or by a consideration of matter, we cannot give the reason for the laws of motion discovered in our time, some of which I myself have discovered. For I found that we must have recourse to *final causes* for this, and that these laws do not depend upon the *principle of necessity*, as do logical, arithmetical, and geometrical truths, but upon the *principle of fitness*, that is, upon the choice of wisdom. And this is one of the most effective and most evident proofs of the existence of God for those who can delve deeply into these matters.[28]

If there was any doubt of the depth of abyss that divides Newton and Leibniz, it is dispelled by this statement. Anyone who maintains the traditional appeal to final causes would trouble, and be troubled by, Newton and the Newtonians. The fact that Leibniz even bothers to address the question of the existence of God is also a point of severe division. Newton does not need to prove God, for God is already implicitly proven by the existence of absolute space. The rest is a matter for mathematical physics.

For Leibniz, on the other hand, these philosophical and natural questions cannot ever be absolutely segregated from science. The new science must present not only a mathematically profound account of nature, but must also show the justice, the sufficient reason, of this account. Any science that does not acknowledge the essential moral implications of nature is guilty both of bad philosophy and flawed observation: "In Leibniz's view, traces of divine wisdom can be discerned throughout created nature, down to the level of phenomena. It follows that in physics, as in all branches of natural philosophy, we are obliged to approach nature under the assumption that it has been arranged according to the architectonic of wisdom. This requires that we suppose nature acts in the fittest and most orderly manner possible."[29] Like a chasm, this principle of the "fitness" of nature separates Leibniz from Newtonian science. Remarkable mathematician that he is, Leibniz denies the primacy of mathematical thought. He asserts a form of thought other than mathematical which makes mathematical thinking possible, a thinking of ethical and metaphysical fitness.[30]

It is on the basis of this thinking of fitness that Leibniz challenges the essential Newtonian claim concerning the manner in which natural phenomena and structures are radically dependent upon God's substantial presence. It is not that Leibniz questions the need for God to have an active role in the world, but he cannot accept God as some spiritual power source which keeps the entire world machine moving. If the world is to be thought of as a machine, then Leibniz thinks it should be a machine, or better a work of art, that has intrinsic reasons for being what it is and not being what it is not, in short, without need of extraneous forces or powers:

> It is *nature* taken as a whole which is, I would say, a work of art of God, and from this each natural machine (here lies the true but rarely noted *difference* between *nature and art*) is composed of an infinity of organs and consequently stands in need of the infinite wisdom and power of that which created and governs it. This is why I believe Hippocrates' *omniscient warmth*, Avicenna's *Cholcodean* donor to souls, the purportedly omniscient *plastic virtue* of Scaliger and others, and Henry More's *hylarchic principle*, are all either impossible or superfluous. It suffices that the world machine could be constructed with such great wisdom that all these marvels are produced by its own functioning and that organic bodies in particular develop, its seems to me, beginning with a sort of preformation.[31]

The world according to Leibniz is a work of art composed of natural machines as opposed to unnatural machines. Such a world has built into itself active as well as quiescent qualities which by themselves can account for its fullness and self-completeness. This self-sufficiency of the world does not render God a fable to be forgotten, but rather verifies the undeniable necessity of a singular power and wisdom great enough to make such a world not only possible, but the only world that can exist with its own self-sufficient grounds. For Leibniz, God's infinity stems from the knowledge and power to perform a self-sufficient world out of nothing rather than the power to create just any world out of nothing. Ultimately, Leibniz agrees with the Newtonian point that the world is essentially dependent on God's infinite essence. However, he makes it clear that this dependency is not to be confused with something like the world's incompleteness or inadequacy as a natural whole, but rather the world is radically dependent on God for its rational coherence, its fullness, and its beauty.

The fundamental disagreement between Leibniz and the Newtonians concerning God's role in the natural world is usually characterized in terms of the well-known image of the clockmaker and the clock. Leibniz claims that God has enriched his clock with possibility so that it will be able to adjust its workings naturally whenever the need may arise. Newton claims that this exorcizes God from the world altogether, when in fact God's presence is not only apparent to the careful observer but also theologically necessary. It is because of this difference in perspective that I define Leibniz's image of God "poetic" or "artistic" and Newton's image of God "technical." These terms are borne out by the rhetorical differences found in the correspondence between Leibniz and Clarke, as well as

Newton's and Leibniz's own independent writings. This distinction sheds light on the way in which the theological and scientific differences between Newton and Leibniz stem from the same fundamental difference: Newton's technical authority of God versus Leibniz's artistic authority of God. This difference centers around another difference (or lack of difference): the fundamental difference between (or essential sameness of) natural things and human machines.

In his challenge to the basic trajectory of the modern science, Leibniz is reminiscent of Bacon. Unlike Bacon, however, he poses his objections not as the new science is only beginning to assert itself, but rather at the moment modern science has found its dominant practice and voice. Most crucially, Leibniz focuses his challenge precisely on the issue that links Bacon to Descartes and Descartes to Newton, the resonance of artificial and natural machines. By questioning the sameness of human and natural machines, Leibniz stands alone against a basic principle that binds together virtually every other figure on the modern scene:

> I am as willing as any man to give the moderns their due; but I think they have carried reform too far, among other things in confusing the natural and the artificial, through not having had sufficiently exalted ideas of the majesty of Nature. They conceive that the difference between her machines and ours is but the difference between the great and the small. . . . This difference is one not merely of degree, but of kind also. It must be recognized that Nature's machines possess a truly infinite number of organs, and are so well protected and armed against all accidents, that it is not possible to destroy them. A natural machine still remains a machine in its least parts, and, what is more, it always remains the very same machine that it was, being merely transformed by the different foldings it receives, and being sometimes stretched, sometimes contracted and as it were concentrated, when we think that it is destroyed.[32]

In the first sentence Leibniz separates himself from the moderns. Who is he, if not one of these moderns? Leibniz's own answer to this question is found in his commitment to the difference between natural things and artificial bodies. In this renewal of the strict borders between the artificial and the natural, Leibniz demonstrates his distance from virtually all of his modern contemporaries and predecessors. He stakes his identity to this difference which the moderns had all but convinced themselves did not exist. Leibniz's new science begins and ends with the difference between technical and natural things, and, as a result, his science is not modern science.

He asserts a science which is rigorously philosophical, and in so doing he distances himself from the modern scientific project as it was coming to be. Unlike Bacon, Leibniz maintains the radical difference between natural and artificial things. Unlike Descartes, Leibniz asserts a concept of nature that is more than mechanical and mathematical. Unlike Newton, Leibniz insists that space must have its reasons. All three of these Leibnizian positions are basic to his view of the rational and sufficient character of nature. In this view of nature he embraces the traditional bond between philosophy and science, eschewing strictly mechanical philosophy as the latest expression of an ancient defunct scientific project:

> There was a time when I believed that all the phenomena of motion could be explained on purely geometrical principles. . . . But, through more profound meditations, I discovered that this is impossible, and I learned a truth higher than all mechanics, namely that everything in nature can indeed be explained mechanically, but that the principles of mechanics themselves depend on metaphysical and, in a sense, moral principles, that is, on the contemplation of the most perfectly effectual [*operans*], efficient and final cause, namely, *God*, and cannot in any way be deduced from the blind composition of motions. And thus, I learned that it is impossible for there to be nothing in the world except matter and its variations, as the Epicureans held.[33]

Leibniz turns the tables on the moderns. He accuses them of subscribing to a refined and mathematically refined Epicureanism. For him, blind nature is not nature at all. Nature is more than mechanical, because natural things are more than machines. This being the case, the truly new science must be more than a mathematical account of an essentially mechanical structure. What is needed is a form of science that is still philosophical in its aims.

Leibniz's overriding concern with rational grounds obliges him to conclude that space can only be natural space if it is fundamentally associated with material things. For Leibniz, a world created without built-in, essentially rational structures, including an abiding distinction between matter and spirit and the recognition of the codependence of matter and space, would not be a world at all; for Newton, such concerns are tangential at best. For the latter, God establishes the requisite lawful structures through his infinite emanative power, his only intermediate agents being of a like substance, invisible forces and forms (e.g., attraction and absolute space and time) that penetrate the entire world without direct empirical manifestation or any justification which is strictly intrinsic to nature. From the Leibnizian perspective, such an appeal renders the world an opaque fact and denies that human rationality has been sanctioned by the world out of which it has emerged:

> Leibniz insists that the very order that human reason claims to find in reality embodies the qualities that divine reason had to give to its work. The controversy here is no longer about the problem of the arrangement of the world to suit the requirements of human life but rather about the question of the effectiveness of the human reason that has to assert its own laws as the laws of the world. The rational dependability of the world, the condition of the possibility of all theory, is the remnant of the teleological order that Leibniz defends. On the other hand, absolute will, as a metaphysical principle, is the equivalent of the assertion that the dependability of the world cannot be proved and is therefore a mere fact, always subject to revocation at any time.[34]

Leibniz is committed to a world grounded in inherent rational structures. No other kind of world will support the consistent development of theoretical understanding (or moral knowledge). Further, where Newton suggests that the present world order may undergo some future transformation, Leibniz does not see how any other world can testify to the full perfection of God, a being of infinite Power and infinite Knowledge, than one which is ordered according to its own fundamental reasons.

The Technical Visibility of the Invisible and the Divine Propriety of Newtonian Science

In the view of Samuel Clarke, Leibniz's objections to the Newtonian conception of absolute space miss the point in a very telling manner. Leibniz is a representative of the old science, a science built for the most part on the rigid edifice of Aristotelian formalism and Cartesian abstraction. Where Newton grasps the purity of will necessary to bring the world into ordered creation, Leibniz compromises the God of infinite power in the name of an outmoded rational principle. Where the former discovers the basic physical principles of absolute space and attraction, the latter peevishly complains that these notions upset the traditional order of things. Clarke concludes that since it lacks the necessarily profound conceptions of both God and the natural world he willed into creation, such a tradition-bound scientific system can in no way produce a natural philosophy to rival that of Newton.

Clarke levels these charges against Leibniz in the most explicit terms, aiming in particular to show that the principle of sufficient reason is antithetical to the essence of true natural philosophy and natural theology. Clarke's criticism seeks to place Leibniz in the company of the ancient pagan thinkers he so highly honors insofar as most of these thinkers knew nothing of the nature of the true God: "This Notion [of sufficient reason] leads to universal *Necessity and Fate*, by supposing that *Motives* have the same relation to the *Will of an Intelligent Agent*, as *Weights* have to a *Balance*; so that of *two* things absolutely indifferent, an Intelligent Agent can no more choose *Either*, than a balance can move itself when the Weights on both sides are Equal."[35] According to Clarke, the Leibnizian conception of sufficient reason reduces God to the rank of logical principle, while the Newtonian view grants God the full measure of his perfection and power. What is more, the Leibnizian denial of the fundamental nature of space is a denial of divine presence in the world, for "space and duration are not *hors de Dieu*, but are caused by, and are immediate and necessary consequences of his existence."[36]

For Clarke, the Leibnizian argument amounts to an Aristotelian recidivism, denying the scientific view most capable of correcting the excesses of the tradition and setting human perception back on its naturally solid footing. By his reference to "Necessity and Fate," Clarke accuses Leibniz of having the audacity to place God within the order of nature, and thus to render what is most certain—the movement of corpuscular bodies against and within the frame of a single space and time generated by God—questionable. For Clarke, this Leibnizian misrepresentation of absolute space as a being rivaling God stands as primary evidence of Leibniz's attempt to undermine the only true science, that is, Newton's natural philosophy. Further, Clarke's concerns are not simply those of a pious Anglican, but rather expose the fundamental link between theological impulse and scientific commitment that grounds the emergence of early modern science. Indeed, the "scientist was more a theologian than the philosopher,"[37] because philosophy itself must be called into question and subsequently "converted" to better support the project of Newtonian science.

As we have already seen, in Newton's view, absolute space (and absolute time) are not substances, as Leibniz claims, but rather direct properties or expressions of God's infinite productivity. At the same time, any crude identification of them with God, rather than as an unlimited product of this infinite source, implies a restriction of this radical generativity, a restriction which could only be perpetrated by a *nullibist*: "He is not duration, or space, but He endures and is present. He endures forever, and is everywhere present, and by existing always and everywhere He constitutes duration and space. Since every particle of space is *always*, and every indivisible moment of duration is *everywhere*, certainly the Maker and Lord of all things cannot be *never* and *nowhere*."[38] Newton's evidence for God's omnipresence in the world always comes back to what he sees as empirically apparent. If we grant that space and time are apparent (and Newton does not understand how such obvious qualities can possibly be denied), then we must grant that divine presence is equally if not more apparent.

The exchange between Clarke (and Newton) and Leibniz again leads one to recall the exchange between More and Descartes. Descartes had argued that God's existence and nature were not knowable through the study of material things, that is, of motion and extension, although the power of divine creativity was to some extent revealed in such study. Newton says something quite different, maintaining instead that we can be sure of God's presence everywhere and at every moment, precisely because of the empirically certain phenomena of the spatial and temporal sensoria. In other words, it is not a question of abstraction for Newton; we know God acts everywhere because we see it, both literally and mentally. If, in fact, such a revelatory vision is not visibly operant, it is because traditional philosophical attitudes have stultified it.

In Newton's view, anything like Cartesian skepsis with regard to God's agency is unwarranted. To prove God's existence in Descartes's manner is to ignore the most natural and easily accessible proof imaginable: all one has to do is look at the world, specifically the motions of comets and other bodies, to see the propriety of God, a propriety manifested in the mathematical force of attraction and in absolute space and time—the very essence of what is and what can be: "God, being omnipresent, is really present to every thing, essentially and substantially. His presence manifests itself indeed by its operation, but it could not operate if it was not there."[39] The issue of theological presence is connected to the question of natural operations, the latter being most apparent empirically but the former more real or essential. The functioning of nature arises only as a result of God's sanctioning presence via space and time; the former depends directly and continuously upon the latter.

As Clarke points out repeatedly to Leibniz, God is no ordinary technician, but a technician who also creates the material laws and powers which all technical activity requires ("the author and continual preserver of their original forces or moving powers").[40] Further, it is a fuller recognition of God's technical authority that makes Newtonian science the most proper scientific approach; it takes most directly and openly into account the divine productivity and craftsmanship upon which the natural world depends:

> The *active forces*, which are in the universe, diminishing themselves so as
> to stand in need of new impressions; is no inconvenience, no disorder, no
> imperfection in the workmanship of the universe; but is the consequence
> of the nature of dependent things. Which dependency of things, is not
> a matter that wants to be rectified. The case of the human workman
> making a machine, is quite another thing: because the powers or forces
> by which the machine continues to move, are altogether independent on
> the artificer.[41]

God is the technician who makes nature and technology possible, establishing the distinctions between the natural and the technical (as
humanly known) by a supreme technical act. All of the powers, forces,
and structures which comprise the world, as well as its actual contents,
stem from the will of this *technica supramundana*. The machine of the
world operates according to a system (*systema mundi*) which is innately
engendered by a divine technical power.

On the basis of this image, one must again ask what Newton's "the
things themselves" refers to, the contents of the world machine or the
"powers or forces by which the machine continues to move," or both?
Given Clarke's notion of absolute dependency the answer seems to be
clear: the "things themselves," those empirically evident entities to which
Newton appeals, are in fact not ordinary things, but theoretical amalgams,
that is, hierarchical complexes which are comprised of everyday things
encased in the structure of powers and forces which gives rise to them.
Newton is indeed committed to empirical research, but the nature of
empirical reality has been redefined to include those invisible structures
which give the "things themselves" their lawful lives.

Newton's fundamental project revolves around this "discovery" of
the invisible structures imbedded in physical entities. The conception
of absolute space as a divine sensorium serves as one of the linchpins
of this project of discovery, for by it (and companion concepts such as
attraction, aetherial fluid, and so forth) Newton claims to be able to show
that such structures have always been at play in nature. Absolute space,
then, comprises part of the chassis or blueprint of the system of the world
machine. Faithful to the technical image, Newton states that even if the
machine should undergo improvement or replenishment the invisible
chassis, the "frame of Nature," remains essentially the same. Indeed, even
the specific laws and forces may be altered but the fundamental forms
(of space, time, attraction, etc.) continue to function:

> it is unphilosophical to pretend that [the order of the world] might arise
> out of a chaos by the mere laws of nature, though being once formed it

> may continue by those laws for many ages. . . . And since space is divisible *in infinitum* and matter is not necessarily in all places, it may be also allowed that God is able to create particles of matter of several sizes and figures, and in several proportions to space, and perhaps of different densities and forces, and thereby to vary the laws of nature and make worlds of several sorts in several parts of the universe. At least, I see nothing of contradiction in all this.[42]

Several worlds could exist alongside one another in this Newtonian universe, because each of them is grounded in a divine technical pattern. What is for Leibniz the ultimate irrational framework, a plurality of worlds or (even worse) a series of worlds each replacing its now worn-out predecessor, is for Newton the most compelling of images, indeed a compelling truth which engenders the possibility of all revealed knowledge.

If Leibniz and Newton both subscribe to the image of the world machine, one crucial difference must be noticed: for the former the world is a singular form, while for the latter the world is a device which can and more than likely will need replenishment or replacement. The Leibnizian position is that the world is the beginning and end of the possibility of natural science, indeed of science as the quintessential rational pursuit. Thus, even if the world is a grand machine, the image is not terribly informative, for one can never step outside its confines to compare it to another. The study of nature must accept the sufficient reason of the natural world or abandon its project altogether; reason finds its beginning in the world and from the world. Or to maintain the image of the world machine, one could say that the fundamental technical workings of nature, its rational pattern, is the same as the structures which human rationality depends upon in its pursuit of all rational knowledge. The "technology of nature" and the "technology of the mind" are analogous structures which reflect their common divine source. This fundamental analogy grounds the authentic project of natural science in the material world; mind and matter are twins whose possibilities are born together out of divine thought and power.

For Newton, the image of the world machine means something strikingly different. If one seeks to discover the fundamental structures of the natural world, one must always have one eye on the natural phenomenon and one eye on the technical pattern which precedes and will survive after this world has crumbled to dust. The propriety of this double vision is found in Newton's call to obey the wisdom of the things themselves. In the unpublished Fifth Rule at the beginning of Section Three of the *Principia* we find a summation of this decision:

Rule V: Whatever is not derived from things themselves, whether by the external senses or by the sensation of internal thoughts, is to be taken for a hypothesis. Thus I sense that I am thinking, which could not happen unless at the same time I were to sense that I am. But I do not sense that any idea whatever may be innate. And I do not take for a phenomenon only that which is made known to us by the five external senses, but also that which we contemplate with our minds when thinking: such as, I am, I believe, I understand, I remember, I think, I wish, I am unwilling, I am thirsty, I am hungry, I rejoice, I suffer, etc. And those things which neither can be demonstrated from the phenomenon nor follow from it by the argument of induction, I hold as hypotheses.[43]

It is, as Koyré tells us, a remarkable statement on the part of Newton, because it "offers us a confession of purely *philosophical* faith."[44] This faith calls into question all others, because it demands a new form of empiricism, a new form of hypothetical and theoretical thinking, indeed a new form of experience.

All of this is intimately caught up with Newton's appeal to the techno-theological forms which both underlay and exceed this world we live and perceive. Absolute space is the emblem for the entire Newtonian project, for by it Newton points to something which has no place in this world and yet grounds the possibility of this world and all the others. The world is revealed by what lies beyond itself, and true, fundamental knowledge of this world is to be found there as well. Newton's appeal is theological, not simply because he was a pious man, but because he saw no conclusive grounds *within the world* for scientific knowledge as such:

For basically there was no worldly knowledge. The so-called natural knowledge not based upon any revelation, therefore, did not have its own form of intelligibility or grounds for itself, let alone from out of itself. Thus, what is decisive for the history of science is not that all truth of natural knowledge was measured by the supernatural. Rather it is that this natural knowledge, disregarding this criterion, arrived at no independent foundation and character out of itself.[45]

The world needs theoretical legitimation which cannot be found within it. Newton finds this support for the world in the technical patterns engendered by the productive will of God. These invisible structures form the theoretical and metaphysical underpinnings of Newtonian science which establishes its priority by its success in bridging the seemingly abysmal gap between the mechanical/mathematical rigor of Cartesian science and the quest for empirical truth called for by Bacon and Boyle.

This success is built upon the double vision of Newton science, one eye on the world, the other on its invisible precedents.

The best, most essential science must take into account this hierarchy of technical creation. Newtonian science claims to be an empirical science, one which is committed to an ongoing experimental research project. However, it also claims to have discovered certain fundamental physical principles, either mathematical or mathematically renderable, which are invisible, even nonempirical. What brings these at least potentially contradictory commitments into accord is the Newtonian transformation of the visibly empirical realm into a site which is more directly inhabitable by invisible structures. All of this is facilitated, perhaps inevitably, by Newton's image of a willful God whose power is essentially and infinitely technological.

Leibniz's objections to the "occult" flavor of Newtonian science and to its extremely problematic theological imagery is warranted, but ultimately represents a misunderstanding of the still emerging essence of modern science and the new nature of nature. Leibniz assumed before the fact that his discourse with Newton would be an engagement with a kindred rational thinker, another natural philosopher. He did not understand that there was and is more at stake in science than rational grounds and consistent causal explanations. Despite his considerable reading of Bacon, Leibniz did not see the similarity between Bacon and Newton. Newtonian science indeed seems far removed from the crude scientific efforts of Bacon, but the fact is that Newton is deeply committed to the basic techno-theological vision of Baconian science. The theoretical edge of Newton will serve to take this vision to new heights of conviction and power. Its explanatory force and its technological potential fulfilled the re-creative role that Bacon said humanity should serve at the same time that it provides almost indisputable evidence of the rightfulness, the divine propriety, of Newton's science.

9

Theoretical Embodiment: The Technical Authority of Newtonian Time and Space

I n the first eight chapters of this project I have attempted to show how the collaboration of a sometimes conflicting set of theological commitments and technical impulses contribute to the grounds of Newtonian science. It is my contention that Newtonian science represents the fulfillment of modern science because it so richly embodies this conflicting play, but also because it so carefully conceals its debt to these troubling precedents. The fact that the tremendous success and achievement of Newton's work has rendered these theological and technical elements so difficult to trace should not be taken as a coincidence. In short, the inverse ratio between bold scientific success and muted nonscientific prerequisites can tell us much about the nature of Newtonian thought. Ironically, without the silent, but crucially productive conflicts of these various theological and technical forms, Newtonian science would not have had the grounds necessary to claim that its scientific vision was *the* scientific vision.

And yet, these divergent commitments and impulses which I claim lie at the heart of the Newton's project do not seem essential to the actual science that comes to be called Newtonian science. That is, aside from questions involving the religious preoccupations and professional pride of Newton, one might fairly ask if these factors actually have any *direct* and crucial influence on the scientific work that emerges with, and in the wake of, the Newtonian visions of nature and science. Or, to use the distinctions that Newton and his followers were fond of, are these concerns *merely metaphysical* or do they in fact bear on the true scientific weight and scope of this work? If my approach is tenable, then surely some trace of this Newtonian theo-technological vision ought to be identifiable in the practice of modern science. The task of this ninth and last chapter is to show this elusive trace, and to show why it is not a tangential (or "merely metaphysical") concern, but rather that it exists as the concrete heart of the sciences that finds their beginnings and ends in Newtonianism. Indeed, our difficulty in perceiving these impulses has much to do with their remarkable concreteness, their blatantly or crudely overt appearance. The unprecedented theoretical prowess of Newtonian science stems from the new, more subtle bodies to which it gives birth.

The Theoretical Rebirth of Perception in the Authority of Newtonianism

For Newton, all that we perceive is made possible and comprehensible on the divinely established grounds of the physical laws of absolute space and time, the hyperphysical force of attraction, and the corporeal nature of entities. Perception is a lesser recapitulation of the infinite sensorium of God and what appears perceptually is real insofar as it has always already been subjected to an absolute perception which renders it up to us spatio-temporally, and mathematically. On the basis of the structural relationship between these two perceptions, Newton proclaims the arrival of the new empiricism, and in so doing vows to eliminate the residual difficulties of abstraction and skepsis left over from the old science and philosophy, particularly as embodied in Cartesianism. In this way, he promises to guide mathematical and natural philosophy to its long-promised place of honor and power.

In 1620, Bacon made a similar promise, though without the pronounced mathematical aspect: the new science will methodically detect the divine marks and signatures and, thus, do away with the idols which have plagued human knowledge for so long. He also proclaimed a new empiricism, though somewhat naively, and this proclamation was certainly not lost on Newton or the other members of the early Royal Society.

However, as I have argued in the second section of this project, Bacon's actual scientific work had little in common with the science which was actually to appear. The Newtonian conception of science, at once corpuscular and mathesical, draws on the Baconian vision, but at the same time establishes a quite different schema of perceptual priorities. In the Newtonian scheme of things, sense perception will not guide the understanding, but rather will be subjugated to it. Newton himself states that his science depends upon to the authority of "the things themselves," but as we have seen this does not mean that Newtonian truth is framed by the same sort of empirical factuality that defines Bacon's approach. Indeed, perception takes on a new identity with modern science, and Newton represents the fulfillment of this transformative definition.

The concepts of the mind and the senses as two lesser recapitulations of the divine sensoria, that is, their status as two coordinated levels representing secondary and tertiary recapitulations of absolute space and time, are crucial to the modern transformation of perception. In its Newtonian form, this perceptual transformation follows from the Cartesian effort to rework perception, but in such a way that an, at least, apparently clear difference exists between the two sciences. Just as in Descartes's philosophical justifications, where the human mind is described as a minor expression of the infinite intellectual substance, Newton speaks of the way in which the human mind reflects in miniature the qualities of divine mentality. At the same time, however, Newton is careful to stress the importance of the sensory level of this reflectivity, doing so, at least, in part, to demonstrate the "non-Cartesian" nature of his scientific philosophy.

It is, of course, quite apparent that the sensory level of this recapitulation is dependent upon the mental aspect. In short, at the very same moment that Newton emphasizes the important role of sense experience in the human recapitulation of the divine sensoria, he is also reinforcing, even deepening, the Cartesian commitment to a scientific primacy of intellectual perception. And yet, the Newtonian claim to be thoroughly committed to "the things themselves" is curious, for it is born of a scientific philosophy that rejects the abstract and skeptical philosophy of Cartesianism by more thoroughly articulating the structures which define science as even more fiercely theoretical. All the more curious is the fact that Newtonian science can indeed claim superiority over Bacon and Descartes both in terms of its theoretical and experimental commitments. It is this double accomplishment which makes Newton's declaration concerning his new and well-founded empiricism all the more credible and all the more provocative.

The development of this new two-tiered recapitulative structure of thought and sense means that the relation of theory and observation in the new, emergent, and extremely successful physics will also exceed that found in Galileo. The Galilean ambiguity with regard to sense experience that Descartes saw as the Italian's fundamental scientific weakness has been all but expunged, as has the crude analytic mechanism by which Descartes sought to solve and replace it. Without doubt, observation remains a vital component in the Newtonian scientific project, but both its role and its nature have been rewritten: "observation and experience—in the meaning of the brute, common-sense observation and experience—

had a very small part in the edification of modern science; one could even say that they constituted the chief obstacles that it encountered in its way. It was not *experience*, but *experiment* that had nourished its growth and decided the struggle: the empiricism of the modern science is not *experiential*; it is *experimental*."[1] What Koyré argues here involves the much discussed principle of the "theory-ladenness" of scientific experimentation and observation. If one compares the work of Bacon to that of Newton, both self-professed devotees of the experimental aspect of science, one sees something of the striking shift from experiment grounded in commonsense experience to that form of experiment which sees quotidian experience as something which must be overcome.

One also finds this shift in the nature of experimentation at play in the respective positions of Galileo and Descartes, the former a more sophisticated experimentalist than Bacon and the latter paying only slightly more than lip service to the importance of experimental work. Newton is a strange sort of hybrid of these two traits, fiercely theoretical in his scientific outlook but adept at devising at least imaginary experiments to support or undercut theories. Newton believes that many of the experiments which he devised but never fully implemented (e.g., his notebook drawings) nonetheless serve as empirical validation or invalidation of certain hypothetical stances. It is as if the diagram of a possible experiment is virtually the same as the experiment itself. The sketch of an experiment, its theoretical plan, is particularly effective in uncovering the prejudices inherent in those theories which begin with and never go beyond common everyday experience.

And yet this overcoming of everyday experience is constantly accompanied by the claim that science is pursuing the real, the worldly, the "things themselves." Newton, like Descartes and Bacon before him, speaks of the "vulgar" or "common" conceptions of physical factors such as time, space, and motion as "prejudices" to be overcome, so that the "absolute," the "true," and the "mathematical" may be uncovered.[2] His project is by almost all accounts an effort to develop a "Platonizing theory," one which establishes the absolute, true, and mathematical as the gauge or gauges by which ordinary things are to be measured.[3] In other words, the Newtonian scientific project can be described as "Platonizing" insofar as it seeks to reveal the forms which give common experience its real substance, forms largely lost in the shuffle of everyday experience.

And yet Newton did not see the "uncommon" factors of space, time, and attraction as *merely theoretical*, but rather as those invisibly present forms and forces that make matter live. He always emphasized that his work was founded rigorously on what is actively present, though largely unseen, in the universe. Although his work is without doubt fiercely theoretical in outlook, Newton claims time and again that he seeks a science committed above all to the empirically real world.[4] By taking on the traits of both the fiercely theoretical and the fiercely empirical science, Newtonian science offers a solution to the increasingly troubling dilemma of real phenomena. However, the degree to which this achievement is self-fulfilling can only be assessed if one takes into account the aforementioned shift in experience from a quotidian base to experimental grounds. In short, Newton's claim of total commitment to empirical truth is honest and accurate precisely because his project punctuates the early modern rewriting of the nature of empirical reality by rewriting the perceptual structures by which it grasps nature. In this view, Newtonian science would represent a the fulfillment of a prolonged global shift in the manner in which the world (and the world's observer) is grasped.

Koyré terms this global shift the "destruction of the cosmos." This destruction is also a "construction," one that alters the shape of scientific perception and, thus, stands as the overt moment of transformation of modern scientific perception in general. This constructive movement involves the supervision of the everyday world by a new form of thought and action that sees with eyes of precision, eyes which can detect what is most real behind what is only qualitatively obvious. More than a simple mind set or weltanschauung, this new experiential dimension represents a force capable of populating the world with new things that confirm its perceptual power and its experiential legitimacy. In an examination of how these new things come to be one can see the destructive/constructive shift of which Koyré speaks. At the same time, in the examination of these new things it may be possible to discern how the new perceptual authority of Newtonianism takes hold so pervasively, influencing any number of nonscientific realms and pursuits. Let us begin by examining the efforts which give rise to precision timepieces and scopes, to the first modern scientific things, the first things born of modern scientific theory.

From Galileo to Huygens: The Birth of the Modern Scientific Thing

The Clock

Following Koyré's lead, I wish to explore an episode in seventeenth-century mechanics, the advent of the precision scientific clock.[5] This episode involves Huygens's attempt to arrive at a more precise measure of the acceleration of gravity. Despite Huygens's own increasingly critical view of Cartesian philosophy and science, he had grave doubts about the Newtonian concept of absolute space/time, although not to the degree of Leibniz. Perhaps more than any other seventeenth-century scientist (with the possible exception of Newton himself) Huygens embodied the talent and commitment of both a gifted experimentalist and a remarkable mathematician. Thus, he represents a sort of second convergence of many of the most significant themes of early modern science.

In the attempt to measure gravitational acceleration, Huygens's work follows a long line of experimental efforts, including those of Galileo, Mersenne, and Riccioli.[6] As Koyré points out, Galileo's attempts at experimental measurement of the acceleration of a falling (or rather, rolling) body were greatly hampered by the simple and crude nature of his devices: a piece of picture frame lined with smooth parchment, a bronze ball, and so forth. However, Koyré identifies the absence of a precise timepiece as the chief factor that impeded Galileo's efforts. In these attempts at precise measurement, Galileo used a water clock, or alternatively, a human clock, though never the pendulum clock which he himself had helped to develop.[7] Needless to say, given the approach and the "instruments," his measurements and subsequent calculations could result only in rough approximations susceptible to no more than minor improvements.

In the wake of Galileo's work, and the many subsequent efforts, such as those of Marin Mersenne and Johannes Baptista Riccioli (an anti-Copernican professor of philosophy from Bologna, who applied the simplest of pendulum clocks to the problem and achieved significantly improved measurements), Huygens seeks to determine a precise measurement of gravity's acceleration. Or more specifically, he intends to establish the gravitational *constant*. Huygens, seeking to measure the acceleration of gravity, begins with very much the same equipment as his predecessors, recapitulating with slight improvements the Mersennian attempts which he had studied so carefully. However, after numerous, perhaps modestly more successful, efforts, Huygens, like Riccioli, recognizes that the essential problem involves the nature of the measuring device, in this case, the pendulum clock.

Huygens goes on rather quickly to identify the problem as one of *perfecting* rather than simply improving the clock. A radically new kind of timepiece is necessary, one which Huygens proceeds to invent, not as he had previously attempted to do by a process of trial and error, but now by an essentially mathematical determination. The key to the problem of a perfect clock lies in establishing a new mathematics, not in experimenting with clocks containing pendulums of various lengths and springs of different sizes.[8] Perfection is a product of *anticipatory precision,* not of a posteriori corrections or adaptations.

Through his mathematical research much more than his experimentation, then, Huygens builds the first precision timepiece, one which will allow him to measure accurately the time it takes an object to fall a given distance. With this new form of clock, a truly automated device, Huygens is now ready to fulfill the empirical quest for precise measurements. Yet, as Koyré points out, Huygens "never tried to perform them. This because the construction of the pendulum-clock put into his hands a much better procedure."[9] The very same vision which gave rise to this new and precise measuring device transforms the very meaning of measurement from the means of determining with increasing accuracy the acceleration of gravity into an activity for verifying after the fact the mathematical discovery of the gravitational constant. The answer to the Galilean problem is not found in rounder and rounder bronze balls rolling down smoother and smoother wooden troughs, but in determining the equation for the cycloid described by the "falling" pendulum. What Koyré calls the "truly scientific experiment" refers to experimentation couched in terms of the imperatives of modern science: to experiment no longer means to "save the phenomena," that is, to tolerate in an ad hoc fashion the conflicting demands inherent in a mathematically precise description of a profound and diffuse phenomenon, but rather to transform the things themselves at the very moment that one appeals to their primacy. Thus, Koyré's assertion that Huygens's clock is the very embodiment of this new and dominant scientific style is much more than a figure of speech.

As Koyré points out, the crucial gap that separates Galilean science from the territory of true, rather than virtual, modern science is dramatized by this difference in style of experimental procedure. Indeed, although the mark of Cartesian science manifests itself in Huygens's approach, it too seems a remote precedent when evaluated alongside the productive work of the latter. Huygens's style reveals to us the transformation of the still empirical or semi-empirical experiences of Mersenne and Riccioli into a truly scientific experiment; it imparts to us, too, a very important lesson, namely, that in scientific investigations the direct approach is by no means the best and easiest one, and that empirical facts are to be reached only by using a theoretical circuit.[10]

What Huygens shows is that science can and should be both actively experimental and fiercely theoretical. On the surface, these two traits do not seem a novel revelation. However, Huygens's work shows that the two commitments are, in fact, two sides of a single commitment. In other words, as embodied by Huygens, active experimentation is theoretical by its very nature. Both how one imagines or constructs one's experiments *and* the instruments one must make or modify for these experiments presuppose the field of play opened by the "theoretical circuit." At the same time, one's theoretical commitments only reach the level of full articulation with the sort of productive moment exemplified by Huygens's breakthrough timepiece.

Thus, it is not accidental that one of the episodes in early modern science which best symbolizes the decisive turn toward theoretical embodiment should involve the birth of a new technical entity, the precision timepiece. Further, the symbolic importance of this episode of "experimental" discovery in modern science for the issues of perception and natural appearance cannot be sufficiently stressed. Koyré suggests that this episode shows how the new science is essentially characterized by a double movement, one which diverges significantly from the usual description of the play of theory and experiment. At the end of his essay on the episode of the scientific clock, Koyré delineates the distinction between theory and experiment as in fact the play of theory and "theory incarnate."

> The moral of this history of the determination of the acceleration constant is thus rather curious. We have seen Galileo, Mersenne, and Riccioli endeavoring to construct a timekeeper in order to be able to make an experimental measure of the speed of the fall. We have seen Huygens succeed, where his predecessors had failed, and by his very success, dispense with making the actual measurement. This, because his timekeeper is, so to say, a measurement in itself; the determination of its exact period is already a much more precise and refined experiment than all those that Mersenne and Riccioli have ever thought of. The meaning and value of the Huygenian circuit—which finally revealed itself as a shortcut— is therefore clear: not only are good experiments based upon theory, but even the means to perform them are nothing else than theory incarnate.[11]

Indeed, Huygens's shortcut to the gravitational constant redefines what experimentation is, though not necessarily what it claims to do. By defining modern scientific experimentation as "theory incarnate," Koyré points beyond the idea of the experiment as a distinct, but subsidiary, component of mathematical science. Koyré's notion exposes the way in which the modern scientific experiment arises as the other of modern scientific theory, that is, as the material vehicle by which modern science represents that remarkable moment where theoretical science and productive science no longer stand against one another, but now have become a single project.

Huygens's work on the modern scientific clock serves to show how this feat of the new science is accomplished. Only once Huygens recognizes that experimentation is of limited use in the study of questions such as the gravitational constant, does he then proceed in an entirely different direction from the experimenters who came before him. He sees that one must stop thinking of experimentation as the first step toward scientific truth. The first step must be preparation for the experiment, preparation of instruments, but also preparation of the scientist himself. When Koyré writes of "theory incarnate" one can understand this as the embodiment of theory both in the new devices of the new science *and* in the approach taken by the new science's new scientist. Thus, Koyré's notion of "theory incarnate" speaks to the way in which the experimental site of modern science always begins with a preparation, not only of its equipment but equally how this equipment is viewed and how its results are interpreted.[12]

Thus, Koyré claims that theoretical science achieves an entirely new level of legitimation through the development of new scientific instrumentation. By examining the way in which modern scientific experimentation is as much the manner in which modern scientific theory comes to embody itself as it is the practical testing grounds of theory, Koyré opens the way for a different approach to the study of the emergent nature of early modern science. I would argue that this approach is particularly important if we are to understand the new science as it takes on a more mature and established shape in the full Newtonian project. In addition to this new relationship of theory and practice, I believe this episode also reveals a new relationship of perception and natural appearance, one by which early modern science stakes its authoritative claim as the only true science.

The Scope

Is this theoretical anticipation only an anecdote bound up with the development of the precision clock or does it extend to other scientific equipment, such as the telescope and microscope, which were emerging in roughly the same period? As many scholars have demonstrated, the materials required for the invention of the telescope existed hundreds of, perhaps even a thousand, years before Galileo.[13] And yet it was not until Galileo constructed his telescope for the purpose of turning a critical gaze upon certain heavenly bodies that the telescope can be said in a crucial sense to exist. Likewise, the lenses needed for the examination of microscopic phenomena were available long before Leeuwenhoek, but it was left to him (or someone like him) to undertake the first research project involving the microscope.[14] Thus, one must conclude that while material and technical requirements are necessary conditions for such technological breakthroughs, something else must be at play as well. Koyré, for one, is not satisfied with the Marxist claim that certain forces of production are the crucial factor in such discoveries, since the industrial revolutions trail along so far behind them. The missing impulse, as Koyré sees it, is a theoretical commitment which goes beyond its classical forms. Koyré suggests that this commitment requires that theoretical understanding give rise to an unprecedented material embodiment of itself, that is, an incarnate verification and legitimation of its truth.

However, the production of instruments per se is not the sole "benchmark" of this embodying fulfillment of the modern theoretical impulse. That is, the design and implementation of a precision telescope does not by itself account for the direction and movement of this impulse. In addition to, even prior to, this process, there must be the impression of a need to develop such an instrument; a "theoretical pressure" must demand the existence of such devices as a means of bringing the theory itself into true or legitimate existence. It is this almost parthogenetic movement which Koyré is alluding to in his discussion of the Galilean reception of the news of the telescope: "as soon as Galileo received news of the Dutch telescope he constructed a theory. And it is in setting out from this theory, undoubtedly insufficient but *theory* all the same, and pushing always further the precision and power of his lenses, he built a series of *perspicilles* which delivered the immensity of the sky to his eyes."[15] Thus, Galileo's theoretical project at once *guided* and was *guided by* the development of his telescope. A certain technological know-how sprang from, but also shaped or influenced, Galilean science; a new instrument and a new set of theoretical possibilities were born out of one another.

Again, it is not simply a question of a scientist in possession of a pure scientific theory seeking the tools necessary to detect the phenomena that the theory has already discovered. But neither is it a question of fabricating theoretical entities which are then placed in the world only to be claimed to have existed in it all along. Rather, the telescope as an embodiment of theory places Galileo the scientist in the obligatory position of reconciling what is seen *within* it with what is seen without it. In other words, the telescope offers a different perspective which can only be reconciled with the everyday world if a new schema is established. This new ordering of experience is doubly initiated by Galileo: by his intimate efforts with the telescope and by his recognition of the unparalleled importance of the Copernican image. Thus, Galileo comes to claim that the telescope's "superior and better sense" must be honored above quotidian perception.[16] Telescopic vision, though just having come into existence, indeed precisely because it has just emerged, takes primacy over older forms of vision.

This argument by Feyerabend runs close to that of Koyré in many respects, particularly in the emphasis both place on the manner in which theoretical work, initially sparked by a technological "incident," then subsequently claims both explanatory priority over the technology in question *and* the undeniable superiority of the new theoretical vision. Old theoretical understanding, especially the sort that endeavored to reconcile itself to what was perceived, is no match for this new vision. Indeed, it is in terms of one of the oldest of these perceptually reconciled theoretical notions that Feyerabend discusses Galileo's struggle to bring the full meaning of the telescope into being: the essential disparity between terrestrial and heavenly phenomena. Here Feyerabend emphasizes a point made repeatedly by Koyré, an point ignored by many historians and philosophers, which provides a basic frame for the Galilean question: Just what is it the telescope reveals? "Only a new theory of vision, containing both hypotheses concerning the behavior of light within the telescope as well as hypotheses concerning the reaction of the eye under exceptional circumstances could have bridged the gulf between the heavens and the earth that was, and still is, an obvious fact of physics and of astronomical observation."[17] The new, telescopic vision reveals that the "obvious fact" of earth and sky must be neutralized. The new science reconciles this ancient division of earth and sky, because the "obvious fact" of this division is now seen as something in dire need of reconciliation. And yet, this new form of theoretical reconciliation goes against the older effort to reconcile what one thinks with what one sees. Now one seeks to render what is seen by what is thought; the telescope is the basis for this new possibility of theoretical conversion.

The new science is a science of conversion: the obvious must be rendered nonobvious. The new science embodies this drive to do away with obvious experiential fact, but not by a simple obscuring of the obvious. Instead, it operates by a kind of replacement or substitution: the new obvious, the theoretically perceivable entity, dwarfs what is merely straightforwardly perceivable. The urgency of this removal of the distinction of earth and sky is not arbitrary, is not undertaken simply because it is possible, but rather represents both a prerequisite and a consequence of the appearance of the modern scientific telescope.[18]

The emergence of the other modern scientific scope, the microscope, reveals another aspect of this theoretical technology of conversion.

Alongside the realm of the telescope another kind of space exists, not the expansive space of the heavens but a vast and minute space, that of the microscopic realm. The development of the microscope is akin to that of the telescope. The lens becomes an modern scientific instrument only when there is something demanding attention, something in need of being detected. As Koyré puts it, Leeuwenhoek's discovery, the discovery of the modern microscope, "consists principally in his decision to gaze."[19] Something is there: an obvious but previously unseen fact. However, this decision is not an empty theoretical urge, but a theoretical decision to use available instruments as modern technology so that one may see what has become obvious.

Thus, the technological decision which is the telescope and the microscope stems from the compulsion to bring about that which has become theoretically apparent. At the same time, this theoretical compulsion stems from the drive to bring to appearance what is inspired by the vision of the world as subject to intervention and manipulation. Or as Koyré so powerfully puts it, it is an impulse which sees a world that needs to be "infected by the spirit of precision."[20] What in fact had never been seen, what had never been an "obvious fact," becomes the now visible body of this spirit of precision. This infecting force is fundamental to both kinds of modern scientific scope, and if the telescope comes of age scientifically speaking prior to the microscope, perhaps it is because the perceptual raw material to be infected (the "obvious fact") is more readily available in the case of the former. In other words, the distinction of earth and sky has already been theoretically cast, already theoretically prepared for yet another more intense form of theoretical conversion. The microscopic realm still requires a more thorough theoretical preparation.

Both the telescope and the microscope do more than make already existent entities and structures accessible to the human eye. They make what was invisible visible by giving what was imperceivable, the terribly distant star and the terribly small microorganism, a new space in which to exist. These spaces are neither merely theoretical nor simply technological effects, but rather theoretically instigated forms that appear as and through the modern scientific scope. At the same time, what had been eminently visible things are rendered less apparent by the technological successes of this new theoretical vision. The heavens are no longer seen as radically distinct from earthly phenomenon and what was considered by the eyes to be the smallest now has worlds within it. The thoroughly visible has become thoroughly questionable. Only by this calling into question of these previously acceptable facts is room created for the new space(s) of things. The convicting power of the modern scientific telescope and microscope by which the very distant star and local phenomena, and the things of the quotidian world and the realm of minutia, come to participate in a single common reality, depends upon the increasing questionableness of perceptually commonplace phenomena.

Thus, when read together, Koyré's notion of "theory incarnate" and Feyerabend's complementary arguments suggest that the early modern scientific discoveries of the scopes and the clock involve a recognition of the new powers of experimentation, powers which arise out of the redefining of the experiment in relation to the new definition of theoretical science. These new definitions offer the means to resolve problems which had previously not even been problems. Huygens's discovery of the clock as the embodiment of gravity's constant and Galileo's recognition that the telescope harbored within it a new theory of light and vision both point to the way in which modern science emerges as a new form of embodiment.

Although the movement toward these new clocks and new scopes begins long before Newton, they only find their full articulation in Newtonian science. However, it is clearly not the creation of straightforward instrumental bodies, but some much more complex, even ambiguous, entity. To address the question of this strange notion of embodiment, one must examine those principles that are being given new bodies, namely, time and space. To do this, we must move beyond the work of Newton and into the work of those who saw in Newtonianism an entirely new authority of theoretical and scientific things, but also the stuff of a new philosophy and theology.

The Modern Measure of Preparation: The Theoretical Authority of Time and Space

Time incarnate and space incarnate, that is what the scientific timepiece and the scientific scopes are. Or should one say time and space *reincarnate*, since they surely enjoyed some less rigorous form of embodiment long before the arrival of early modern science. In either case, the appearance of the modern clock and scopes is a dramatic event. Through these modern instruments, time and space have finally been discovered for what they always have been. Now they can be seen as they should have been all along. In short, thanks to the modern discovery of the common truth of these primordial categories, all things, large and small, earthly and heavenly, will now come to be known for what they are, rather than what they are not.

Little wonder that on the heels of its discovery of true space and time, Newtonian science is granted of an unprecedented legitimacy. The new science embodies new powers, powers no previous theoretical science has ever possessed. The authority of this new science is built largely upon the notions of time and space discovered *as* and *through* the first modern scientific instruments. However, it was assumed by both the practitioners and the admirers of Newtonian science that a sort of pure theoretical power gave rise to the necessary instruments as well as the finished theories of the new science. In other words, it was supposed that the intellectual force of Newtonian thought had created the experiments, the instruments, and the initial hypotheses. Because Newtonian thinking apparently gives rise to the material and theoretical aspects of its own methodical culmination, new scientific instruments are recognized merely as the outcome of this thinking. They are not perceived as having any influence upon this new form of thought.

It is difficult to miss the mark of Descartes on this prevailing attitude toward the self-originating power of Newtonian theoretical science. An attitude very much like that expressed by the Cartesian primacy of intellectual substance is at work in the essentially positive response to Newtonian science. In the Cartesian schema, material things are what they are because they are idea-things; from the Newtonian point of view, they are theoretically shaped bodies. The difference between these two views is significant but hardly overwhelming. For Descartes, the primacy of idea-things stems from their source, infinite mental substance. The primacy of the former is guaranteed by the power of the latter and therefore lies in their intellectual existence. However, Descartes argues that this does not make material things any less real. In short, a tension exists between the purely intellectual source of material things and their own mixed nature.

The Newtonian commitment to the primacy of theoretical bodies resolves this tension, for as theoretical bodies they are framed by the force of absolute space and time but comprised of fundamental material stuff. The source in this case is not infinite mental substance but rather the worldly emanations of it (e.g., space and time). Thus, Newton inserts a third term into the Cartesian primacy of the idea-thing; space and time are of this world but as immanent theoretical structures. This means that Newton and his followers can appeal to a more radical form of material self-origination without calling into question the primacy of mental substance. Their appeal is not to God as the source of idea-things, but rather to a being that emanates structures which theoretically condition the possibility of all material entities, both those which now exist and those which should exist. This normative principle of existence is already provisionally at work in the advent of the clock and scopes, and it represents a kind of bodily fulfillment of the Cartesian notion of the idea-thing.

Of course, to have recognized that the new scientific instruments were theoretical embodiments would not have meant for Descartes and Newton what Koyré is suggesting by his assertion. For, despite the many differences between Descartes and Newton, those both real and imagined, they agreed entirely on at least one point: the human body, like all natural bodies, can only act, indeed, only has life, if motivated by the will and the mind. Instruments, like the human body, are bodies in no more than this sense. Thus, if instruments have any influences it is only negative, only a function of the bad functioning of the device in question (e.g., refractory distortion or hallucinations). The influence was seen as unidirectional, flowing from thinking minds to plastic bodies. In the wake of the Newtonian scientific successes, embodiment does not represent a theoretically productive possibility, but rather shows in a conclusive manner the legitimate power of Newtonian science. The new science is the right science, to play on Descartes's play of words.

The singular legitimacy of Newtonian science is not confined to the realm of physics, nor is it as quickly surpassed as the Cartesian form. Newtonian thinking continues to shape both scientific and philosophical discourse well into the nineteenth century. However, this lasting influence is perhaps nowhere better seen than in Kant's *Inaugural Dissertation* (1770). In this project, in which he seeks to describe the necessary conditions whereby a world can exist, Kant demonstrates his profound commitment to the essential tenets of Newtonian thinking: "These formal principles of the *phenomenal universe*, absolutely primary, catholic and moreover as it were schemata and conditions of anything sensitive in human cognition, I shall now show to be two, namely space and time."[21]

The younger Kant provides Newtonian thought with a broad and thorough philosophical platform, chiefly by demonstrating that time and space are "*formal principle[s] of the sensible world,* which [are] absolutely first."[22] In doing this, Kant follows Newton's lead in the manner in which he analyzes the form of the intelligible world. The unmistakable link is evidenced by a passage from Kant's Scholium to Section IV, a passage in which he allows himself to speculate:

> For indeed the human mind is not affected by external things and the world is not open to inspection by it to infinity, except *in as much as the mind itself together with all other things is sustained by the same infinite force of one being.* Hence the mind only senses external things through the presence of the same common sustaining cause. And so space, which is the sensitively

cognised universal and necessary condition of the co-presence of all things, can be called PHENOMENAL OMNIPRESENCE.[23]

Newton's God is very close to this "PHENOMENAL OMNIPRESENCE," although Kant does not cite Newton explicitly. However, after describing time as "phenomenal eternity," Kant ends the Scholium by issuing a warning to the reader and himself: "But it seems more advisable to keep close to the shore of the cognitions granted to us by the mediocrity of our intellect rather than to put out into the deep sea of mystical investigations of that kind as Malebranche did. For his view is least distant from the one which is here being expounded, *namely that we intuit all things in God.*" Kant could just as easily have cited Newton as Malebranche in critical account. Newton's appeal to the principle of *Makom*, as well as to Paul's statement "For in him we live, and move, and have our being," were surely well known to Kant.[24] And yet, Kant does not identify his own brief venture into "mystical investigations" with Newton, but rather with the neo-Cartesian Malebranche. For Kant, like so many before and after him, Newton the scientist is one thing, Newton the mystical investigator something else entirely.

Kant's God is, of course, more than this "Phenomenal Omnipresence," being as he points out earlier in this same text, "NOUMENAL PERFECTION."[25] Newton is not Kant's precedent in this matter. However, the purpose of the *Inaugural Dissertation* is to describe forms, conditions, and structures that are necessary for there to be a world, that is, phenomenal reality. God is only discussed, therefore, as that which is necessary for there to be a world, as a single and sustaining "infinite force of one being." Having granted the noumenal essence of God several pages earlier, Kant is free to identify time as "phenomenal eternity" and space as "phenomenal omnipresence." In other words, Kant feels free to endorse, firmly and without hesitation, the phenomenally absolute nature of Newtonian space and time.

If one reflects upon the aforementioned new scientific bodies in the light of Kant's subsequent validation of Newtonian scientific philosophy, a common theme emerges. These new bodies appear in their full meaning with the recognition of the singular principle of body. Interestingly, the grave tension that existed between Descartes's theological appeal to infinite intellectual substance and More's subsequent vision of the world as God's extended body is resolved in Kant's work as the difference between the noumenal essence and the phenomenal presence of God. God has a body, a phenomenal presence, inasmuch as time and space are indisputable structures of the world. Further, insofar as these temporal and spatial principles are also conditions of human experience, Kant has little or no difficulty (keeping in mind his emphasis on God's noumenal essence) endorsing Newton's comparison of the divine and human sensoria, of the will of God to move the world and the human will to move the human body. In fact, Kant's work reveals the decisive and intimate link that exists between the accomplishment of the new science of Newtonianism and a new vision and reality of embodiment.

What was for Leibniz a sophisticated form of animism, a sort of high-tech animus mundi, has now become in the early work of Kant the double condition and structure that makes all the things of the world, and the mind which grasps them, possible. Absolute time and space not only grant to things their worldly context, but these forms also lie at the structural heart of human experience. Newton had said as much himself: to know how the world operates is no more and no less mysterious than understanding how a man can will his hand to move. In fact, it now amounts to the same problem. In Kant's terms, and by way of a refinement of Newton's position, one finds a validation of the "intuitively given possibility of universal coordination" between the intellectual and sensory forms of experience and the respective forms of the sensible and intelligible worlds.[26] The matter and form of the world and the double aspect of human experience stem from the same source, namely God, and are structured by the same expressions of this source, namely time and space. What had so troubled Leibniz about the Newtonian worldview— the pivotal notions of time and space, and their metaphysical proximity to God—have become, thanks to a Kantian modification, a necessary and indispensable expression of the maturing modern scientific endeavor *and* its philosophical shadow.

Indeed, it is this philosophical shadow, and the nonscientific implications so forcefully sanctioned by Newtonian science, that most troubled Leibniz. To put it differently, the promise of a total explanatory framework, of a single scientific method and outlook which could account not only for physical events but also for social and moral events, was more like a threat to Leibniz. He does not discount the importance of Newton's scientific accomplishments, but rather feels that the dangerous implications of Newton's metaphysical claims must be pointed out. He rejects Newton's claim of the singularity of bodies, the assertion of the sameness of heavenly bodies and human bodies, of divine will and human will, because these are not, rightfully, scientific assertions. Thus, Leibniz believes that Newton, while at the same time claiming his concerns are only scientific, steps outside the realm of science by making such assertions. As a result, Leibniz fears that the nonscientific implications of Newtonian science will not be seen for what they are.

These Leibnizian fears have not been put to rest. And yet, the battle over absolute space and time gets "resolved" in the new scientific bodies of clock and scope. The sense of urgency expressed in Leibniz's objections rapidly diminishes with the many successes which these instruments help to bring about. In an important sense, however, Leibniz's concerns are validated by these very successes, for included in these many successes are some fundamental changes in how nature and the human mind and body are seen. Newtonian time and space are not merely theoretical conceptions, but also essential expressions of a new, highly productive form of scientific ambition. What Leibniz does not grasp is that the new science will be judged not by its allegiance to a thoroughgoing and traditionally rational understanding of nature, but rather by the transformative force which it can engender in bringing its new theoretical vision into reality. Indeed, the full authority of modern science comes to pass when this transformative embodiment of space and time, not only in the world but also in the mind, has been silently but effectively accomplished.

Epilogue

On the one hand, one could describe the movement of modern science in terms of an effort to develop a purely mechanical philosophy. Once this movement had achieved a certain level of success, it then proceeded to bring other (nonmathematical and nonmechanical) entities and forces into play and account. According to this reading, Newton and the Newtonians succeeded in transforming early modern science into a powerful, even hegemonical, discursive structure, but one which was deserving of its unchallenged position.

On the other hand, one can understand the emergence of Newtonian science as a highly productive *deferment* of the question of the propriety of nonmechanical forces and entities in favor of a theo-technological appeal which renders such entities and forces appropriate, even necessary, for the new physics. This transformative appeal itself is the outcome of a productive struggle between certain Baconian and Cartesian scientific commitments. The chief opponent of this appeal is Leibniz, who finds it unacceptable to import anything occult into the new scientific discourse. Further, while Clarke and Newton vociferously deny the fairness of Leibniz's characterization, it is in fact Newton's ability to convert the "occult" force of attraction into a real nonphysical principle, to render it a scientifically legitimate and appropriate law, that makes his science the new intellectual authority.

The movement from the naive perceptual faiths of Galileo and Bacon to the radical visions of Descartes and Newton represents a wholesale shift in the nature of what there is to perceive and how it ought to be perceived. What I have attempted to show in this project is the way in which the emergence of early modern science involves a struggle between perceptual forms and practices.

On the one hand, there is the Cartesian quest for a realm of certainty beyond the sensible, beyond the realm of appearance which engenders vividness only at the price of illusion and error. Provisionally in Descartes, then in a more definitive manner in Newton, this quest for the supersensible both achieves and expresses itself in the mounting primacy of a new mathematical realm. The primacy of this mathematical realm, however, is much larger in scope and greater in consequence than that sustained by the older, auxiliary science of mathematics. The development of this new mathematical space is the very essence of the new science, for whatever is placed within it is automatically reworked and transformed. Newton's unparalleled role in bringing this new mathematical space into existence links him to Descartes, for this new transformative space gives an entirely new level of legitimacy to the Cartesian rectification of natural appearance. Rather than being superseded, Newton secures this movement of rectification, placing it at the very heart of the new mathematical science.

The Cartesian and Newtonian appeals to God represent pathways for the articulation of this mathematical space of transformation. The ultimate goal of their common quest is the discovery of the things themselves, of those fundamental entities generated and sustained by the motion and space provided through the omniscient power of God. Thus, it is as much a rediscovery of what has always already been at work in things as it is a correction or rectification of the ignorance of traditional science. Both figures seek to show that the ignorance of past science is at once theological and scientific in character. The early modern scientific project can claim authority over past science not because it now uses mathematics to describe nature (a project which is after all quite ancient), but rather because its mathematical commitments are driven by the need to move beyond a description of nature, indeed to move beyond nature altogether, at least as it was formerly conceived and experienced. Early modern science deserves the title of the new science not so much because it is offers a new way of applying mathematics to scientific questions, but rather because of the manner in which it radically combines certain mathematical and theological principles to bring about a new view of nature and the world.

The creation of this new view of nature and the world also requires the creation of a new scientific vision. Perception may involve the five senses for Newton (as it obviously did for Descartes), but it is the internal sensorium—the mind—which most closely resembles the perceptual authority of the divine sensoria.[1] Only a science which fully takes into account the replicant nature of the mind, its limited, but productive talent for emulating pure intellectual substance, can hope to claim a privileged place. The project to establish a new vision of nature and the world must, therefore, also be the project to establish the nature of true mind and true perception. Having accomplished this preparatory project, the search for the things themselves no longer represents an epic or mythical effort. In short, to know how we perceive is to know what we perceive; to know how we have access to the real is to know what the real is. Nature can only be properly perceived and then described if the science which undertakes this task already properly understands the source and the relation of its own perceptual and conceptual powers.

On the other hand, and in apparent opposition to this Cartesian and Newtonian quest, stand the Baconian and Galilean convictions regarding the danger of overlooking the empirical. Bacon asserts that in succumbing to the apparent authority of an overly theoretical science we risk being blinded to what lies most directly before us. Galileo may not fear that the empirical realm is in danger of being lost, but he recognizes the increasing difficulty task of remaining committed to empirical study. Both respect the contribution which mathematics can make to the new science (though Bacon obviously less than Galileo). However, neither understands that mathematics must become more than mathematics nor that scientific thought must reshape itself and its project accordingly. Both Bacon and Galileo (and their scientific followers, such as Boyle and Gassendi) proclaim commitment to experimentation to be at least as essential to the founding of the new science as the development of new calculative forms.

These apparently conflicting positions, however, do not so much comprise opposite camps as the divergent sides which constitute the preparation for the perceptual decisions of early modern science. What will finally arise out of this play is the basic shape of the new science, a science at once fiercely mathematical and strongly committed to experimental practice. Bacon's call had been for a new science based on experience. In his view, human life was imbued with an innate though as yet only quiescent perceptual power capable of piercing the secrets of the things themselves. Bacon called for the full realization of this largely untapped human resource. Newton answered that call by transforming the very nature of perceptual experience. The transformation of perception which comes onto the scene with Newton, Huygens, and all the rest answered this call with all the force necessary for the revolution of which Bacon had but dreamed, and, indeed, with a kind of force that even Bacon may not have imagined. If it is not the revolution which Bacon had sought, it is only because he could not articulate what he saw on the horizon, because in fact he stood only ambiguously in the light of this new way of seeing the world, unlike Newton who was virtually bound by the clarity of the possibility of this new and pure perception.

Further, it is my claim that Bacon's call for a new science of power and productivity was also answered. Huygens's creation of the first precision clock offers an example of the profound interrelation of technical development and theoretical breakthrough. However, early modern science does much more than emulate the productive arts; it gives them another goal, another purpose. Like everything else, how machines are perceived is appropriated and transformed in this new vision of the world. *Techne*, the most ancient of traditions with its crafts, its artisanry, its five simple machines, had enjoyed significant, but restrained, development during the preceding fifteen hundred years. However, with the emergence of early modern science comes modern technology, the latter arising as both the reason and result of the birth of the former. To build with one's hands is, after all, as natural as seeing with one's eyes, but to build precise, even perfectible, devices is a daring act, one only imaginable when both hands and eyes have been created anew.

Koyré's notion of "theory incarnate" reveals something crucial about the movement which brings about this new perceptual authority: theory incarnate is also essentially technical embodiment. The intermingling of the technical and the theoretical (as seen, for example, in the mathematical embodiment of time accomplished by Huygens) is a collusion which symbolizes the strange quadruple reconciliation of perceptual faith and mathesical will, of a physics with Democritean aspirations and a mechanics with Archimedean aspirations. This productive collusion signals the advent of a new perceptual form, one which springs from the fact that technical devices that extend perception also transform perception. As such, the roots of this new technical perception lie not only in the past which it appropriates as its own, but also in the future, whose appearance is granted by the obscure and transformative power which throws this modern perceptual power onto the scene.

The transformation of perception and the transformation of the technical realm arise from the same earth-shattering insight. *Techne*, savoir-faire, "know-how," one of the primordial forms of human knowing and doing, cannot be revolutionary in its import unless it is accompanied, or rather guided, by "know-what," by an anticipatory framing of what one is dealing with in its essence. Perception remains an approximating art if appearance, its "raw material," is not rigorously harnessed: only in achieving a new and fundamental recognition of the nature of appearance—one which lends itself, at least fitfully, to something like a technological perception, a perception of precision—can Newton claim double title as the most faithful of empiricists and the most exact of theoreticians. To accomplish this paradoxical enterprise, Newton needed, on the one hand, a natural history and an experimental history, and, on the other hand, he required both a trustworthy sensory realm and a certain mental realm. The preparations of these two divergent concerns are found in Bacon and Descartes, respectively, but the first accomplishment of modern science is found in Newton, precisely because he makes these concerns two inseparable, bifurcated aspects of the same project: the things themselves, positioned within the context of motion, space, time, and attraction, guide the mind and the senses by the irrefutable evidence of their divine origins. Mathematical precision is the only form which this perfect relation of mind and matter could possibly take.

Within this Newtonian decision lies the uneasy double hierarchy of the new perceptual authority: the mental over the sensory, and the experimental (the theoretically incarnate) over the natural. I say "uneasy," because something strange lies at the bottom of this decision, perhaps the fundamental ambiguity of early modern science. This new perceptual form claims to be the most natural, the most proper, of visions, and yet in order to legitimately deserve this title it must rework the meaning of nature and the meaning of vision. Newton grants without hesitation that it is God alone that sees all, and it is through His power that we can have perceptual faith in the world's lawfulness and regularity. In Newton, there is a concession to the perceptual authority of God, an authority which we discern in nature. On the basis of this authority, Newton stakes the human claim to a secondary authority, one which depends upon the divine sensor and his sensoria. But having conceded this dependency (or rather by appealing to it), the Newtonian project can proceed, knowing with the utmost confidence that it is the way of the highest human knowledge and endeavor, for it and it alone best reveals the trace of that singular infinite and creative force in the apparent world.

A half century after Newton, Kant demonstrates the lasting quality of Newton's science. God is still part of the discourse, but primarily through his sensoria of time and space. There is little to be said about the noumenal essence of God. A hundred years after the *Principia*, Laplace's removal of the purportedly solid and necessary divine foundation of the new perception will provoke little more than the slightest reaction. The philosophical grounds by which the new scientific perception claimed its rights as the only legitimate scientific power are less clear, but also less important. The theological underpinnings of the new science have served their purpose; the new science no longer needs any nonscientific backing. Its clarity and its power are its more than sufficient, self-grounding principles. It has no need of any other hypothesis.

Notes

1. One is reminded of Heidegger's dilemma in the sixth section of the introduction to *Being and Time*. He "solves" the problem of reading the history of ontology by undertaking a "destruction" of the tradition, by stretching its connections and junctures in order to see the constructions that make up much of our received knowledge of what has been. At least in style, I have followed Heidegger's approach by attempting to stretch the structures of early modern science so as to gain a better sense of the complicated and often concealing impulses that comprise it.

2. This is not to minimize the importance of the other writers I draw upon, but only to indicate the origin and trajectory of this project. In my study of the work of scholars such as Marion, Grimaldi, Rees, Rossi, and Blumenberg, I found projects that were, at the very least, resonant with Koyré's own efforts.

3. By his orientation, Koyré bears the mark of his phenomenological upbringing. Even when seen against this background, Koyré's careful and concrete study is unusual. Unlike Husserl or Heidegger, his work involves prolonged and concrete historical studies. Unlike Cassirer, whose work is more consistently concrete, Koyré's work is not confined to intellectual history or the history of philosophy. Finally, where Bachelard's work is centered on science, it tends to assume the primacy of scientific, especially later than modern scientific, thought. In fact, despite important and obvious differences, the work of Foucault and Serres is probably closer to that of Koyré than any of the above. Those of us who follow in the wake of this very mixed and complex tradition bear an even more mixed and complex "birthmark."

Chapter 1

1. René Descartes, *Descartes: Correspondance*, VII, ed. Charles Adam and Gerard Milhaud (Paris: Presses Universitaires de France, 1963), pp. 121–22. All quotations from this text are my own translations.

2. Jean-Luc Marion's notion of "gray ontology" provides an account of the price Descartes must pay for his project of total epistemology, a project that dates from the *Regulae*. See his *Sur l'ontologie grise de Descartes: science cartésienne et savoir aristotelicien dans les Regulae* (Paris: J. Vrin, 1975).

3. Alexandre Koyré, *Etudes galiléenes* (Paris: Hermann, 1966), p. 131. All quotations from this text are based on my own translations. For another English translation, see *Galilean Studies*, trans. J. Mephan (Atlantic Highlands, N.J.: Humanities Press, 1978).

4. Alexandre Koyré, *Entretiens sur Descartes* (New York: Brentano, 1944), p. 80. All quotations from this text are based on my own translations.

5. René Descartes, *The Philosophical Writings of Descartes*, vol. I, trans. J. Cottingham, R. Stoothoff, and D. Murdoch (New York: Cambridge University Press, 1985), p. 44. Also see Descartes, *Oeuvres philosophiques*, I, ed. F. Alquié (Paris: Editions Garnier Frères, 1963), p. 145.

6. See Aristotle, *The Basic Works of Aristotle*, ed. Richard McKeon (New York: Random House, 1941), p. 40. It was Tom Sheehan's lectures on the question of *logos* in Aristotle and Heidegger at the Collegium Phaenomenologicum (summer 1986, Perugia, Italy) that made the rich meaning of this schemata clear to me.

7. *Basic Works of Aristotle*, p. 566.

8. Martin Heidegger, *Die Zeit des Weltbildes* (Frankfurt: Klostermann, 1980), pp. 88–89; my translation. For another translation of this passage, see "The Age of the World Picture" in Martin Heidegger, *The Question Concerning Technology and Other Essays*, trans. William Lovitt (New York: Harper and Row, 1977), p. 131.

9. Pierre Duhem and Alexandre Koyré have both pointed to the fact that Aristotelian physics is in many ways much more compatible with everyday experience than that of modern science. See Duhem's *Le système du monde*, I (Paris: Hermann, 1915), pp. 194 ff.; and Koyré's *Metaphysics and Measurement: Essays in Scientific Revolution* (Cambridge, Mass.: Harvard University Press, 1968), chs. 1 and 2.

This is, of course, not to say that Aristotelian physics is merely a systematized version of quotidian perception. Such a view would be questionable for at least two reasons. First, Aristotle's physics is a rich theoretical structure and as such makes explanatory appeals which are to some extent counterintuitive. Thus, the influence, for example, which the fourteenth-century impetus theory of Buridan and Oresme had on the emergence of early modern physics stems from the appeal to everyday perception which the former makes against the Aristotelian schema. The second, and much more profound reason, has to do with the fact that quotidian perception is not some fixed ahistorical treasure which can be summoned up to oppose science, art, religion, etc. Rather, and this is the crux of my project, perception is an essentially historical phenomenon, linked intimately to the preoccupations of a given culture and time, colluding constantly with its art, its science, its theology, and its technology.

10. See Alexandre Koyré, *From Closed World to Infinite Universe* (Baltimore: Johns Hopkins University Press, 1968).

11. See *Les Méditations* in *Oeuvres philosophiques*, II, p. 414. All quotations from this text are my own translations and are based on the original French translation which Descartes had himself reviewed and approved. For another translation see *Philosophical Writings of Descartes*, p. 16.

12. Along with Marjorie Grene and others, I find it highly unlikely that Descartes is simply trying to avoid dangerously provoking the Church by a

cursory appeal to God. See Marjorie Grene, *Descartes* (Minneapolis: University of Minnesota Press, 1985), p. 8.

13. As Koyré points out, it also frees Descartes from criticism by the learned doctors, though Descartes obviously did not feel sufficiently protected since he hesitates to publish *Le monde*. See Koyré's *Newtonian Studies* (Chicago: University of Chicago Press, 1968), pp. 70–72.

14. *Les météores*, in *Oeuvres philosophiques*, I, p. 719.

15. Plato, *The Republic of Plato*, trans. Allan Bloom (New York: Basic Books, 1968), p. 188.

16. *The Republic of Plato*, p. 189.

17. *Le monde, ou, traité de la lumière*, in *Oeuvres philosophiques*, I, p. 375. All translations from this text are my own. Descartes had at least apparently planned to include two additional chapters in this text which would have served as a bridge to his *L'homme*. Nothing else is known of their contents. Perhaps they would have resembled the part of the *Timaeus* entitled "The Cooperation of Reason and Necessity" which leads to a description of anatomy.

18. See Descartes's preface to the French edition of *Les principes de la philosophie*, in *Oeuvres philosophiques*, III, p. 67.

19. Descartes is, of course, taking up the already established appropriation of Aristotle by the Schoolmen. It is to their reading of the Prime Mover as the God of Creation that Descartes is indebted. This debt is seen clearly in a number of ways, the Cartesian revival of the Anselmian and Bonaventurian proofs of God and his appeal to something like Cusa's indefinite and mathematizable universe to name only two. These Cartesian appropriations of older appropriations are of crucial importance, although it is my determination that a full account of them lies beyond the scope of this project. See Koyré's *Essai sur l'idée de Dieu et les preuves de son existence chez Descartes* (Paris: Editions Ernest Leroux, 1922) and Jean-Luc Marion's *Sur la théologie blanche de Descartes* (Paris: Presses Universitaires de France, 1981) for major studies of Descartes's appropriation and its precedents.

20. *Metaphysics* VII, 1072b 23–29, in *Basic Works of Aristotle*, p. 880.

21. *Basic Works of Aristotle*, p. 779.

22. Hans-Georg Gadamer, *The Idea of the Good in Platonic-Aristotelian Philosophy*, trans. P. Christopher Smith (New Haven: Yale University Press, 1986), p. 132. A significant number of scholars maintain that Plato's position on the relation of the visible and the intelligible is not so straightforward. Gadamer, for example, argues that Aristotle skews Plato's argument concerning the ontological status of the highest good in order to render his own position distinct. Without conceding Gadamer's point entirely one can agree that Plato presents more than one argument on the matter. My claim simply extends what Gadamer himself points out: Aristotle seeks to hold the intelligible and mathematical accountable to and within the phenomenal realm. Aristotle's notion of *to theon* represents the "acid test" of this project.

23. *Basic Works of Aristotle*, pp. 402–3.

24. *Basic Works of Aristotle*, p. 779.

25. *Oeuvres philosophiques*, II, p. 475. See *Philosophical Writings of Descartes*, II, p. 47, for another translation of the same passage.

26. *Oeuvres philosophiques*, II, pp. 491–92. See *Philosophical Writings of Descartes*, p. 56, for another translation of the same passage.

27. I take up the distinction between the natural and the technical realms much more fully in the second section of this project. See chapter 5 in particular.

28. *Le monde*, in *Oeuvres philosophiques*, I, p. 325.

29. Letter to More, April 15, 1949, in *Oeuvres philosophiques*, III, pp. 910–11.

30. *Principles of Philosophy*, in *Philosophical Writings of Descartes*, I, p. 248.

31. Letter to Mersenne, May 27, 1938, in *Descartes: Correspondance*, I, p. 102.

32. On the other hand, it can be claimed that the Cartesian God *cannot* be anywhere, his own infinite perfection thus being a limitation. It was on the basis of this logical conclusion of Descartes's portrayal of God's relation to the world—that God resides nowhere, *nullibi*—that the Newtonians sarcastically referred to the Cartesians as *nullibists*.

33. Koyré, *Closed World*, p. 122.

Chapter 2

1. It is, of course, not the Greek cosmos which is directly under attack by the vision which propels early modern science, but rather the medieval Christian world. If I seem to appeal to the former more than the latter, it is only to stress the profound perceptual and ontological transformation which early modern science represents. The fact remains that early modern science embodies a transformative achievement which renders the important differences which exist between the ancient and medieval worlds almost insignificant in comparison. This dwarfing of previously crucial distinctions is a fundamental trait of modern perception.

2. Koyré, *Metaphysics and Measurement*, p. 20.

3. Plato, *Timaeus*, 47e–48a, in *The Collected Dialogues of Plato*, ed. E. Hamilton and H. Cairns (Princeton, N.J.: Princeton University Press, 1987), p. 1175.

4. Galileo Galilei, *Dialogue Concerning the Two Chief World Systems*, trans. Stillman Drake (Berkeley: University of California Press, 1967), p. 103. I have revised the translation slightly.

5. *Dialogue*, p. 16.

6. Koyré, *Entretiens sur Descartes*, p. 56.

7. Descartes's letter to Mersenne, October 11, 1938, in *Oeuvres philosophiques*, II, p. 91.

8. See the quotation from Galileo's *Dialogue* at n. 4.

9. Letter to More, February 5, 1649, in *Descartes: Correspondance*, VIII, pp. 131–32.

10. Letter to More, August 1649, in *Descartes: Correspondance*, VII, p. 263.

11. Henry More, *An Antidote against Atheism*, in *The Philosophical Writings of Henry More*, ed. F. MacKinnon (New York: AMS Press, 1969), p. 33. More is quoting the *Iliad*.

12. Nicolas Grimaldi, *L'expérience de la pensée dans la philosophie de Descartes* (Paris: J. Vrin, 1978), p. 86. All translations from this text are my own.

13. *Oeuvres philosophiques*, II, pp. 489–90. The fact that Descartes felt compelled to add the phrase "insofar as I am only a thinking thing" in his review of the 1642 French translation is a very telling point regarding this notion of "precision." See *Philosophical Writings of Descartes*, II, pp. 54–55, for another translation of this passage.

14. Of course, corporeal appearance would not be simultaneously so appealing and deceiving were our human essence comprised solely of pure mind. However, as Descartes is pained to report in Meditation VI the human essence is a double one: mind and mind-body. It is the latter, our hybrid aspect, that leaves us open to the dangers of misunderstanding bodies, a misunderstanding which begins with our own corporeal existence. The direction of the Cartesian project to clarify the structure of corporeal nature is laid out quite clearly at the conclusion of the *Meditations* where Descartes describes the mechanistic essence of the human nervous system and bemoans the "necessity of everyday life" and the "feebleness of our nature" (*Oeuvres philosophiques*, II, p. 505).

15. Descartes, *Principes*, in *Oeuvres philosophiques*, III, p. 520. Again, we find the Cartesian warning concerning the power of the imperceivably minute; this time it is directly tied to the image of the machine. As I will show in chapter 9, this connection is not accidental, but instead represents a crucial issue in the development of early modern science. See *Philosophical Writings of Descartes*, p. 288, for another translation of this passage.

16. *L'expérience de la pensée*, p. 147.

17. *Les méditations*, in *Oeuvres philosophiques*, II, p. 491.

18. *L'expérience de la pensée*, p. 148.

19. *L'expérience de la pensée*, pp. 150–51.

20. *Sur l'ontologie grise de Descartes*, p. 186.

21. Thus, as Hans Blumenberg shows, Descartes wants nothing to do with Galileo's "naive" form of theoretical curiosity that believes it must balance its theories "against objective irritations." Blumenberg claims that Descartes operates according to a sort of "intrascientific morality, a rigorism of systematic logic, to which the unbridled appetite for knowledge is bound to be suspect." This morality, which Blumenberg later terms "definitive," seems close to what might be called, in my sense of the term, "technological morality." Such a morality could also be called a morality of power-knowledge. See Blumenberg's *The Legitimacy of the Modern Age*, trans. R. Wallace (Cambridge, Mass.: MIT Press, 1983), p. 391.

Chapter 3

1. It could, of course, be argued that Descartes has no intention of ever leaving his temporary domicile, that this is a rhetorical move designed to appease certain authorities. Undoubtedly, as seen by his decision to leave *The World* unpublished, Descartes is sensitive to such pressures. Treating Descartes's image

of the temporary shelter in this way makes the most sense in terms of his ethical and political concerns. For example, see Pierre Guezancia's *Descartes et l'ordre politique* (Paris: Presses Universitaires de France, 1986). However, as far as Descartes's metaphysical and epistemological commitments go, *doxa* is not to be abided, except for certain controlled forms.

2. See Zeno Vendler's "Descartes's Exercises," *Canadian Journal of Philosophy*, 19, no. 2 (June 1989), pp. 193–224. As Vendler himself states, many scholars have suggested the influence of St. Ignatius of Loyola on Descartes, particularly in terms of literary style. However, Vendler goes further than most by trying to show how the *Meditations* bear more than a literary similarity to the *Spiritual Exercises* and that Descartes's method central involves a project of intellectual conversion that owes much to the Ignatian precedent.

3. In the *Discourse*, Descartes makes it clear that he believes his scientific path will eventually lead to new approaches to justice and ethics, leading to their improvement or perfection just as it has led to the improvement of the sciences of mechanics and optics.

4. This circle of pure doubt and pure space is the almost constant companion of the circle that Descartes draws in his argument concerning God's existence and the existence of material things.

5. I take up Newton's criticism of Cartesian space in chapters 7 and 8 of this project.

6. See Paul Feyerabend, *Against Method* (London: Verso, 1975), particularly chapters 8 and 9.

7. This sensitivity to the phenomenal realm makes it difficult to accept wholeheartedly the description of Galileo as the "father" of modern science, at least, if what one calls modern science involves in some fundamental manner the mathesical vision that drives the Cartesian project.

8. *Dialogue Concerning the Two Chief World Systems*, p. 19.

9. Salviati makes this clear in the same passage. "If [straight motion] were the motion which naturally suited it, then at the beginning it was not in its proper place. So then the parts of the world were not disposed in perfect order. But we are assuming them to be perfectly in order" (*Dialogue*, p. 19).

10. *Etudes galiléennes*, p. 211.

11. *Etudes galiléennes*, p. 329.

12. The special form of mathesical vision which someone like Heidegger claims is the hallmark of early modern science can thus be described in terms of the new relation of mind and space which Descartes struggles to enunciate. See Heidegger's *What Is a Thing*, trans. W. B. Barton Jr. and V. Deutsch (South Bend, Ind.: Regnery/Gateway, 1987), pp. 70–79, 91–92. Blumenberg, Grimaldi, Marion, and, to some extent, Koyré are examples of those who follow Heidegger in pointing to the primacy of *mathesis* in the emergence of early modern science. Other scholars, including J.-P. Weber and John A. Schuster, wish to be more cautious, claiming that Descartes's concern with *mathesis universalis* is not consistently systemic in both his early and later writings. The difference in position on the matter is largely one of a difference in perspective on Descartes's overall project.

While the second group tends to read the Cartesian project as chiefly scientific and mathematical in the limited sense, the first group sees it as an effort that aims at something more global, transforming the nature of human apprehension both in and beyond the scientific project. The work of someone like Foucault, who unfortunately wrote precious little on Descartes (at least directly), might be seen as exploring the subtle connections between these two seemingly opposed camps. Some of Michel Serres's work might also be classed in this third group.

13. *Le monde*, in *Oeuvres philosophiques*, I, pp. 361–62. See Koyré's seminal and profound work on this Cartesian pun in his essay "Descartes and Newton," in *Newtonian Studies*, pp. 70–71.

14. Koyré, *Metaphysics and Measurement*, p. 20. This notion is one which Koyré dwells upon in any number of texts. Because this notion seems such an obvious point, I suspect it is rarely taken as seriously as it ought to be.

15. See Alexandre Koyré, "Du monde de l' 'à-peu-près' à l'univers de la précision," in *Etudes d'histoire de la pensée philosophique* (Paris: Gallimard, 1971), pp. 341–62.

16. Koyré, *Metaphysics and Measurement*, p. 15.

17. Letter to Mersenne, 11 October 1638, in *Oeuvres philosophiques*, II, p. 91.

18. Grimaldi, *L'expérience de la pensée*, pp. 164–65.

19. It is to the Sparta of Lycurgus, and not the Athens of Pericles or Plato, that Descartes appeals in the *Discourse*. Whatever other reasons he may have had for this slight, clearly the fact that the design and operation of a city-state by a single individual comes closer to being realized in Sparta than in Athens is an important issue. Of course, if the universe is like Sparta for Descartes, it is a very technical Sparta.

20. *Metaphysics and Measurement*, pp. 20–21.

21. See the quotation at n. 1, in chapter 1.

22. Gaston Bachelard, *La formation de l'esprit scientifique* (Paris: J. Vrin, 1986), p. 241; my translation.

23. Grimaldi, *L'expérience de la pensée*, p. 173.

Chapter 4

1. *Metaphysics and Measurement*, p. 17. Bacon also called himself the herald of the new science, though it is not clear that he and Koyré mean the same thing. In *Etudes galiléenes* (p. 12ff.), Koyré is much more harsh toward Bacon, apparently dismissing him from modern science altogether and placing him squarely within that strain of Renaissance science which embraced alchemy and magic. It is not an entirely excessive criticism, since such influences do find their way into Bacon's work, but I take the fact that Koyré later softens his view by confirming Bacon's self-image to be a highly significant fact. Dijksterhuis is, on the other hand, more severe than most in his criticism of Bacon. See his *The Mechanization of the World Picture*, trans. C. Dikshoorn (New York: Oxford University Press, 1969).

2. Thus, B. F. Farrington's definition of Bacon as the "philosopher of industrial science" is illustrative but not accurate, since this so-called industrial

science is for Bacon a by-product of his scientific project, not its essential goal. See his *Francis Bacon: Philosopher of Industrial Science* (New York: H. Schuman, 1949).

3. Francis Bacon, *The Advancement of Learning*, in *The Philosophical Works of Francis Bacon*, ed. J. Robertson (Freeport, N.Y.: Books for Libraries Press, 1970), p. 91.

4. Fulton Anderson, *The Philosophy of Francis Bacon* (Chicago: University of Chicago, 1948), p. 57. See also the discussion of Bacon's essay "Sphynx or Science" later in this chapter.

5. Paoli Rossi, *Francis Bacon: From Magic to Science*, trans. Sacha Rabinovitch (Chicago: University of Chicago Press, 1968), p. 80. Among the texts which deal directly with mythical truth is *The Advancement of Learning*. Further, one finds less numerous but still significant references to myth and fable in many other texts, such as the *New Atlantis* and the *New Organon*.

6. *De Sapienta Veterum*, in *The Philosophical Works of Francis Bacon*, p. 822.

7. *Francis Bacon*, p. 76.

8. *Francis Bacon*, p. 88.

9. *De Sapienta Veterum*, in *The Philosophical Writings of Francis Bacon*, p. 840. I take up the issue of Bacon's atomistic convictions in more detail in the third section of this chapter, as well as in the third section of chapter 5.

10. Giambattista Vico, probably Bacon's most overt modern admirer, offered a reading of the significance of ancient myth and knowledge that went beyond Bacon's assessment. Vico did not think that ancient myth and poetry was merely a clear-eyed but primitive vision of nature. He maintained that the common wisdom of ancient lawgivers and poets must be taken much more on its own merits, and that the interpretations of this wisdom by the earliest philosophers and scientific thinkers was not to be trusted more than the myth and poetry it claimed to clarify. Thus, where Bacon tends to see early naturalists as a kind of key to understanding myth, Vico is more suspicious. Vico was convinced that the roughness and richness of ancient myth and poetry was more than a simple and clear hint of the secrets of nature; he saw its fuzzy depth as a culture-instituting force.

The sense of debt Vico felt toward Bacon, as well as the critical distance he put between them, can be seen in a passage from the second edition of the *New Science*: "Hence in Book Two, which makes almost the entire body of this work, a discovery is made which is just the opposite of that of Bacon in his *Novus orbis scientiarum*, or New World of Sciences, where he considers how the sciences as they now stand may be carried on to their perfection. This work of ours discovers the ancient world of the science, how rough they had to be at birth, and how gradually refined, until they reached the form in which we have received them" (*The New Science of Giambattista Vico*, trans. T. Bergin and M. Fisch [New York: Anchor Books, 1961], p. xlviii). As one might imagine, Vico's concept of the new science is significantly different from Bacon's own. And yet, even the decidedly more political and cultural emphasis of Vico's *New Science* can be seen as the other side of what Bacon proposes in texts like the *New Atlantis* and *Advancement of Learning*. Rossi, in particular, stresses the troubling absence of work on the complex connection between Bacon and Vico.

11. Bacon will maintain the superiority of the modern epoch's access to such knowledge based on the geographical and technical discoveries of the fifteenth and sixteenth centuries. For him, these discoveries are breakthroughs which can and should allow moderns to go much further than people of any other historical period. The implications of this view are crucial for his scientific vision, as I will attempt to show later in this chapter.

12. B. F. Farrington, *The Philosophy of Francis Bacon: An Essay on Its Development from 1603 to 1609, with New Translation of Fundamental Texts* (Liverpool: Liverpool University Press, 1964), pp. 120–21.

13. For example, Bacon lauds Aristotle for his biological observations, while criticizing him for his emphasis of the hylomorphic distinction. See the next section of this chapter.

14. *Against Method*, pp. 73–77.

15. *Against Method*, p. 77.

16. *Against Method*, p. 77.

17. A strict line divides the Cartesian and the Baconian views on perception, largely because the question of interpretation rarely if ever enters Descartes's overt discourse. Linked to this is the fact that Bacon's theoretical commitments are less than explicitly stated. Indeed, compared to Descartes (and Newton), Bacon's theoretical biases are superficial, because Bacon is still operating in an experiential experimental framework rather than the still emerging mathematical experimental frame. In other words, Bacon's theoretical biases are *extrinsic*, those of Descartes, *intrinsic*. The question of Bacon's theoretical biases is only now being examined more carefully by certain scholars. See, for example, Graham Rees's "Francis Bacon's Semi-Paracelsian Cosmology and the *Great Instauration*," *Ambix* 22 (1975), pp. 81–101.

18. Bacon sees the latter-day Platonists as following the early Platonists in this crucial conflation of nature and mysticism. The distinction between two Platonisms—one involving a sort of mystical numerology and the other a mathesical idealism—does not seem to be at play in Bacon's view. Of course, the Platonism of Descartes is still on the horizon. I discuss Bacon's reorganization of traditional science and knowledge later in this section.

19. Thus, as Rossi points out, even those like Fulton Anderson who see beyond the Baconian polemic against the two great ancient Greek philosophers fail to recognize "how pointless it is to search for Bacon's Platonic derivations if one does not consider simultaneously the historical importance of the hermetic and rhetorical Platonism Bacon is attacking" (*Francis Bacon*, p. 67). Bacon's ambiguous relation to Plato (and Aristotle) is reminiscent of the two conflicting Platonisms discussed in the first section of this study, those of Descartes and More.

20. *De Principiis atque Originibus*, in *The Philosophical Works of Francis Bacon*, p. 651.

21. Rossi, *Francis Bacon*, p. 59.

22. Indeed, it is tempting to recall Descartes's famous stopping of the ears and eyes when one reads Bacon's criticism of the deafness of Platonism.

23. As Feyerabend points out, this "peeling away" is not an easy or even feasible project. However, he does not seem fully cognizant of the extremes to

which Bacon goes in his efforts. It is not simply a question of eliminating natural interpretations "until the sensory core of every observation is laid bare" (*Against Method*, p. 76). Bacon is not seeking the bare sensory core, but rather the form of the phenomenon. Such a form would not be a purely sensory, but rather a cosmologically situated, being.

24. *New Organon*, p. 61.

25. See Fulton Anderson's *The Philosophy of Francis Bacon*, p. 192.

26. *New Organon*, p. 60.

27. *New Organon*, p. 61.

28. The distinction between the subject matter of metaphysics and physics is symbolized for Bacon as the difference between Pan, universal nature, and Cupid, nature in its material workings. Anderson calls Bacon's notion of metaphysics, "extended physics" (see *The Philosophy of Francis Bacon*, p. 193).

29. *The Philosophical Writings of Francis Bacon*, p. 472.

30. *The Philosophical Writings of Francis Bacon*, p. 472.

31. The preface to *De Sapienta Veterum*, in *The Philosophical Works of Francis Bacon*, pp. 823–24.

32. Indeed, one can see Bacon's extensive reading of myth, fables, and parables as an attempt to recapture this baseline experientio-natural truth. More than this, Bacon seems to believe that the new science must recapitulate this early comprehension of natural truth before it can proceed to its full-fledged business. This is why Rossi, Rees, and others believe any full account of the Baconian scientific project must recognize the essential role of myth.

33. *The Works of Francis Bacon*, III, ed. J. Spedding, R. Ellis, and D. Heath (Claire Shores, Mich.: Scholarly Press, 1976), p. 358.

34. Bacon sees this overriding principle of self-projection as the most troubling legacy of the tradition. The issue of self-projection lies at the heart of his discourse on the idols. See chapter 5 for a discussion of the problem of anthropomorphic self-projection with regard to Bacon's creative science.

35. Rossi, *Francis Bacon*, p. 123. See chapter 5 for an extensive account of Bacon's quasi-atomistic commitments.

36. *De Principiis*, in *The Philosophical Writings of Francis Bacon*, p. 656. See also Rossi, *Francis Bacon*, p. 124.

37. From Bacon's *The Masculine Birth of Time*, in Farrington's *The Philosophy of Francis Bacon*, p. 63.

38. Rossi, *Francis Bacon*, p. 54.

39. *New Organon*, I, 48, pp. 51–52.

40. *New Organon*, p. 92. This passage is foreshadowed by a passage in *Valerius Terminus* which Bacon wrote more than fifteen years earlier. Interestingly, the later, more comprehensive account of Bacon's scientific project includes a slight change in tone, particularly in terms of the increased stress on the force of Providence and the stronger hint at apocalypse: "for to my understanding it is not violent to the letter, and safe now after the event, so to interpret that place in the prophecy of Daniel where speaking of the latter times it is said, *Many shall pass to and fro, and science shall be increased*; as if the opening of the world by navigation

and commerce and the further discovery of knowledge should meet in one time or age" (*The Philosophical Writings of Francis Bacon*, p. 188).

41. *New Organon*, pp. 69–70.

42. *New Organon*, p. 71.

43. *New Organon*, pp. 90–91. Of course, Columbus also included a religious commitment among the reasons that he gave for his desire to set out to find a new route to the East: the opportunity to bring Christianity to the emperor of China, who was said to be interested in it.

44. Michèle le Doeuff cites Marta Fattori's book *Lessico del Novum Organum* in which the latter counts at least sixty-three instances of *spes* and *sperare* in the Bacon's text. See le Doeuff's essay, "L'espérance dans la science," in *Francis Bacon: science et méthode*, ed. Michel Malherbe and Jean-Marie Pousseur (Paris: J. Vrin, 1985), p. 39. All translations from this text are my own.

45. "L'espérance dans la science," p. 38.

Chapter 5

1. *New Organon*, pp. 126–27. One can see the interesting resonance between Bacon's claim and Descartes's appeal to invisible things in his letter to More (see the beginning of chapter 1). This connection is taken up more fully in the second and third sections of this chapter.

2. *New Organon*, p. 122.

3. In fact, this reaffirmation of the proper place of humans is actually a *new place*. Like Bacon's reading of the history of naturalism and science, this proper human position is situated between the theologically sanctioned past and future, between early insights and powers and the hope of an only emergent science and technology. While I would not go so far as to claim that Descartes is undertaking his own philosophical anthropology, it is interesting that he feels the need to remind his reader from time to time of the special position of the human, at least as finite mental substance. Jean-Luc Marion seems to be treading this path in his "Generosity and Phenomenology: Remarks on Michel Henry's Interpretation of the Cartesian *Cogito*," in *Essays on the Philosophy and Science of René Descartes*, ed. Stephen Voss (New York: Oxford University Press, 1993).

4. *The Works of Francis Bacon*, V, p. 132. Cited by Rossi in his *Francis Bacon*, p. 129.

5. This Fall is actually more than double as Hans Blumenberg points out. One can take into the account not only the Human Fall, but also the Fall of the Angels: "The relation between the two events lies in the interchange of the motivations appropriate to the behavior of each species, motivations that thereby become culpable: the angels, destined for the pure contemplation of the divine truth, aspired to power; men, equipped in their paradisiacal condition with power over nature, aspired to the pure and hidden knowledge" (*Legitimacy of the Modern Age*, p. 386). The implications of this merger of the two Falls, of angels and humans, can be seen in the quoted passage.

6. *Francis Bacon*, p. 58.

7. *The Philosophical Works of Francis Bacon*, p. 474. As Ellis points out, the phrase *Magnalia naturae*, translated as "wonderful works of nature," was often used by Paracelsus, whom Bacon harshly criticizes in *The Masculine Birth of Time*.

8. *New Organon*, p. 72. Bacon spends a great deal of time and space distancing his notion of magic from natural magic. As Rossi notes, Bacon does not disagree so much with their aims as with their means, particularly their appeals to supernatural intervention in natural phenomena (see his *Francis Bacon*, p. 105). As for what Bacon calls "superstitious magic," the very term suggests he discounts it altogether. See Aphorism 85 of the *New Organon* (pp. 83–84).

9. Frances A. Yates, "The Hermetic Tradition in Renaissance Science," in *Art, Science and History in the Renaissance*, ed. Charles S. Singleton (Baltimore: Johns Hopkins University Press, 1967), pp. 267–68.

10. *The Masculine Birth of Time*, in Farrington, *The Philosophy of Francis Bacon*, p. 66.

11. *Legitimacy of the Modern Age*, p. 384.

12. *New Organon*, pp. 88–89.

13. *New Organon*, pp. 117–18.

14. Indeed, it is to something like God as Unmade Maker, and not the Aristotelian Unmoved Mover, that Bacon appeals. The distinction between these two principle has vast implications. Bacon's Unmade Maker stress the intentionality of God, the willfulness of God, while the Aristotelian principle of Unmoved Mover is an empty but necessary principle.

15. *New Organon*, p. 86.

16. Lisa Jardine, *Francis Bacon: Discovery and the Art of Discourse* (Cambridge: Cambridge University Press, 1974), p. 116.

17. Francis Bacon, pp. 115–16. Jardine cites Rossi's *I filosofi e le macchine (1400–1700)* (translated as *Philosophy, Technology, and the Arts in the Early Modern Era*), although she criticizes Rossi's conclusion that scientific truth and operational skill, knowledge and power, "involves not two processes but only one, because theoretical research and practical application are but 'the same experience which constituted in two different ways.'" See Rossi, *Philosophy, Technology, and the Arts in the Early Modern Era*, ed. B. Nelson, trans. S. Attanasio (New York: Harper and Row, 1970), p. 161.

18. *Philosophy, Technology, and the Arts*, p. 160. This quotation represents Rossi's attempt to rework the difficult passage in Aphorism 124 of the *New Organon*.

19. Descartes, *Principes*, in *Oeuvres philosophiques*, III, p. 520. See the third section of chapter 2 for a discussion of Descartes's views on the similarities of natural and artificial objects.

20. Jean-Claude Margolin, "L'idée de nouveauté et ses points d'application dans le Novum Organum de Bacon," in *Francis Bacon: science et méthode*, p. 24. I take the term "frontiers" to be extremely apt, since Aristotle never asserted this as a "hard and fast" distinction. Instead, he acknowledges that this distinction is a frontier fraught with tensions and exchanges. Bacon, however, promotes the almost total conflation of these two realms of things.

21. Aristotle, *Physics*, 193b 8–9, in *Aristotle IV: Physics, Books I–IV*, trans. Philip H. Wicksteed and Francis M. Cornford (Cambridge, Mass.: Harvard University Press, 1980), pp. 114–15. I have altered the given translation of the term *genetai* from "propagate" to "generate."

22. See the quotation from Heidegger's "The Age of the World Picture" concerning the Greek experience of appearance at n. 8 in chapter 1.

23. On a related plane, Aristotle calls into question the notion that the essence of human life is "demiurgic" in the fourth chapter of Book Six of the *Nicomachean Ethics* where he distinguishes the two activities or capacities relating to the temporally dynamic realm, making and acting. Aristotle's claim that cultures are themselves natural rather than technical in their essence addresses this ambiguity in yet another important manner.

24. *Physics*, 193b 12, in *Aristotle: Physics I–IV*, p. 115.

25. A number of feminist thinkers have stressed the general tendency on the part of Bacon and other early modern scientific philosophers to view nature as "feminine," as compliant and yielding, or petulant and unyielding. The importance of such feminist accounts is undeniable, and while my own project moves in a somewhat different direction, I believe our approaches are much more than compatible. See Carolyn Merchant's *The Death of Nature* (New York: Harper and Row, 1980) and Evelyn Fox Keller's *Reflections on Gender and Science* (New Haven: Yale University Press, 1985).

26. *De Augmentis Scientiarum*, in *The Philosophical Works of Francis Bacon*, p. 427.

27. See Bacon's subsequent criticism of Aristotle in the same text, *De Augmentis Scientiarum*, in *The Philosophical Works of Francis Bacon*, p. 472.

28. *Preparative toward Natural and Experimental History*, in *New Organon*, p. 284.

29. Again, although I believe Lisa Jardine is correct to call into the question the labeling of Bacon as some champion of a crude technological movement, a deeper, more significant, movement of technology is clearly launched in Bacon's work.

30. Rossi, *Philosophy, Technology, and the Arts*, p. 142.

31. *New Organon*, p. 180.

32. As Blumenberg points out, the misunderstanding of this short phrase has obscured Bacon's project for a very long time. He suggests that this misreading stems from the assumption that Bacon is committed to the "thoroughgoing lawful determination of nature," that "nature commanded" and "nature obeyed" spring from "one and the same aspect of law." My point runs parallel to Blumenberg's own, although I stress the connection between this double nature and the technical reproduction of nature more than Blumenberg. See *Legitimacy of the Modern Age*, pp. 383–84.

33. Leibniz, who considered Bacon's physical theory "profound," extends this Baconian line of thought in an essay which discusses "slumbering things." See Leibniz's "De la production originelle des choses prise à sa racine," in *Opuscules philosophiques choisis* (Paris: J. Vrin, 1978), pp. 83–92. An English translation is

found in G. W. Leibniz, *Philosophical Essays*, ed. and trans. R. Ariew and D. Garber (Indianapolis: Hackett, 1989), pp. 149–55.

34. Blumenberg, *Legitimacy of the Modern Age*, p. 387. Bacon's allusion to Solomon in the New Organon regarding the "glory of discovery" (see the first section of this chapter) substantiates Blumenberg's claim.

35. Graham Rees, "Atomism and 'Subtlety' in Francis Bacon's Philosophy," *Annals of Science*, 37 (1980), p. 565.

36. Bacon must go to the margins of the scientific tradition to find his precedent, because his project seeks to establish a naturalistic base for science. This move to the questionable figure or the questionable position is one which Bacon makes not only in his scientific project, but also in terms of his philosophical, social, and theological concerns as well. After all, Bacon is not only calling for a new naturalism, but also for a new humanism and a new theism. As we have seen, Bacon is also well aware of his own marginal status, at least if one takes the term "*Buccinator*" seriously.

37. Indeed, the number of historians of science who place Bacon firmly within the atomist school makes for a formidable list. Rees's work goes against this commonly held and extremely convenient position. For examples of this large group of historians, see R. H. Kargon's *Atomism in England from Hariot to Newton* (Oxford: Clarendon Press, 1966); Marie Boas's "The Establishment of the Mechanical Philosophy," *Osiris* 10 (1952), pp. 412–541; and Mary Hesse's "Francis Bacon's Philosophy of Science," in *Essential Articles for the Study of Francis Bacon*, ed. Brian Vickers (Hamden, Conn.: Archon Books, 1968), pp. 114–39.

38. As Betty Jo Teeter Dobbs points out, More follows Descartes in maintaining the fundamental distinction between matter and spirit, though More "allowed for the *action* of spirit on all kinds of matter." Still, since More's concept of spirit is defined by an essential "indiscerpability," there does not seem to be any room for Bacon's theory of tangible and pneumatic forms of matter. See Betty Jo Teeter Dobbs, *The Foundations of Newton's Alchemy or "The Hunting of the Greene Lyon"* (Cambridge: Cambridge University Press, 1975), p. 105.

39. Rees, "Atomism and the 'Subtlety' of Francis Bacon's Philosophy," p. 553.

40. The fact that Bacon seeks to show how spirits do not simply visit matter, but in fact reside within it, has caused tremendous difficulties for historians of science. How can one take such discussions as a part of serious science? Much of the problem has to do with the language that Bacon is obliged to use. He must depend in large part on Paracelsian terminology, though his pneumatic theory of matter represents a dramatic recasting of Paracelsian views. Bacon's quest for a more rigorous scientific language is difficult to deny (e.g., one has only to consider his extensive criticism of Gilbert's magnetic theories). Indeed, like his own contemporaries, it may be that the critical use of this Paracelsian language has led most historians of science to question the seriousness of Bacon's scientific views when taken as a whole. The problem with this attitude is that one does not recognize the limited number of discursive options open to Bacon nor does one grant that Bacon may have perceived that certain aspects

of Paracelsian thought, once rectified, contained something important for the new science.

Much more significant for this project, however, is the general tendency to see Bacon as somehow caught between a commitment to the establishment of basic scientific principles and a commitment to a cosmology that detracts from this solid scientific endeavor. Given the unfinished nature of Bacon's Great Instauration, this attitude is to a certain extent understandable. Yet the convenience of this view, like so many other convenient stories found within the history of science, stems more from the shortcomings of the reading than the flaws or incompleteness of the writer's project.

41. In other words, historians of science tend to separate Bacon's work into two distinct parts: what they see as a reasonable (contiguous) anticipation of the modern scientific view of matter and what they perceive to be far more speculative theory of material nature. Rees calls into question these "popular" parameters of inclusion and exclusion.

42. "Atomism and 'Subtlety' in Francis Bacon's Philosophy," p. 571.

43. The tendency to read Bacon as partially touched by the outmoded or outlandish theories of thinkers like Paracelsus and Telesius and partially a herald of the new science is not a new one. It begins in the years immediately following Bacon's death and still continues to exercise influence even today. See Rees's "The Fate of Bacon's Cosmology in the Seventeenth Century," *Ambix* 24 (1977), pp. 27–38.

44. Graham Rees, "Francis Bacon's Semi-Paracelsian Cosmology and the Great Instauration," p. 173.

Chapter 6

1. *New Organon*, p. 22.

2. Descartes's early flirtation with natural magic, as found in some of his most youthful writings, does suggest some similarities. Nonetheless, Descartes ceases to refer to this tradition, at least, in any direct manner, in his more mature work. See *Philosophical Writings of Descartes*, I, pp. 1–5.

3. One could of course claim that all of Bacon's accentuation of the underutilized status of perception is just so much rhetoric. However, if this is the case, then all of Bacon's appeals to the fundamental scientific inspiration of the early Greek naturalists would make very little sense. The efforts of Rees, Rossi, and others have shown how very crucial and very real the influence of early naturalism is on Bacon's vision of the new science.

4. *De Sapientia Veterum*, in *The Philosophical Works of Francis Bacon*, p. 850.

5. Ernst Cassirer, *The Platonic Renaissance in England*, trans. James P. Pettegrove (Austin: University of Texas, 1953), p. 53.

6. Further, one of the direct consequences of this total naturalization of the natural light involves the commitment to an open community of science rather than a closed circle of initiates. Bacon is especially critical of Paracelsus and others

for this hermetic trait, although his own notion of the "high priest of the sense" seems ill-chosen from this perspective.

7. *The Masculine Birth of Time*, in *The Philosophy of Francis Bacon*, p. 67.

8. See Bacon's discussion of the "riches of Solomon's House" in the *New Atlantis*, in *The Philosophical Works of Francis Bacon*, p. 731.

9. Margolin, "L'idée de nouveauté," p. 24. The term "technological initiative" is very significant for my project. The reader will notice that I have to this point discussed Baconian science in terms of its technical (rather than technological) commitments because one of my main objectives is to show how modern technology shows itself only with the dramatic theoretical and theological mutations which Bacon announces, but does not fully achieve. I have been more free with the term in the first section of this book, because Descartes represents the first basic merger of theological and theoretical impulses. Much of this chapter involves the question of Bacon's quasi-technological initiative. His status as only half-modern may have more to do with the question of his limited technological vision than anything else.

10. *New Organon*, pp. 205–6.

11. See *New Organon*, pp. 213–14, for Bacon's anticipatory account of the Cartesian problem.

12. When compared to the Baconian notion of natural light offered by this reading, Descartes's natural light suddenly seems less supernatural.

13. See the quotation from the *New Organon* at n. 40 in chapter 4.

14. Alfred North Whitehead, *Science and the Modern World* (New York: Free Press, 1953), p. 96. Whitehead's description clearly points to the central role a certain form of theological impulse will play in modern scientific and philosophical thought. As I will show in the following chapter, this question of the theological position of the modern individual is not a spurious one for modern science, something simply peculiar to Bacon and Descartes, but rather an issue central to its formation and development, particularly in its first accomplishment with Newton.

15. *Preparative towards a Natural and Experimental History*, in *Philosophical Works of Francis Bacon*, p. 403.

16. See *Discourse on Method*, in *The Philosophical Writings of Descartes*, I, p. 143.

17. "Francis Bacon's Semi-Paracelsian Cosmology and the *Great Instauration*," pp. 170–71.

18. To conclude that Bacon's vision of science is nonmodern because his experimental method seems crude is to overlook the notion of technology that is coming into being with Baconian science. Bacon's commitment to experimental history, to *technical* natural history, paves the way for a secondary form of technology, but a secondary form that will occlude its progenitor insofar as it will claim its own unprecedented nature. The theoretical aspect of Baconian science is covered up in the very same movement, the movement of overt early modern science.

19. Rees, "Francis Bacon's Semi-Paracelsian Cosmology and the *Great Instauration*," p. 173.

20. *New Organon*, p. 54; my italics. It is important to note that Bacon places

the magnet in the Prerogative Instances of the thirteenth place, *Instances of Alliance or Union*. Bacon defines them as the sort of instances that "mingle and unite natures supposed to be heterogeneous, and marked and set down as such in the received divisions" (*New Organon*, p. 186).

21. See, e.g., William Whewell's *On the Philosophy of Discovery* (New York: B. Franklin, 1971), Koyré's *Etudes histoires de la pensée philosophiques*, and Mary Hesse's *Forces and Fields* (Westport, Conn.: Greenwood Press, 1970).

22. *The Legitimacy of the Modern Age*, p. 390; my italics.

23. Indeed, Bacon's three great epochs of human achievement line up closely with historical moments in which new civil constitutions are established (i.e., Athens, Rome, and England). This is another intimate link between Bacon's scientific and social concerns. One also finds here another Baconian anticipation of Vico's *New Science*.

24. *Preparative towards a Natural and Experimental History*, in *New Organon*, p. 273.

25. In a similar way, Bacon's pneumatic theory is not guided by a theory of atoms so much as what a quasi-atomic view makes possible. In other words, Bacon seeks to lay out a new theoretical rhetoric by the selective appropriation of traditional scientific notions.

26. "Sphinx or Science," in *Selected Writings of Francis Bacon* (New York: Modern Library, 1960), p. 419.

27. It is important to note that in the "Catalogue of Particular Histories" Bacon includes two histories of "Pure Mathematics" as the very last entries, histories 129 and 130 (*Parasceve*, in *The Philosophical Works of Francis Bacon*, p. 412). He also points out that these are "observations rather than experiments," thus emphasizing the restricted role mathematics enjoys in his scientific scheme.

28. Carol Merchant's *Death of Nature* dedicates an entire chapter to Bacon's scientific vision. Her chapter on Newton in the same text suggests just how influential Merchant believes this Baconian vision was on the "true" fathers of modern science. Again, I believe my project comes to many of the same conclusions, though without a directly feminist edge. Indeed, Merchant alludes to the famous quote about "chaste and holy wedlock," but within Bacon's extensive work on myth there lies a huge, largely untouched resource for such feminist readings.

29. Perhaps this is because Bacon does not imagine, or at least chooses not to profess the merits of, a moment at which technical creation will begin to occlude the creation that went before, namely nature.

30. Michel Foucault, *The Order of Things* (New York: Vintage, 1970), p. 128.

31. C. S. Peirce, *Writings of Charles S. Peirce* (Bloomington: Indiana University Press, 1982), vol. I, p. 113.

Chapter 7

1. The tendency of Bacon and others to conflate the views of Lucretius and Democritus is relevant, since it demonstrates the sort of appropriation of the

ancients which modern science undertakes, an appropriation that will preserve or re-create only those distinctions which further its own transformative project. As an example of this conflation, see *The Works of Francis Bacon*, II, p. 83. It is of course an appropriative technique which Newton will perfect by bringing it to bear on more contemporaneous writings, particularly those of Descartes.

2. David Gregory notes that Newton declared that the "philosophy of Epicurus and Lucretius is true and old, but was wrongly interpreted by the ancients as atheism." See *The Correspondence of Isaac Newton*, ed. H. W. Turnbull (Cambridge: Cambridge University Press, 1961), vol. III, p. 338.

3. Marie Boas's "The Establishment of Mechanical Philosophy" offers an excellent account of Boyle's struggle to produce a full-fledged corpuscular philosophy which at the same time did not violate the principles of a rigorous mechanical philosophy. As Boas points out, this struggle lays much of the groundwork for Newton's own decisions concerning the same issues.

4. *Metaphysics and Measurement*, p. 16.

5. Compare Newton's title to the title of Descartes's *Principia Philosophiae*. Interestingly, Newton often referred to his own work as "my *Principia Philosophiae*." In his "Newton in the Light of Recent Scholarship" (*Isis* 51, 1960, pp. 489–514), I. B. Cohen suggests that this fact further emphasizes Newton's anti-Cartesianism. While Cohen's point is well taken, it should also be obvious that Newton is linking his project to that of Descartes. Newton may oppose any number of specific Cartesian claims in his *Principia*, but in terms of the scope and ambition of his project he positions his text right alongside the *Principia* of Descartes.

6. Sir Isaac Newton, *Principia*, trans. Andrew Motte, rev. Florian Cajori (Berkeley: University of California Press, 1962), vol. I, p. xxxii. This passage is actually part of Roger Cotes's "Preface to the Second Edition," but the care which Newton took editing and overseeing Cotes's preparation of the second edition of the *Principia* is well known (see, e.g., *Newtonian Studies*, pp. 31, 142, 160). We can take these words as more than merely acceptable to Newton.

7. A number of scholars have shown that Newton does, in fact, rely upon certain "fabulous stories" in the development of his science of nature, most notably certain alchemical and mythical forms. See, for example, I. B. Cohen, "Newton in the Light of Recent Scholarship"; Richard Westfall, "The Role of Alchemy in Newton's Career," and Marie Boas Hall, "Newton's Voyage on the Strange Seas of Alchemy," both in *Reason, Experiment, and Mysticism in the Scientific Revolution*, eds. M. L. R. Bonelli and W. R. Shea (New York: Science History Publications, 1975); see also Betty Jo Teeter Dobbs, *The Foundations of Newton's Alchemy*.

8. Recall that Descartes had cited the convicting power of appearance, albeit in a more pejorative sense than Newton apparently does.

9. Samuel Clarke, *The Leibniz-Clarke Correspondence*, trans. H. Alexander (New York: Barnes and Noble, 1984), p. 12.

10. *The Leibniz-Clarke Correspondence*, p. 15.

11. Martial Gueroult, *Dynamique et métaphysique leibniziennes* (Paris: Les Belles Lettres, 1934), p. 100; my translation.

12. The differences between the Cartesian and Newtonian mathematical

projects have by no means been fully explored. However, my aim is to show how the development of new mathematical entities advances alongside the development of new natural entities. Seen against the backdrop of this concern, the differences between the Newtonian and Cartesian mathematical projects are overshadowed by the similarities, if you will, the mathesical sameness, of their overall projects.

13. Voltaire, *Lettres philosophiques*, ed. G. Lanson (Paris: Cornely, 1924), vol. II, p. 7. The translation is taken from Koyré's *Newtonian Studies*, p. 61.

14. Leibniz, "Preface to the New Essays," in *Philosophical Essays*, pp. 304–5.

15. Quoted in J. E. McGuire's article, "Force, Active Principles, and Newton's Invisible Realm," *Ambix* 15 (1968), p. 179.

16. *Leibniz-Clarke Correspondence*, p. 94.

17. Scholars such as Koyré and Cohen feel certain that Leibniz either wrote or contributed to this review. See Alexandre Koyré and I. B. Cohen, "Newton and the Leibniz-Clarke Correspondence," *Archives Internationales d'histoire des Sciences* 15 (1962), pp. 68, 88. This essay by Koyré and Cohen is by far the best assessment of the Leibniz-Clarke correspondence. It is especially invaluable for an understanding of Newton's role in this correspondence.

18. *Acta Eruditorum* (1714), p. 141. See "Newton and the Leibniz-Clarke Correspondence," pp. 68, 88.

19. "Newton and the Leibniz-Clarke Correspondence," p. 88n.

20. "Newton's 'Account of the Book entitled *Commercium Epistolicum*'" is included as an appendix to A. Rupert Hall's *Philosophers at War* (Cambridge: Cambridge University Press, 1980), p. 314.

21. *Philosophers at War*, p. 95.

22. *Philosophers at War*, p. 119. The controversy involving Newton's voluntarist theology and Leibniz's commitment to the principle of sufficient reason is taken up directly in chapter 8.

23. Isaac Newton, *Opticks*, trans. I. Bernard Cohen (New York: Dover, 1952), p. 542.

24. Koyré, *Newtonian Studies*, p. 10.

25. Koyré and Cohen's point concerning the fact that "Newton's conception of Space cannot be fitted into the traditional ontology—nor, to tell the truth, can that of Leibniz" can be said of their respective philosophical projects as well. See Koyré and Cohen, "Newton and Leibniz-Clarke Correspondence," p. 93.

26. Leibniz, *Opuscules philosophique choisis*, p. 92.

27. Koyré uses this term in the title of one of his chapters on Newton and Leibniz in *From the Closed World to the Infinite Universe*, "The Work-Day God and the God of the Sabbath."

28. The next chapter is largely devoted to the Newton-Leibniz debate concerning the notions of absolute space and time.

29. Stephen Toulmin, "Criticism in the History of Science: Newton on Absolute Space, Time, and Motion," *Philosophical Review* 68 (1959), p. 20.

30. Leibniz's fourth paper, in *Leibniz-Clarke Correspondence*, p. 39.

31. McGuire, "Force, Active Principles, and Newton's Invisible Realm," p. 206. McGuire is quoting from a letter from Newton to Thomas Burnett.

32. Here Newton is using something like Descartes's play of worlds of *The World*. Notice, however, that where Descartes asserted the other world as an imaginary experiment, Newton's play has a more apocalyptic edge. I would suggest that this play of worlds has a great deal to do with the project of the mathematical transformation of nature shared by these two figures. It seems to be, if you will, a mathesical "habit."

33. John Locke, *Mr. Locke's Reply to the Right Reverend Lord Bishop of Worcester, Answer to his Second Letter* (London, 1699). Cited in Koyré's *Newtonian Studies* (Chicago: University of Chicago Press, 1965), p. 155.

Chapter 8

1. "Is not universal space the Sensorium of an Incorporeal, Living, and Intelligent Being, which discerns and completes all things in themselves and profoundly perceives things as present in itself; that which thinks and feels and thinks in us contemplates only images of this [sensorium] in the brain?" (my translation). Quoted from the original page 315 of Newton's *Optice*, 1706. Reprinted in Koyré and Cohen, "The Case of the Missing *Tanquam*," *Isis* 52 (1961), p. 564.

2. As Koyré and Cohen have shown, Newton (probably with Clarke's encouragement) substituted a revised page 315 with the qualifying *tanquam* for the original in the 1706 *Optice* after the volume had been printed, but before binding. However, at least a few volumes slipped through unchanged, that is, with the more straightforward, less ambiguous, statement concerning the *sensorium dei*. Koyré and Cohen suggest that Leibniz may have seen one of these unchanged copies of the *Optice* and thus found Clarke's insistence on the "as it were" of the sensoria image to be an avoidance tactic. See Koyré and Cohen, "The Case of the Missing *Tanquam*," pp. 555–66.

3. Much work has appeared in the last thirty years or so on the question of the connection of religion and science in the seventeenth century. There seem to be three distinct positions on the matter: (1) religion and science are utterly separate issues which should not be treated in mixed company; (2) developments in religion cause scientific change or revolutions in science cause shifts in religious commitments; or (3) the relationship between religion and science is one of mutual inspiration and stimulation that exceeds the language of cause and effect. It is the last position which has given rise to the most exciting work in the field of late. See, for example, Barbara Shapiro, "Latitudinarianism and Science in Seventeenth Century England," *Past and Present* 40 (1968), pp. 16–41; James R. Jacob and Margaret C. Jacob, "The Anglican Origins of Modern Science: The Metaphysical Foundations of the Whig Constitution," *Isis* 71 (1980), pp. 251–67. Perhaps most significantly, work in the third category does not restrict us to a two-term debate, but rather brings other issues (e.g., social and political concerns) into the mix of questions. Within the philosophical context, the work of Hans Blumenberg serves to show the merits of a similar approach.

4. From Newton's *De Gravitatione et Aequipondio Fluidorum*, c. 1668. Translated in *Unpublished Scientific Papers of Isaac Newton*, ed. A. Hall and M. Hall (Cambridge: Cambridge University Press, 1962), p. 136.

5. Newton, *Opticks*, p. 369; my italics.

6. *Unpublished Scientific Papers of Isaac Newton*, p. 131.

7. *Unpublished Scientific Papers of Isaac Newton*, p. 136.

8. Leibniz's fifth paper, in *Leibniz-Clarke Correspondence*, p. 72. The comparison between More and Newton had already been made in the review of the *Principia* published in the 1714 *Acta Eruditorum*.

9. Quoted from the fourth draft of *Advertissement au Lecteur* which Newton prepared for des Maizeaux's French edition of the Leibniz-Clarke correspondence (Draft D, Cambridge University Library, Add. 3965, fol. 289) which is quoted in its entirety in Koyré and Cohen's "Newton and the Leibniz-Clarke Correspondence," p. 99. Clarke's fifth reply to Leibniz includes the same quote from Acts 17:27–28 (see *Leibniz-Clarke Correspondence*, p. 103). As Koyré and Cohen point out, the overlap between the language used in Newton's several drafts of the *Advertissement* and Clarke's responses to Leibniz makes the claim that Clarke was acting as a "loose cannon" without Newton's knowledge virtually untenable. It is of interest that Clarke (more than likely with Newton's approval) amends the quote from Acts to read "for in him we (and all things) live and move and have our being."

10. *Enchiridion Metaphysicum*, in *The Philosophical Writings of Henry More*. See "Newton and Leibniz-Clarke Correspondence," pp. 87–88.

11. Quoted and discussed by Koyré in *Closed World*, pp. 194–96.

12. *Closed World*, p. 205

13. *Closed World*, p. 200.

14. J. E. McGuire, "Newton on Place, Time and God: An Unpublished Source," *British Journal for the History of Science* 11 (1978), p. 117. The bracketed interpolations are McGuire's.

15. The appeal to the Platonic tradition is never a univocal appeal. As Koyré has pointed out, one must "recognize the existence of *two* (and not one) Platonic traditions, that of mystical arithmology, and that of mathematical science" (*Metaphysics and Measurement*, p. 40, n. 2). These two traditions rarely appear independently of one another, either in a clear-cut fashion or as two distinct aspects of one given project. Newton's project does not seem to be an exception.

16. McGuire, "Newton on Place, Time, and God," p. 123.

17. Blumenberg, *The Legitimacy of the Modern Age*, pp. 80–81.

18. *Newtonian Studies*, p. 13n.

19. Leibniz's third letter, in *Leibniz-Clarke Correspondence*, p. 26.

20. Leibniz's fourth paper, in *Leibniz-Clarke Correspondence*, p. 42.

21. Leibniz's second paper, in *Leibniz-Clarke Correspondence*, p. 18.

22. The quotation is from the Halls's translation of Newton's manuscript "De Gravitatione et Aequipondio Fluidorum," in *Unpublished Scientific Papers of Isaac Newton*, p. 141. The bracketed interpolation is mine. Newton makes a similar

statement in the 1692–93 manuscript on place, time, and God: "The most perfect idea of God is that he be one substance, simple indivisible, live and making live, necessarily existing everywhere and always, understanding everything to the utmost, freely willing good things, by his will effecting all possible things, and containing all other substances in Him as their underlying principle and place; a substance which by his own presence discerns and rules all things, just as the cognitive part of man perceives the forms of things brought into the brain, and thereby governs his own body" (J. E. McGuire, "Newton on Place, Time and God: An Unpublished Source," p. 123).

23. Given the fact that alchemical practices and discourse were still fairly prevalent in his time, it is not surprising that Leibniz should have already perceived what many historians of science now concede, namely, the influence of alchemy on Newton.

24. Blumenberg, *The Legitimacy of the Modern Age*, p. 149.

25. Leibniz's fifth paper, in *Leibniz-Clarke Correspondence*, p. 72.

26. Leibniz's fifth paper, in *Leibniz-Clarke Correspondence*, p. 81.

27. Leibniz's fifth paper, in *Leibniz-Clarke Correspondence*, p. 77.

28. Leibniz, *Philosophical Essays*, pp. 210–11.

29. Donald Rutherford, *Leibniz and the Rational Order of Nature* (New York: Cambridge University Press, 1995), p. 239.

30. It might be argued that Newton also asserts a nonmathematical thinking as prior to mathematical thought, and yet such metaphysical discourse serves a temporary support for an essentially mathematical and physical discourse. The insertion of the *tanquam* is a symbol of this Newtonian practice of asserting a never more than temporarily essential metaphysical frame.

31. *Opuscules philosophiques choisis*, p. 94.

32. G. E. Leibniz, *Exposition and Defence of the New System*, in *Leibniz: Philosophical Writings*, trans. M. Morris (New York: Dutton, 1965), pp. 102–3.

33. "On the Nature of Body and the Laws of Motion," in *Philosophical Essays*, pp. 245–46.

34. Blumenberg, *Legitimacy of the Modern Age*, p. 149.

35. Clarke's fourth reply, in *Leibniz-Clarke Correspondence*, p. 45. The argument involving the weights and balances was initiated by Leibniz in his second paper (p. 16) where he cites Archimedes as an ancient precedent for the venerable history of his principle of sufficient reason: "Archimedes being to proceed from mathematics to natural philosophy, in his book *De Æquilibrio*, was obliged to make use of a particular example of the great principle of a sufficient reason. He takes it for granted, that if there be a balance, in which everything is alike on both sides, and if equal weights are hung on the two ends of that balance, the whole will be at rest. 'Tis because no reason can be given, why one side should weigh down, rather than the other. Now, by that single principle, viz. that there ought to be a sufficient reason why things should be so, and not otherwise, one may demonstrate the being of a God, and all the other parts of metaphysics and natural theology; and even, in some measure, those principles of natural philosophy, that

are independent upon mathematics: I mean, the dynamical principles, or the principles of force."

Thus, Leibniz concludes that theoretical investigation should always be guided by the question of whether one's position affirms the singularity of the phenomenon (its reasons for necessarily being what it is), rather than pursuing rash speculations which lead to the conclusion that a given phenomenon could just as easily not be what it is or even not exist to begin with. Mathematics has purview only over those natural phenomena which can be treated mathematically *by their intrinsic nature.*

Leibniz is making almost classic Aristotelian points here. Most importantly, he is challenging the idea that the world and its elements are radically contingent. The world can and does evolve, the sleeping things awake, but it cannot be apocalyptically shifted or undone. It is also interesting that Leibniz cites Archimedes, the patron saint of modern mathematical philosophy. He seems to be claiming that Archimedes had commitments more essential than mathematics, that his mathematical impulses were superseded by his obedience to the principle of sufficient reason. All of this is to say that Leibniz considers Archimedes to have been a good ancient.

36. Leibniz's fifth paper, in *Leibniz-Clarke Correspondence*, p. 47.

37. *Unpublished Scientific Papers of Isaac Newton*, p. 81. This statement by the Halls in their introduction to the "Mechanics" section of the book is made in the context of a comparison of Newton and Berkeley, but the general point also bears on the difference between Newton and Leibniz.

38. Newton, *Principia*, II, p. 545.

39. Clarke's third reply, in *Leibniz-Clarke Correspondence*, p. 34. Again, there is strong evidence to support that position that Clarke showed his letters to Newton before sending them off. The language here is akin to that of the General Scholium of Newton's *Principia*, as Clarke's own footnoted reference demonstrates (footnote a, p. 34): "God is omnipresent, not only virtually, but substantially; for powers cannot subsist without a substance."

40. Clarke's first reply, in *Leibniz-Clarke Correspondence*, p. 14.

41. Clarke's third reply, in *Leibniz-Clarke Correspondence*, p. 34.

42. From Query 31 of the *Opticks*, pp. 542–43.

43. Quoted and translated by Koyré in his *Newtonian Studies*, p. 272.

44. *Newtonian Studies*, p. 272. Koyré's contribution to the study of the variations and emendations in Newton's *Principia* and other writings is without peer. It is safe to say that he almost single-handedly stimulated the tremendous amount of subsequent study in this area.

45. Martin Heidegger, *What Is a Thing?* p. 96.

Chapter 9

1. Koyré, *Metaphysics and Measurement*, p. 90.

2. The words are quoted from the General Scholium of the *Principia*, I,

p. 6. Stephen Toulmin, for example, takes Koyré to task for reading too much into Newton's use of the term "common." He claims that Koyré sees a "scornful" edge to Newton's use of the term. In fact, it seems to me that Newton is only following what had already become the modern scientific "tradition" of placing those notions which one opposed on the everyday side of the ledger. Toulmin is critical of efforts in the history and philosophy of science which challenge the "internal integrity" of science. However, his criticism of Koyré is to some extent offset by his own arguments, which move in much the same direction as those of Koyré. See Stephen Toulmin, "Criticism in the History of Science: Newton on Absolute Space, Time, and Motion," *Philosophical Review* 68 (1959), p. 11.

3. *Principia*, I, p. 21. Again, Toulmin is suspicious of any reading of Newton which makes him out to be more (or less) than a scientific thinker. Thus, Toulmin writes of the top half of "Newton's dividing-line" as involving "not the most perfect measures one could conceive, but rather the theoretical ideals to which all relative measures are more or less good approximations." This reading seems to fly in the face of much of Newton's mainstream scientific discourse.

4. In fact, the Newtonian commitment to the primacy of empirical phenomena was so convincing that philosophers like Hume and Comte could claim that it supported an antitheoretical approach. See Ian Hacking, *Representing and Intervening* (Cambridge: Cambridge University Press, 1983), pp. 48–49.

5. In this section, I draw extensively and intensively from Koyré's essay "An Experiment in Measurement," which offers an account of the protracted efforts to measure the acceleration of gravity. See *Metaphysics and Measurement*, pp. 89–117.

6. Koyré's essay "An Experiment in Measurement" was originally written in English. In its subsequent translation into French (as part of the posthumous *Etudes d'histoire de la pensée scientifique*, Presses Universitaires de France, 1966) the title was rendered as "*Une experience de measure.*" However, it is doubtful whether the ambiguity of the French title (i.e., "*experience*" rather than "experiment") could be justifiably exploited. I take the more conservative point of view here, despite the fact that the shift from experience to experiment was not an infrequent concern in Koyré's writings.

7. One might be tempted to read into this oversight on Galileo's part something more significant than just a curious lapse. If such is the case, that is, if Galileo suffers from some blindness to the possibility that his pendulum clock might hold the key to measuring gravity's effect, it is not a possibility which is "right in front of him." Rather, this possibility has yet to be made apparent, has yet to be "invented." Its emergence requires a reconfiguration of relationships deriving from a certain still nascent theoretical vision.

8. Huygens, in fact, established the theory of evolutes of geometrical curves. See Koyré's *Metaphysics and Measurement*, p. 111.

9. *Metaphysics and Measurement*, p. 111.

10. *Metaphysics and Measurement*, p. 108.

11. *Metaphysics and Measurement*, pp. 112–13.

12. Indeed, Koyré's work helps us to see that modern science embodies a double vision of new things, of new equipment and the new entities which this equipment brings to view.

13. See J. D. Bernal's *Science in History*, vol. I (Cambridge, Mass.: MIT Press, 1971) about the existence of lens technology in the Middle Ages.

14. Hacking is correct to question the apocryphal title of "first microscopist" generally accorded to Leeuwenhoek, but I believe it is fair to say that he was one of the first to do ongoing research with the single lens microscope. See *Representing and Intervening*, pp. 192–93. See my discussion of the microscopic event below. See also Brian J. Ford's *Single Lens: The Story of the Simple Microscope* (New York: Harper and Row, 1985) and Catherine Wilson's *The Invisible World: Early Modern Philosophy and the Invention of the Microscope* (Princeton: Princeton University Press, 1995) for prolonged examinations of Leeuwenhoek's importance.

15. "Du monde de l' 'à-peu-près' à l'univers de la précision," p. 352.

16. Feyerabend, *Against Method*, p. 138.

17. *Against Method*, 122.

18. Galileo, of course, will not relinquish the experiential aspects of experimental study altogether. Perhaps this is why Galileo's work with the telescope is only a preface to the telescope as a modern scientific instrument, leaving for Newton and others to pronounce its arrival by their theoretical work. Still, in his efforts to establish the modern telescope, Galileo seems to express more fully the spirit and approach of modern science than he does in other places. It is as if the device itself, or at least its possibilities, allows him to be more daringly theoretical, to leave behind at least provisionally many of the traditional scientific preoccupations which normally entangle him.

19. "Du monde de l' 'à-peu-près' à l'univers de la précision," p. 351, n. 2.

20. "Du monde de l' 'à-peu-près' à l'univers de la précision," p. 361.

21. Immanuel Kant, *The Inaugural Dissertation*, in *Kant: Selected Pre-Critical Writings* (New York: Barnes and Noble, 1968), p. 63. A brief comparison of this line and certain passages from the "General Scholium" of the *Principia*, as well as certain sections of the Leibniz-Clarke correspondence, reveals interesting resemblances.

22. *The Inaugural Dissertation*, pp. 68, 72. Indeed, although Kant is clearly critical of certain "philosophers of the English," he does not mention Newton by name in these critical passages. He does, however, criticize Leibniz directly. Further, in the footnote on p. 66 he concurs with Newton by borrowing the latter's phrase, the "ubiquity of time."

23. *The Inaugural Dissertation*, pp. 78–79.

24. This curious similarity between the views Kant identifies as Malebranche's and those publicly espoused by Newton is accentuated by Clarke's amended form of the quote from Acts: "for in him we (*and all things*) live and move and have our being" (Clarke's emphasis). See Clarke's fifth reply to Leibniz (*Leibniz-Clarke Correspondence*, p. 103). Also see the first section of chapter 8 for a lengthy discussion of these issues.

25. *Leibniz-Clarke Correspondence*, p. 59. One page earlier, Kant bemoans the

lost "noble institution of antiquity, the discussion of the character of *phenomena and noumena.*" He marks Christian Wolff as chiefly responsible for this "abolition."
    26. *Leibniz-Clarke Correspondence,* p. 74.

Epilogue

1. See the quotation from the unpublished Fifth Rule at n. 43 in chapter 8.

Index